D1086726

GANGS OF LONDON

GANGS OF LONDON

100 Years of Mob Warfare

BRIAN McDONALD

MILO BOOKS LTD

Published in October 2010 by Milo Books

Copyright © 2010 Brian McDonald

The moral right of the author has been asserted.

All rights reserved. No part of this publication may be
reproduced in any form or by any means without
permission in writing from the publisher, nor be otherwise
circulated in any form of binding or cover other than that in
which it is published and without a similar condition being
imposed on the subsequent purchaser.

ISBN 978 1 903854 91 4

Printed in Great Britain by
CPI Cox & Wyman, Reading, Berkshire

MILO BOOKS LTD
The Old Weighbridge
Station Road
Wrea Green
Lancs PR4 2PH
United Kingdom
www.milobooks.com

'Take that … and that … and here's another.'

The Sabini gang, 1922.

Brian McDonald was born in 1937 and grew up in Kennington and Borough, south London. His uncles were leaders of the Elephant and Castle gang. In 1960, he married and moved to Kent. He became production manager for a weekly newspaper and a lecturer in business. He is the author of *Elephant Boys*.

Contents

Introduction

IT MAY BE a need to belong, as much as a need for protection, that brings young men, and sometimes women, together in a gang. It is also a foundation for learning for youths who desire to become streetwise, that magical state that places them in strata much like taking a position in a pride of lions. In deprived areas, 'belonging' flattens out the bumpy terrain: you have found a place in your local society. If you grow up in a privileged area, there is a reciprocal understanding: whoever first said 'You scratch my back and I will scratch yours' put this very well.

Most people do not live in a privileged environment and so must carve a pathway for themselves. Some do it alone and to them must go the greatest credit and respect; for others, perhaps less talented or less well educated, there is the need for support of a backing group. In place of opportunity, the application of force is used to get on. Here respect is given to leaders, often courageous in the way they take on society, too often doomed to take a criminal route to success. When will society learn that equal opportunity for all from birth is the only way to achieve a settled society? We must allow people to find their own level, and resist propping up the privileged and treading down the underprivileged.

Gangs have a structure. At the top is always a tough guy, 'puncher' or fearless individual who overcomes lack of muscle by sheer determination. Someone once said of 'Mad' Frankie Fraser, all five feet six inches of him, 'If you tell him you are going to have a go at someone you had better do it, for he will expect you to.' Gang leaders like Fraser do not fear the consequences of their actions: those that do never remain long at the top. The problems of leadership of a criminal gang are considerable, making it certain they must eventually fail; they are against the law and so must lose. They may be kept in existence by corrupt police officers, but when things become tight they are left to get on with it, the wolves gather and gangs are eaten up. A classic example is the Richardson gang of south London, led by brothers Charlie and Eddie Richardson, both ferocious fighters who existed on fear and respect in the 1950s and 1960s. When their police protectors deserted them, they were left to the legal wolfpack and, although they had made money, they went to prison for long terms. Not only were they prosecuted for what they had done, they were crucified on concocted evidence and exaggerated stories to be ruthlessly destroyed by their own legend.

In the ranks of gangs live weaker members, shrewd operators and frustrated entrepreneurs who, instead of becoming legitimate business leaders, become conmen, long-firm fraudsters and crooked businessmen; they have business acumen without education and opportunity. Gangsters regard their enterprise as 'their business' and see no reason to regret or to apologise for it. In place of the business contract, they are bound by violence.

What is the difference between a gang on the streets of Chicago or New York and those inhabiting Birmingham or London? Take away the use of firearms and they become remarkably similar. Toss in an ingredient such as unregulated racecourse activity in Britain and Prohibition in America and it can be seen how gangs adapt to their own specialities. It would have made no difference if American gangs had fought over racecourse pitches and British ones had had the opportunity of sanctimonious temperance thrust upon them. Each would have used their untutored entrepreneurial skills to make money.

'Down these mean streets a man must go': I quoted this

famous Raymond Chandler line in my book *Elephant Boys: Tales of London and Los Angeles Underworlds*, which went from London to LA and back again, taking in assorted gangsters and scoundrels along the way. Hidden in Britain's underworld are characters and little known gangsters who have received only fleeting comments on their careers. How much do we know of Dodger Mullins, Tommy Benneworth and others like them, who appear as bit players among the cast of better-known villains such as Darby Sabini, Frankie Fraser, Billy Hill, Jack Spot and the Krays? How much do we know about the violent mobs who fought in London's streets at the end of the Victorian era?

I have been digging to uncover the story of some of the supporting cast in the annals of British crime. Far from being sidemen, some of these villains deserved starring roles, not to be relegated to the footnotes of history. Some, of course, preferred to avoid the limelight. Others had a fleeting glimpse of fame before departing in a puff of smoke, accompanied by a loud bang, or took up long-term lodgings in Their Majesties' accommodation. Yet, others did reform. I have also uncovered previously overlooked details of better-known gangsters.

I am a south Londoner, descended from a celebrated family that inhabited Lambeth and Southwark between the wars and in the years following World War Two, when criminal enterprise had some strange respectability. We knew our villains, even paid homage to some of them, and most people, including the police, accepted them. They were easy to find, although usually left alone as long as they fought only amongst themselves and kept us entertained through the local and Sunday newspapers. I played a part myself, sometimes helping to put the boot in (well, you had to). After surreptitious involvement, and because I had no interest in getting caught, I quickly joined the crowd of onlookers, gratified that my anonymous appearance allowed me to blend into the curious spectators. One rule for the survival of a villain is never to look like one. Mostly I watched and made notes.

I have picked up on some characters you will find mentioned in other books on crime in Britain's early twentieth century: south London yes, and north London, and the Birmingham allies of the London gangs, and so on. At times, I attempt to make sense of what makes a gangster what he (or she) is. I have not neglected the women. I dare not, as one of the Forty Elephants might come back and get me. Some of these terrors were as tough as the men they worked for and protected.

Some gangs used colourful names, such as the Titanic, the Watney Streeters, the Forties, and Abbey Street Boys from London's East End, and the Silver Hatchets from Islington, but when naming a gang, alliteration often came into play. Names that roll off the tongue seem to make a gang's title more memorable. 'Boys' is used extensively in gang nomenclature and, when it coincides with a district commencing with 'B', they go nicely together.

1

MASTER CRIMINALS

Prime Players in London's Early Gangland

The Original Wild One

JONATHAN WILD WAS born in Wolverhampton, Staffordshire, in 1683 and arrived in London in his mid-twenties. He became an immediate burden on businesses in the capital, obtaining goods on credit and defaulting on payment for large orders, thereby proving that long-firm fraud is not solely a product of modern times. Soon he was running prostitutes and operating gangs of thieves and receivers. Most probably, he was the archetype for Charles Dickens's Fagin.

Wild was recruited as a thief taker, or bounty hunter, by Charles Hitchin, a corrupt libertine who had bought the position of Under City Marshal with his wife's inheritance, a position he abused with great abandon. This association afforded Wild protection and opportunity to expand his empire. The pair fell out when Hitchin became jealous of Wild's success, and both published leaflets accusing each other of a raft of criminal activity,. This included an assertion that Hitchin was a sodomite, something that later proved to be true, and saw Hitchin fined, kicked out of office and put in the Strand pillory. There he was severely injured by stones from an angry crowd, before being imprisoned in Newgate for six months.

Wild survived Hitchin's allegations to become Thief Taker General, a sort of private detective sanctioned by the law to track down thieves and recover their loot for a percentage of its value. It was only a small step from there to commiting thefts himself and selling goods back to victims. He also began contriving evidence against innocent people, arresting them and claiming the £40 reward for each that dangled from a rope, an enormous sum at the time. Wild and other thief takers sent many an innocent wretch to the gallows, yet the practice of thief taking, although in disrepute, continued until the formation of an official police force in 1829. Theft was a capital offence and men, women and children were hanged for small larcenies.

The origins of many familiar brands of crime can be traced back to Wild: protection, extortion, corruption, fraud, receiving, and what would become insurance fraud as soon as that industry was invented. He did not shrink at murder, at times removing rivals or dissenters that he had failed to get imprisoned or executed by corrupt authorities. He was a master of the bribe. Success bred a gang of huge proportions – so large he split it into district gangs under sub-chieftains. Returns were spectacular: the best in wine, women, revelling and, the byword of today's crime lords, 'respect'. Wild lived with five women, at least one of whom had a child by him. At the same time, Londoners admired him for his stand against criminals. He owned a large house in St. Andrew's, near today's Holborn Circus, where his servants lavishly entertained his benefactors and cronies. He wore the finest clothes to cover up his otherwise coarse appearance.

However, not everyone was fooled. Honest lawyers suspected Wild and contrived to change the laws he used to protect himself from prosecution. They succeeded in making it illegal to recover goods for profit. Wild responded by using his powers to persuade less scrupulous lawyers and government officials to reverse the new legislation, after which he carried on with even more exuberance. He bought a ship to transport stolen goods for sale abroad and to return with contraband to be smuggled ashore in Kent.

Wild's only fears stemmed from fellow criminals who envied his rich pickings and political power. A particular thorn was lone wolf robber John 'Jack' Sheppard, an East End lad who was the forerunner of twentieth century villains such as Jack 'Dodger' Mullins and Timmy Hayes. He refused to join Wild's gang and spread it about that Wild was a crook. Systematically, Wild had such enemies put away; framing people is nothing new. Sheppard managed to break jail on four separate occasions, only to be rounded up again to be hanged in 1724.

Wild's reign lasted nearly fourteen years until it suffered its next serious setback. Jack Blake, a highwayman partner of Jack Sheppard, had also refused to join Wild's gang and was informed on by Wild as a punishment. In retaliation, he leapt from the dock of the Old Bailey and slashed Wild's throat with a piece of blunt metal before he could be overpowered. While Wild recovered, Blake – otherwise known as 'Blueskin' due to the knife scar that disfigured his face – told all he knew of Wild's exploits, and in such detail that it overcame efforts to cover up what should already have been obvious. The rushing of Blueskin to the silencing effect of a hangman's rope came too late. Wild was investigated and found to be in possession of a large amount of stolen property. As the loot was identified, it became clear he was at the head of a ring of thieves and murderers.

Public opinion turned against Wild and his accomplices. His protectors, who were unable to prevent his arrest, tried to silence him by smuggling laudanum, an opium-based drug, into his Newgate cell for him to avoid the noose. Wild drank partially from the container, became violently sick and appeared close to death. In order not to be cheated of seeing their nemesis mount the scaffold, his prosecutors contrived to have his execution brought forward. Doubtless, this also suited many worried people in high places.

The gallows at Tyburn Tree, at the spot roughly where Marble Arch stands, had existed from the time of Richard I. Hangings were sometimes followed by drawing and quartering of a half-hanged wretch, watched by gleeful crowds who preferred the spectacle to more genteel forms of public entertainment. The sickly Wild suffered humiliation from the crowd as he was transported by cart to meet his fate. The people who once had revered him pelted him with rubbish. He had sent over 100 men and women to their deaths and many others had been hanged after being named by Wild during and after his trial. He was hanged on 24 May 1725. His nineteen-year-old son was confined during the execution for fear he would launch a serious insurrection and rescue attempt, and Wild's body was later stolen from its grave and sold to surgeons for dissection. His legacy continues all around the world to this day. He was the first boss, don or Mister Big in a long line of successors and criminal organisations.

IN 1862, DURING the American Civil War, the Federal Government swamped America with two commodities that would open up bank robbery as an industry: newly invented greenbacks and government bonds made payable to bearer. Both triggered many a criminal career. Previously banks had hardly been worth robbing; suddenly there was a spate of burglaries and, at the end of the war, bank hold-ups. In the 1870s, Pinkerton investigators came to Britain in pursuit of a flood of New York-based American, German and British crooks, including Adam Worth, Baron Max Shinburn, John Curtin, Charlie Bullard, the Bidwell gang and English Harry, all of whom had substantial pedigrees in crime, from thieving from banks to train robbery, forgery and fraud.

Just as Jonathan Wild had been Dickens's inspiration for Fagin, so Sir Arthur Conan Doyle found Sherlock Holmes's dastardly enemy, Professor Moriarty, in Adam Worth. A German Jew born in 1844, Worth was a true criminal mastermind. In 1869, with his boss Max Shinburn, he rescued Charlie Bullard from New York's White Plains Prison, where Bullard was serving time for bank robbery. After deserting Shinburn, Worth and Bullard burrowed into the vault of a Boston bank and remove close on $500,000 worth of cash and securities. Mission accomplished, they set off to expand their worldly experience.

Arriving in Liverpool in 1870, Worth and Bullard, using aliases, went into the burglary business with zeal, targeting banks and pawnbrokers. They lavished money in the desperately dirty dives of the seaport, where the dross of the world mingled. Soon they met pretty Kitty Flynn, a twenty-year-old barmaid who was attracted to money and to Charlie, whose manner was easier-going than the austere and businesslike Worth. Kitty and Bullard were married in February 1870. Perhaps it was Bullard's talent for tickling the ivories that tilted in his favour – he confessed to being known as 'Piano Charlie' back home. Most likely, the moniker pointed more to his skills as a safecracker than to any mastery of a Strauss waltz.

The newly-married couple and Worth left their digs in Liverpool's Lime Street to travel to London, where they did the rounds of gambling establishments. They set up their own faro bank, a card game in which players bet on the order cards will appear from the top of the deck, which much favours the banker. They were soon swimming in money. Years later, Kitty claimed she was unaware that her husband and Worth were cheating and thieving at every opportunity, although it is difficult to see how she could not have known.

In 1873, after Worth robbed a pawnbroker's shop, the three moved to Paris, where Bullard opened the first Bar American on the Rue Scribe. Things were fine until William Pinkerton, son of the founder of the Pinkerton National Detective Agency, arrived on Bullard's bar stool to inquire about the stolen bonds. In their hurry to elude Pinkerton, Bullard and Worth duped a Frenchman out of thousands of pounds worth of diamonds and left the bar just ahead of the French police, leaving Kitty to sell up. Bullard went to America. According to the Pinkerton files, Worth returned to England and took an expensive apartment in Piccadilly. Strangely, Kitty joined Worth, not her husband, and was said to be living with him at his other home on the edge of Clapham Common.

Worth left England many times to commit frauds in the

West Indies and Europe, always returning to Kitty, who was now the mother of a daughter, Lucy, the child of either Bullard or Worth. In May 1876, Worth broke into a Bond Street exhibition room and stole Thomas Gainsborough's Duchess of Devonshire, a portrait of Georgiana Spencer, an ancestor of Princess Diana. It was worth about £10,000, a tidy sum in 1876. Although it took an American to steal it, he had to stand on the shoulders of an Englishmen, Jack Phillips, to reach the window to break in, while another American, 'Little Joe' Elliott, kept watch. Having done the deed, Worth told Phillips, known as 'Junko' because of the junk bonds he dealt in, that he had parted with the painting for pennies and did not even offer to share those. They had a fight, after which Phillips left for America to continue swindling on both sides of the Pond. He was eventually arrested by Pinkerton agents and jailed.

The Duchess was taken aboard Worth's steam yacht, *Shamrock*, at Cowes. It was intended to be used as a bargaining tool to free a confederate named Thompson (believed to be an alias of Adam's brother John Worth), who had come from New York to join Worth's gang and immediately been arrested for forgery. Thompson was to bargain for his release by giving information about where the painting could be found. When Thompson was freed on appeal, Adam became stuck with a hot painting. He smuggled it to Paris, then to New York, and Kitty and her daughter went with him.

Worth's departure was partly due to a little known murder. On 13 April 1876, a thirty-eight-year-old American, Lydia Chapman, was found dead at her home in Chelsea. Scotland Yard suspected she had been poisoned. Her husband, Joe Chapman, had been jailed in Turkey with Little Joe Elliott and two other Americans for fraud and forgery. Lydia went to Turkey and bribed officials to release the Americans, but failed to free her husband, who was ill. One of the freed prisoners, Carlo Sesicovitch, returned to England and demanded Lydia hand over funds held on behalf of the group. She demurred and the likely outcome is that she was killed because of it. The fact that Worth happened to be in London at the time, there was money to be had, he knew her husband was rotting in a Turkish prison, and that he left hurriedly for New York, suggests he had a hand in her demise. No one ever came to trial for Chapman's murder.

Little Joe Elliott, born around 1851, had embarked early on a career as a thief. He was prosecuted many times for petty thefts, forgery and bank robbery, to a point where he felt picked upon by America's police force. As with a number of experienced American thieves and swindlers, he decided to chance his arm in the safer haven of London, where only Scotland Yard had a belief in its ability to deal with astute criminals. He was one of the three Americans arrested in Turkey and may have been implicated in the murder of Lydia Chapman. Elliott took up with English actress 'Rosie Posey' Kate Castleton, whom he met in 1876 at a music hall benefit. Castleton found her way to New York (perhaps with Joe) later that year, where she appeared in bawdy revues, sometimes accompanied by a giant St. Bernard she had insured for $1,000. Joe, who had hurriedly departed for New York in July 1876, married Kate the next month at the Church of the Transfiguration, known as 'The Little Church Around the Corner', in the Bronx. The marriage record gives their true identities: William Riley, aged twenty-six, and Jennie (Jane) Freeman, twenty-one.

Elliott returned to his previous occupation and was later arrested for bank burglary in New York. He tried to do a deal by blowing the whistle on Worth's theft of the Duchess but still received four years, though he somehow managed to escape. By the time he was recaptured he had chalked up more crimes and his sentence was extended. He was arrested again in 1886 for crimes committed in Rochester, New York, and was sentenced to fifteen years for forgery. He died in New York's Tombs Prison.

Worth returned to England in 1880, where he swindled

banks and investors and became a controller of thieves, taking
a percentage of their ill-gottens for shifting them. He was persuaded to travel to South Africa by London villain 'One-eyed
Charlie' King, from Whitechapel, who regarded pickings to be
of the easy variety. They made two botched attempts to rob a
mail coach carrying packets of diamonds, forcing them to flee
to Turkey, later returning to South Africa under aliases. Worth
managed to steal a packet of diamonds, which he regarded as
his sole property, something Charlie could not accept. They
fell out, causing Worth to run off to France before returning
to England. While attempting to dispose of the diamonds in
London, he was arrested.

The reason Kitty had remained in New York became clear
when a second daughter was born. Her marriage to Bullard
was dissolved and she was free to marry a South American
banker. In London, Scotland Yard and William Pinkerton
interviewed Worth but, as the diamonds could not be traced
to their owner and the painting was not forthcoming, he was
released. He settled down to a life of some style in Mayfair
until his wealth was exhausted by rich living. Kitty died at
her home in New York at the age of forty-one, from Bright's
disease. The death of her second husband had left her a rich
widow, much sought after as a party hostess, and her demise
made headline news.

In 1891, in search of funds, Worth went to Paris then to
Brussels, where he robbed a Belgian mail coach by tricking
his way into the driver's seat and riding off with the mailbag.
He was caught soon after and sentenced to seven years in Louvain Prison. Belgium had a particular attraction for American
thieves. In 1883, Charlie Bullard, much dissipated by drink,
had arrived there and was soon caught bank-burgling in Belgium with 'Baron' Max Shinburn. Shinburn was in Louvain
Prison when Worth arrived there, Bullard having passed away
in his cell in 1888. Shinburn was still smouldering over his
rejection by Worth, but felt much better after he did a deal for

his early release by snitching on Worth's early career. In 1893, Shinburn was released.

WORTH'S ENEMY, MAX Shinburn, known as 'the Baron' through his crooked purchase of a Belgian title, was a robber of Prussian origin. He was most likely Maximilian Schoenbein, who arrived in America in 1861 and whose early crimes were in the United States and Canada, where he was a prolific robber of banks. He robbed an Ontario bank by blowing the safe and escaped in a blizzard across a half-finished plank bridge above Niagara Falls. Arrested and jailed on numerous occasions, he never had much difficulty in escaping from prison cells: on one occasion he picked the lock of his handcuffs while chained to a dozing policeman. He arrived in England in about 1881 with a gang of international criminals that he organised into cells for operations in England and Europe. He took part in swindles from his headquarters in Mayfair, and several bank burglaries through associates in the Whitechapel district of east London, and continued his feud with Worth, before fleeing to Belgium to avoid arrest and making it his home. In September 1883, he and Bullard were arrested for robbery of the Verviers Provincial Bank. Shinburn was jailed for seventeen years and Bullard for sixteen. Shinburn informed on Worth to obtain his own early release. He returned to America, where he found that earlier investments had made him wealthy enough to retire.

On his release from Louvain Prison in 1897, Worth returned to London to commit more frauds, before flitting to Paris to rob a bank. He returned to New York in 1898, where his feud with Max Shinburn continued. Shinburn had worked through his fortune, not least by paying off crooked cops who held old robbery charges over his head, forcing him into another robbery for which he was caught and jailed. Worth had declared his intention of having him killed, but nature and years of dissipation had reduced Shinburn to a shell. Even so, he outlasted Worth, to die in Detroit in 1916.

In his last years, fearing he was near death, Worth negotiated through William Pinkerton for the return of the Duchess of Devonshire in exchange for £2,000 and amnesty in England. The deal worked. In January 1899, twenty-five years after it had been stolen, the painting was returned to William Pinkerton, who shipped it back to England. The American tycoon Pierpont Morgan later bought it. In 1994, the painting returned to England when it was purchased by the Chatsworth Estate.

It seems Worth desperately wanted to return to England. It is said that after Kitty married her millionaire, he had also married in London and now his wife was mentally ill. He was allowed to return in 1901 and soon became ill with suspected tuberculosis. He died penniless on 8 January 1902, aged fifty-six, yet looking much older. His death certificate records heart failure due to disease of the liver and heart, caused by chronic habits of intemperance. Adam Worth, whose last home was at Park Village East, Camden, is buried under one of his aliases, Henry Judson Raymond (it was common practice on both sides of the Atlantic to use aliases also used by other criminals in order to confuse investigation) in the west section of Highgate Cemetery, although his grave is marked with a simple plaque of recent origin. There is no doubt he was a wonderful scoundrel, although evidence suggests tales of his wealth are exaggerated; not so his wild life.

According to Ben Macintyre in *The Napoleon of Crime: The Life and Times of Adam Worth, The Real Moriarty*, Worth married one of the daughters of a Bayswater landlady, where he lodged on one of his returns to London from a foreign venture. In the 1881 census, H.J. Raymond, a thirty-seven-year-old born in the United States, is a lodger at a boarding house at Arundell Street, just around the corner from the American Bar in the Criterion that Worth was known to frequent and close to the flat he once rented in Piccadilly. He is described as a patentee and it is a fact that Worth sometimes described himself as an inventor of security systems. Also at this address is sixteen-year-old Barbara Boljahn, who fits the bill perfectly for the 'wife' of Adam Worth, alias Henry Judson Raymond. She was born Catherine Babetha Boljahn in Westminster to German parents. She died in The Manor Asylum, which housed 700 female lunatics near Epsom, Surrey, in November 1900.

Worth complained that while he was in prison, his wife was seduced by his colleague, the prolific swindler John Curtin, who introduced her to drugs and loose living, resulting in her madness. Curtin was another American, a well-known thief who fled to England in 1886, where he was arrested after sneaking a packet of diamonds into his pocket in a West End jewellery shop. He was jailed for eighteen months. Worth made it his business to provide services for every American crook who visited London.

'English Harry' Howard was sought by Pinkertons for the 1865 robbery of the Concord National Bank in Massachusetts. Howard had teamed up with Langdon Moore, a thirty-five-year-old American bank robber with a history of violence. On this occasion, it was Harry's skills that came into play. Renowned as an expert safecracker and locksmith, he took a wax impression to make a duplicate key to the bank's outer door. Moore had previously sized up the inside of the bank and noticed that the cashier had written the combination on the side of the safe. With Moore keeping watch from a saloon opposite, Harry lounged outside the bank until the cashier left for his lunch in the saloon. Harry used his key to enter, had a bad moment when a customer tried to enter with him, unlocked the safe and removed over $300,000 in US government bonds. Moore stood by the saloon door to prevent the cashier leaving, should it become necessary. It did not: Harry coolly locked the safe and the outer door behind him. Moore joined him and they rode from town in a borrowed horse-drawn phaeton carriage. It was a theft 'as sweet as a nut', hardly demanding the safe-breaking skills of the Englishman.

After selling his share of the bonds to a third party, Harry sailed for his native Liverpool. Langdon Moore, who had not parted with his share of the bonds as he was holding out for a higher price, was arrested trying to enter Canada. He offered to help catch Harry, who he said was in possession of $100,000, in exchange for amnesty. Their means of communicating with each other was through a personal ad in a New York newspaper. Pinkertons placed the ad, not knowing Harry was not in New York to read it. Moore was acquitted and able to continue his career as one of America's most prolific thieves. Naturally, he wrote a book, *His Own Story of His Eventful Life*, published in 1893 and now extremely rare, in which he gives an entirely different version of his life and crimes to that recorded in police files.

Harry mixed into haunts around the London district of Camden, where, in 1870, he was arrested by Scotland Yard detectives for forgery. He escaped from a detention room in Albany Street Police Station by picking the lock. In 1871, two American forgers, Austin and George Bidwell, arrived in London. They got together with George Macdonnell, a naturalised British subject who was born in America, to carry out a series of credit frauds on banks by using a money 'float' to pay money in and make withdrawals at regular intervals. By recycling money, they built up a credit relationship that enabled them to buy goods on the bank's credit, sell them, and skedaddle. This must be one of the earliest examples of long-firm fraud. Among their victims was the Bank of England, which they took for over £100,000 by depositing forged bills of exchange with long expiry dates and cashing them in before the bank realised they were worthless. They were exposed when Macdonnell, in his relish to cheat the Bank of England, failed to date one of the bills.

William Pinkerton traced Austin Bidwell to Cuba, where he was arrested and extradited to England. George Bidwell was traced to Ireland, and then Scotland, where a private detective seeking the reward of £5,000 arrested him. In George's pocket was a notebook containing addresses, one of which was 'Harry H, 13 Brill Row, Somers Town, Euston'. When Scotland Yard detectives knocked on the door it was answered by a young woman, who said she was in the house alone. However, in bed upstairs they found English Harry. He was sentenced, under his real name, Henry Hauck, to six years' for his previous fraud. Just what he had been up to with the Bidwells is not known. He was luckier than they were: in 1873, with Macdonnell, they were sentenced at the Old Bailey to life imprisonment for their swindle on the Bank of England. Many years later, both men did the lecture rounds in America, deploring crime.

Both Bidwells wrote books: *Forging His Chains*, by George, and *From Wall Street to Newgate*, by Austin, 1895. The latter is a good read, although given to much exaggeration and concluding with a bitter diatribe against the British and their system of justice and incarceration.

Consummate Cracksmen

GEORGE INGRAM KEPT his real name secret, although he did claim to be descended from Scottish nobility. Born Alfred Tragheim, at Notting Hill in 1892, he later said his criminal career began in 1922 while he was enrolled at London University to study medicine. He said it was there that he met an established burglar to the landed gentry, George Smithson, who had raided several country houses and was having difficulty placing his loot on London's informal underground market. In fact, it was in Borstal in 1911 that Ingram met Smithson, which blows a hole in his original claims. Ingram, who had served a previous six-week sentence for stealing postal orders, was then serving three years for stealing a bicycle.

Ingram came from a criminal family. His father, also Alfred, had convictions for theft going back to 1904. In April 1910, he was acquitted of stealing a milk churn and seventeen gallons of milk from Paddington Railway Station, the property of Great Western and Metropolitan Dairies. He had sold the full churn to a shop and got off because he claimed it was common practice for churns to be taken from one consignment, sold, and replaced from the next consignment. In 1911, when his son was arrested for theft, he assaulted police and was punished with six weeks' imprisonment.

Later that year, he got together with Henry Pascoe, who had snuggled up to Lucy Bodimead, a servant at the home of Member of Parliament Arthur Steel Maitland. He had elicited information from her about the household and took this information to Ingram. They arranged for Pascoe to take Lucy to the Coliseum cinema on an evening when she was left in sole charge of the house. With the coast clear, Ingram jemmied his way into the unoccupied house at Cadogan Place, Chelsea, and stole jewellery, watches and other valuables. When Pascoe brought Lucy home, she asked him in for cocoa and they discovered the break-in. Pascoe helped search the house for intruders and telephoned the police.

Detectives listened to the story, then worked on Pascoe, who soon told everything. Decently, he said Lucy knew nothing about it. Ingram's home in North Kensington was raided at 3 a.m. While he rubbed his eyes, police looked under his bed and found a little treasure trove and burglar's tools. Pascoe was sentenced to thirteen months' imprisonment; Ingram's sentence was postponed for further inquiries. Poor innocent Lucy got the sack.

In February 1912, Alfred Ingram was charged, along with two accomplices, with three burglaries, all around the Maida Vale area, after they were seen forcing the door of a house. A search of Ingram's flat revealed a cache of stolen property. Before their trial began, Paddington Police Station received a parcel through the post containing more stolen property, in an attempt to halt proceedings. Police described Alfred as the head of a gang who, with other family members also using the name Ingram, comprised a network of thieves and receivers responsible for keeping Paddington's police busy.

George Smithson, the son of a north of England nurseryman, became known as the 'Gentleman Burglar' and 'King of the Cracksmen'. Police said he was the most dangerous burglar since the notorious Sheffield-born Charles Peace, although unlike Peace, Smithson did not murder anyone. In his criminal lifetime, he stole a large fortune but, as with most burglars, money slipped through his fingers and he ended up with next to nothing. Prison terms paid for short-term luxuries. He claimed he never robbed a poor man from the moment he ran away from home, after stealing his father's money. His burgling career began with a raid on a hotel in

Northamptonshire. He often burgled two or three houses a night, becoming bolder with each expedition, plundering over fifty country mansions and taking spoils of over £100,000 in value.

On one occasion, he was almost discovered by departing guests who were taking a stroll in the gardens. But he had become addicted to danger, which led him to go ahead with the burglary. He had a tense time, struggling to open a safe without success, and had to settle for small jewellery items. He later found that the safe had contained several thousand pounds. His secondary hobby was to delight in reading the newspapers to see what he had missed and to discover the value of what he had stolen.

Smithson's prolific robberies were interrupted when he was arrested in June 1910, after he had given a gold musical box to a publican's daughter as a gift before going raiding. When he returned, he learned that a visiting policeman had seen the box, forcing him to go on the run. He was hunted by police from several counties until he was dragged from his bicycle near Epping in Essex. He was nineteen years old. On the plus side, his father forgave him. For burglaries across thirteen counties, his sentence was two terms of three years to run concurrently in a Borstal institution. He was transferred from a holding prison to Borstal, near Rochester, Kent, where he commenced lessons in burglary from more experienced practitioners among the 500 inmates.

Smithson was released in November 1912. After a short spell of work arranged by his father at a garden nursery in Cheshire, he migrated to London to join up with George Ingram. He was determined to become a better burglar. Smithson was quite taken with what he described as the stocky, auburn-haired, blue-eyed, fresh-complexioned 'Adonis in crime', who had an enticing personality in spite of his superficial education (so much for Ingram's claims of a university education). For his part, Smithson came across as an intelligent, mild-looking gentleman, with rimless spectacles, a three-piece suit, starched collar and a prematurely balding pate. In January 1913, he went robbing while Ingram set up a network of fences. They were determined to target isolated country homes. At first, Smithson worked alone, until he was startled by a victim's parrot and decided he needed company.

Although Ingram lived in the North Kensington district of west London, he had developed contacts with a ring of fences in Hoxton, east London, an area he referred to as 'Hell's Kitchen', from whom he bought small items of jewellery to sell around college campuses. He also pawned stolen items through contacts made in this unwholesome neighbourhood. After hearing tales of Smithson's 'countryside business', Ingram decided life would be simpler if he just took what others had acquired. No study was required, just nerve, nimble fingers, a light tread and an ability to climb walls and drainpipes. He abandoned his intention of becoming a doctor and within a short time had found a fence who would handle most of the stolen merchandise: Mike Spellman, an American who had made his home in London. After a few burglaries, Ingram lived a satisfying life and was hooked on his new job and the lure of an undisciplined life. From that point on he was committed to his new profession.

Ingram and Smithson embarked on a series of country house raids with a style developed from meticulous research and patience. They would go though *The Times*, *Debrett's*, *Burke's Landed Gentry* and other upmarket journals to select targets. They searched out information on who lived where and when they would be visiting their country piles, taking their valuables with them for the season. They would then spy out a vicinity and wait, for days if necessary, to find the right moment to enter a country mansion. As many raids failed as were successful, but they were young men learning their trade. They robbed only the rich but they did not give to the poor, instead spending money on a fast time and comfortable living in cosy apartments.

As their skills grew, successes outweighed failures and the money gained from the sale of portable valuables jingled in their pockets. They 'blitzed' houses across the Home Counties and the Midlands. Their *modus operandi* was to rifle through large country houses while the residents were sleeping: the bigger the house, the less likely inhabitants would be alerted to midnight sounds. They were after cash and jewellery, which was generally kept in a bedroom dressing table drawer, and which they had to creep in to get – and they got plenty. They carried only a sparse toolkit, the reason for which was their use of silent, unobtrusive transport: they were 'Bicycle Bandits', who journeyed by train with their cycles in the guard's van. They would raid two or three houses in one night. On one occasion, Ingram was tempted to mount an afternoon sortie, but Smithson's prudence overcame him. They popped off to see a silent film, *The Miracle Man*, about a gang of thieves who reform, starring Lon Chaney, before returning for a successful night raid.

Ingram once related that the hotspots of criminal London were Hoxton, Bethnal Green and the Elephant and Castle. This supports other prominent crooks' recollections of the time. Police designated Hoxton's dubious denizens as 'the Hoxton thief' to denote individuals within teams of shop breakers, burglars, car thieves and smash-and-grab specialists. The district had streets of premises occupied by receivers. When American filmmakers presented Sir Arthur Conan Doyle's Sherlock Holmes masterpiece *The Adventure of the Six Napoleons* (which they re-titled *The Pearl of Death*), they spiced it up by introducing the spine-snapping 'Hoxton Creeper'. Ingram knew Amelia Hill, mother of later notorious gangster Billy Hill, but after attending one of her 'open to all' parties, he decided he did not fit into her riotous lifestyle. His opinion of Amie was that she harboured crooks and informed on their activities to keep the police off her doorstep. He was teetotal, a sensible trait for a midnight creeper.

Ingram's and Smithson also made friends with arch-villain

Alf White, who ran a team of pickpockets. They marvelled at the dippers' dedication to their work, as they practised for hours on each other and used exercises to keep their hands and fingers supple. Ingram noticed that the wives of these pickpockets often belonged to teams of shoplifters. He was taken aback by the brutality that existed in these circles when one of its members was found to be holding out. Ingram had no use for razor thugs; the only thing he learned from White's crowd was the sensible practice of keep-fit exercises. He and Smithson regarded themselves almost as royalty, looking down on lesser individuals, and soon they would become known as the 'Princes of Burglary'. The only other crooks they admired were cardsharps and thimble riggers, who practised their art in the full gaze of their prey. It was the easiest way to make money because mugs, who could not see how it was done, would not believe they were being tricked.

Ingram and Smithson's escapades were not without humour. On one expedition, they burgled a country mansion and took a haul of jewellery and a painting that took Ingram's fancy. On their escape, they espied another manor and decided to take it in. They had placed their haul from the first raid in a canvas holdall, which also held their tools, and took it with them into the manor. Perhaps through over-confidence, they roused someone, forcing them to hide in a room until they realised the rooms were being searched. They locked the door from the inside and left through a window. When they reached their bicycles, something hit them: the bag containing their tools and loot was still in the manor house. Ingram was all for leaving it as a bad job but Smithson thought there were items in the bag that might lead to them. They waited until the lights went out and then stole back into the manor, where they found their bag entirely unmolested. On the way out, they tiptoed past an occupant who was creeping around with a shotgun.

One of Ingram's fencing arrangements was with Isaac Grizard. He had been jailed in 1892, for receiving assorted goods stolen from market traders, and again in 1901 after Detective Tom Divall arrested him, at a coffee shop he owned on Bethnal Green Road, for the theft and receiving of fur coats. Another notorious receiver of stolen goods, Joseph 'Kemmy' Grizzard, was his brother, although he had an extra 'z'. Ingram, who also handled merchandise for other crooks, was turned over by Isaac and, for revenge, he and Smithson burgled the old rogue's home.

The pair set out on a mission to burgle on a colossal scale. Ingram was reluctant to enter houses, often leaving Smithson to go in alone; they argued constantly, but the partnership continued. On one occasion, when they were discovered, Smithson escaped on a horse while Ingram pedalled his cycle furiously after him, followed by the splatter of shotgun's pellets. For a break, they visited Ingram's family in Edinburgh, but left for a hotel when they were not welcomed. Ingram then suggested they should steal the Scottish Crown Jewels from Edinburgh Castle. The regalia consists of a crown of pure gold, encrusted with precious stones. It is believed to have been made for Robert the Bruce and once sat upon the heads of Stuart kings, up to the reign of Charles II. Also included is a royal sceptre, used by Scottish kings to touch the parchment on which new laws were written to give them Royal consent, and a sword of state, nearly five feet long. These made up the 'Honours of Scotland'. They lay on a marble table in the middle of a room with other precious state relics, surrounded by an iron-barred cage. At one time they had been hidden under stones in Kinneff Church to stop Oliver Cromwell getting his hands on them. They were brought out again when King Charles II was crowned. Later they were locked away in Edinburgh Castle to prevent them being taken to England. Almost forgotten, they lay in an iron-banded chest within a sealed room for 110 years until, amid great excitement, the room was opened in 1817 on the orders of the Prince Regent, and they were put on public display.

This time it was Smithson who was scared. Such an auda-
cious theft would have been seen as an attack on Scotland
itself. Nevertheless, 'Doctor' Ingram prepared, making chlo-
roform in their rooms and gassing a cat by accident. It was
intended that Ingram would dope the watchman for Smithson
to open the cabinet and steal the jewels. In the clumsy attempt,
Ingram dropped the bottle and was cursed by the watchman,
who wanted to know what they were up to. They pretended
to be medical students who had accidentally dropped a phial.
Had they been successful in stealing Scotland's Crown Jewels,
there would have been outrage.

Ingram and Smithson often took along pieces of meat to
offer to dogs they might come across outside or inside the
premises. Their experience was that any dog would accept a
treat. Dogs left to roam rooms inside a house welcomed human
companionship and were quite happy to meet a burglar. The
most difficult were small, yapping terriers, big dogs being
mostly docile. On one occasion, Smithson was confronted by
two large hounds, which he easily befriended. They followed
him from room to room, as he pilfered the movables. When it
became time to leave, the dogs left with him and he left them
wandering the grounds. One rule sufficed: if a dog was aggres-
sive, give up and go home. When they raided one home, they
were obliged to stay outside on a stormy night. They struggled
across the grounds, through lashing wind and rain, to a small
building where they sheltered against a wall, before moving
on to the house. There, with great difficulty, they broke open
a window, only to hear a growl. A dog came out of the small
building and watched as they climbed through the window,
then watched them leave with the owner's suitcase filled
with goodies, including a valuable pearl necklace. The owner
sold his useless dog and sacked his nightwatchman, who had
weathered the storm inside the outbuilding instead of doing
the rounds with his dog.

Both Ingram and Smithson were opposed to attacking dogs

and humans. They never found a man to be a problem; women were more dangerous because they had a better feel for the house and were more vigilant. Women were also often brave enough to confront a burglar who, if he had any sense, withdrew. A particular danger was a hysterical woman, who could raise the whole countryside. Servants usually hid if they heard a noise, or would avoid risk by calling out to alert a burglar.

The two Georges enjoyed reading reports of their exploits, especially when victims exaggerated their losses and their own brave actions. Claims of chasing burglars across fields, through hedges and over fences, were mostly invented, although there were times when they were chased. They heard an occasional shotgun blast, but marvelled at tales they had been bloodied when the truth was that the shot was a random one in the air in case they were sheltering nearby and still a possible threat.

The duo preferred to dispose of their plunder through a chain of small receivers who were not professional fences; they were dishonest dealers who dealt within a small circle that was usually safe. The problem with large receivers was that they were always under police suspicion. Worse, if a thief was caught selling them goods, they would certainly carry the can for other stolen property found on their premises, and be charged with burglaries police wanted to clear from their books. Receivers often specialised: some would take clothing, some small household items, while pawnbrokers took jewellery. If caught, they would get a small sentence or fine and were not tempted to 'blow' on their suppliers. They would also claim to have bought in good faith and often get off altogether. All were driven by greed and were inclined to give the least for goods and get the most for them: they would take advantage of a thief's ignorance and insist the loot was far less valuable than it actually was. After one great haul of jewellery by Smithson, who was working alone, Ingram managed to get only about a quarter of its value. Later some of the loot was recovered by police and returned to its owner; the fence was quick to claim he had dealt in good faith and pointed the finger at Ingram. It seems Smithson, who may have been the shrewder of the two, did not deal with receivers and was happy to leave that to his sidekick.

Smithson and Ingram set up hideaway headquarters in a villa at Lacey Green, near West Wycombe, Buckinghamshire, from where they embarked on a further string of burglaries. Smithson, who had been unnerved by the Edinburgh incident, took to carrying a revolver, which he pulled on a maid during one raid. He also slept with it under his pillow. In May 1913, a Kent police constable observed the pair as they walked towards Ashurst Railway Station. He summoned another constable and attempted to arrest the two 'well dressed men' as they bought train tickets. Smithson pulled his loaded revolver from a bag and was jumped on by the constables, who knocked him unconscious and handcuffed him. Ingram fled, but was captured a mile away, still in possession of his bag. They were taken to Tonbridge Police Station, where they were searched and found to have spoils, tools and several hundred keys in their possession, one of which belonged to the safe at Sevenoaks Weald rectory. They became objects of curiosity when they were inspected by victims and visitors. When their villa was searched, a large quantity of property, including jewellery, clocks and silver plate, was recovered.

They were charged with burgling the home of the chairman of the Thames Ironworks of jewellery worth over £3,000. Smithson gave his name as Frank Watson and Ingram as Alfred Carlton. At their trial at Maidstone, a whole bundle of robberies was added to the charges, plus one of sacrilege. The pair pleaded guilty to over fifty burglaries. Ingram received four-and-a-half years' penal servitude and Smithson five years' because he was six months older; the revolver seems to have been forgiven. After a spell in Maidstone Prison, Smithson went to Portland and Ingram to Parkhurst. Smithson was just twenty-two-years of age.

Portland was the perfect location for convicts sentenced to terms with hard labour. Many buildings faced with Portland stone owe their fine visage to the sweat of convicts. Its windswept Dorset promontory is as bleak as Dartmoor. Prisoners were placed in a cell ten feet by seven feet with only a tiny window, high enough to let in a dim light but making outward viewing difficult. First offenders were designated as 'star men' during their first two years,: they were allowed to write and receive only one letter and have one twenty-minute visit within a four-month period. Smithson shared a cell with an American named Sharman, who had robbed the Berkeley Hotel in the West End and viciously beaten the watchman.

In the early hours of 29 May 1913, Stephen Sharman, thirty-nine, and William Fell, thirty-eight, robbed the Berkeley Hotel in Piccadilly of jewellery and cash worth over £6,000. In the process, they wounded the night porter by striking him four times over the head, inflicting cuts to the bone, and by gripping his throat so fiercely that it was crushed. He had been carried to hospital in a collapsed condition, from which he was fortunate to recover.

Bermondsey Boy Fell was a boyhood friend of gangster Eddie Emanuel. He had previous convictions for church breaking, violent theft and receiving. His worst offence was in 1904 when he was arrested as part of a gang of burglars, one armed with a revolver and others carrying ammonia for blinding dogs, and was sentenced to seven years. Fell would leave home dressed as a painter, commit burglaries, then enter a railway carriage only to emerge from the other side dressed as a gentleman returning home from work, in checked cap, frock coat, even an opera hat, before crossing the line to another platform. Stephen Sharman had fled the forces of law and order in the United States and gathered convictions for horse stealing and jail breaking in South Africa and shop breaking in England. The pair were sentenced to fourteen years each for the hotel raid and two hotel employees, including Sharman's brother, James, were also jailed. Fell did his the easy way and earned full remission. Sharman, who was the Mad Frankie Fraser of his day, fought authority all the way and served every day of his sentence.

This robbery featured in a police report of thefts during 1913, a report that highlighted how active jewel thieves were at that time. In June, a packet containing jewellery and silver plate disappeared from the cloakroom at King's Cross Railway Station. In Antwerp, £6,000 was stolen from a strong room, although diamonds worth over £11,000 were left behind when the gang was disturbed; it was thought the stones were destined for the London black market. Also in June occurred what became known as the 'great pearl necklace theft'; August saw jewellery worth over £9,000 stolen from a hotel in Llandudno, Wales; in September, a large amount of sovereigns disappeared between London and Paris. October saw jewellery worth about £8,000 taken from a commercial traveller in Westmoreland, his samples case having been opened and lumps of coal substituted for diamonds and rubies. In November, it was Antwerp again: this time thieves successfully stole £12,000 worth of diamonds. December finished the year, with jewellery worth £4,000 disappearing on a train journey from the Isle of Wight to London. It was reckoned that well over £500,000-worth of jewellery had been taken: a substantial haul.

The year 1914 started with a rash of smash-and-grab raids on pawn and jewellery shops. After one raid in Manchester Square, London, Jimmy Ward was captured after breaking a window and stealing a tray of diamonds. Police could not find the booty on him and he refused to be questioned, shaking his head at attempts to get him to talk. A constable noticed he was clenching his jaw and forced his mouth open, revealing two diamond rings; investigations then became 'alimentary'. When George King, of the Camden Town gang, was acquitted of a smash-and-grab in Essex Road, Islington, he claimed he was a victim of a vendetta by the Titanic crowd from Hoxton.

Also in Portland Prison with Smithson was Bethnal Green gangster Arthur Harding, who was serving time for his part in the East End Vendetta (see pages 87-95). Among other violent men was Jack Allard, an illegitimate child born in the union workhouse in Derbyshire and a one-time Birmingham book-maker, racing man, racecourse tout and thief, brought down by drink; he was serving seven years for manslaughter and taking it too much to heart. Allard would later be jailed for eighteen months for his part in the 1921 Epsom Derby riot, when the Birmingham gang attempted to ambush Italians led by Darby Sabini, and would die soon after his release. Patrick Mahon was another inmate; he later went to the gallows for murdering his sweetheart and cutting her body into chunks. One of Smithson's softer cellmates was Herbert 'Grimmy' Grimshaw, a jockey born in Hungary to British parents from the Elephant and Castle, who had a secret career as a burglar. He had been convicted of stealing a valise containing jewel-lery from a hotel during Ascot Week.

In Parkhurst, on the Isle of Wight, Ingram had company too, in the shape of William Kennedy who, with Frederick Browne, would later hang for murdering PC George Gut-teridge in Essex, in 1927. Beside Gutteridge's body lay his notebook, suggesting he had been interviewing a suspect at the time of his death. The macabre circumstances were that he had been shot four times: two bullets had taken out his eyes. South Londoner Browne denied the killing and named Kennedy as the man who had shot Gutteridge, removing his eyes to prevent his image being engraved on the victim's pupils. Though bizarre, this was believed to have been possible at the time. Kennedy attempted to shoot police who arrested him in Liverpool. He admitted he was present, but said it was Browne who killed the constable, a classic example of recipro-cal blame to confuse prosecutors. It did them no good, as both were hanged.

August 1914 brought the outbreak of World War One and a petition to Home Secretary Reginald McKenna by Smithson for early release to join the forces and go straight to the Front. He drew attention to three years' service as a trooper with C Squadron, Queen's Own Dragoons, at Doncaster. However he had no luck (if it can be called that) and served his five years, less fifteen months' remission, being released in 1917 on a ticket of leave. As part of the arrangement, he was required to join the Royal Marine Light Infantry and was transferred to their barracks at Deal in Kent. Ingram had been released from Parkhurst and, ever the craftier, did not join the forces due to a claim of disability. He was living in 1917 in Notting Hill, where he formed a partnership with Jim Slade, until they were arrested for a series of burglaries in Berkshire. Ingram had taken a box of cigars to Smithson at Deal, and Smithson had written to thank him and say he looked forward to more of the same. The letter was intercepted by police investigating Ingram's burglaries. Smithson deserted at Deal rather than give evidence against Ingram.

On his own, he started burgling again in Scotland and the north of England, this time posing as an Army officer, until arrested at Carlisle wearing a second lieutenant's uniform under his raincoat. He was jailed for five years. Ingram also received five years, at Reading Assizes. In December 1917, Smithson arrived at Parkhurst, where he was locked up with German spies. He met Cubine Williams, an American who later became the lover of notorious international criminal 'Chicago May' Churchill. Released in January 1922, Smithson went to work as a gardener in Liverpool, which had been arranged by an old crony. He returned to form by stealing some British Museum antiquities from Stoke Rochford Hall, near Grantham in Lincolnshire. For the remainder of 1922 he was still burgling, sometimes alone and sometimes with Ingram.

Both burglars took pride in 'jousting with the aristocracy'. They numbered dukes, duchesses, earls, countesses and knights

among their victims and came close to robbing King George
V, who they read planned to stay a few days with Sir William Portal at Leverstoke House, near Whitchurch, Hampshire.
The notion was that the best jewellery would be on show
for a royal visit and they decided to make the raid the day
before, when they believed there would be much swag. After a
dreadful night waiting in pouring rain, they forced a window
and got in to have a rummage around, but found nothing of
value. The King did visit the next day, but only to inspect a
mill in the grounds – there had been no plans to visit the
house. Even crooks should not believe everything they read
in newspapers.

Many more burglaries followed. In 1922, Ingram took a
brief respite by becoming a potato merchant with premises in
Hoxton. He visited Lincolnshire to buy a vanload of spuds and
was promptly arrested and put before an identification parade.
He was not picked out and was released without explanation.
It later emerged that Smithson, who had not taken a sojourn,
had been busy in the vicinity. Ingram made a great fuss about
his treatment, writing letters of complaint to the Chief Constable of Lincolnshire and to the Home Secretary. His indigna-
tion was increased by hints from the police that they knew he
was a crook and were keeping an eye on him. Ingram could be
obstinate when he chose. The spud business folded.

The pair teamed up again to embark on a rash of burglaries
across middle England. Sometimes Smithson raided alone,
but always it fell to Ingram to fence the loot. On 16 March
1923, they perpetrated their most notorious raid, and it would
prove to be one too many. It had not been the intention of
Ingram and Smithson to raid Benham Park: their target had
been Borwood Park, the Wiltshire home of Lord and Lady
Lansdowne. At this time, the duo had forsaken the train for a
motorcycle and sidecar. Ingram was the driver, mechanic and
navigator, and was not very good as any of them. On their way
to Hampshire to carry out a 'recce', they missed their road and

continued in search of it. The paths they travelled were broken and bumpy and the motorcycle began to shake apart, forcing them to stop to make emergency repairs.

Not in the best of spirits, they continued until they burst a tyre. They had forgotten to pack a puncture repair kit. Undaunted, Ingram waited by the side of the road to flag down the first passing motorcycle. None emerged from the darkness, but a faint light signalled the approach of a bicycle. Out stepped Ingram, bringing the bike to a stop, at which a police constable asked what the trouble was. He saw immediately that he was dealing with novice motorcyclists, but he had a solution: he took out his bicycle tyre repair kit, fixed their tyre, and bade them bon voyage. They travelled on.

It was late and they would not now reach Borwood Park at a suitable hour to do the job. Out came their maps and they identified the nearest of previously considered targets: Lord and Lady Lansdowne's good fortune became the Sutton family's misfortune. The motorcycle rattled to a halt and was hidden in bushes. The devious duo climbed a fence and made their way across pleasant acres, landscaped by the famous Capability Brown, to the large sandstone house. Good fortune now came in the form of a ladder that workmen had left leaning against the house. Smithson may have been a poor mechanic, but he was as agile as a cat; he shinned up about thirty feet, gave the glass a little tap and a piece fell out. He was inside in a flash. Ingram waited a torturous fifteen minutes for Smithson to reappear. When he did, it was at a door beneath the portico and Ingram joined him inside.

Benham Park was cluttered with beautiful treasures: wall hangings, paintings, miniatures, objets d'art of all kinds, loose cash and pieces of jewellery and silverware, all easily found. The drawing room was hung with many paintings that were illuminated by security lights. Ingram decided on two small paintings of Sutton ancestors, a man and a woman, which looked valuable, saleable and portable. Ingram carefully cut the canvases from their frames. To celebrate, they sampled the contents of the Sutton's port decanter, after which Smithson crept upstairs to have a nose around while Ingram removed two more canvases. Smithson came down with little else, so they unfastened cushion covers, packed the canvases and other items in them, and departed. The Suttons snoozed on.

The return journey required Smithson to sit on the pillion to allow room in the sidecar for the loot. It was now early dawn and wet. Smithson moaned while Ingram drove doggedly on, until another puncture stopped them. This time they were close to a garage that was just opening and they paid for a repair. But the tyre blew again. Smithson insisted his frugal Scots companion bought a new tyre, and with that they made it home. Smithson was dropped off at his Kensington flat and the loot went with Ingram to his nearby hideaway. He was so weary he could barely carry the goods to his flat. He collapsed on his bed and slept all day.

Ingram awoke on Sunday morning and took a stroll to a newsagents. He had intended to buy one newspaper but, when he saw the headlines, he bought three. He and Smithson were accustomed to their exploits being reported on the inside pages but now they were headline news. 'Two Gainsboroughs stolen,' declared one headline. Back at his flat, he read the articles with mixed feelings of melancholy and pride. There was no sign of Smithson. In the evening, Ingram loaded the loot into his sidecar and went to see his premier fence, Mike Spellman, who, having seen the newspapers, was expecting him. Spellman, being an American, was a sensible choice, as the only possible market for famous paintings was overseas and preferably America. He left the loot with Spellman, who thought he had a likely buyer.

Two weeks passed without news from Spellman. Newspapers rumoured that an American was suspected of taking the paintings out of the country and Ingram worried that Spellman had done the dirty. Then he turned up at Ingram's flat and handed the paintings back: Spellman explained that he was under constant watch and had taken his one chance to retrieve the paintings from a lock-up. He had considered burning them, but decided to hand them back to Ingram.

Ingram's next move was to try to interest country toffs in purchasing the paintings, as he considered they would have the money and might find it humorous to own valuable artwork. This was a mistake. He asked King's Cross gangster Alf White, whom he knew through his Hoxton connections, if he could help. White said he could introduce him to dishonest gentry who would be interested in buying the paintings. White, however, brought racing men dressed as gentlemen to Ingram's flat: they looked over an assortment of merchandise and left without buying anything. Then Ingram found they had spirited away valuable jewellery and taken cash from his bedroom drawer.

Ingram moved from North Kensington to a flat in Islington. Now sought by police, he confined himself to his rooms, cooking his own meals and staring at the walls. He was afraid to go to a bank, for fear his account was being monitored. With what cash he had from items sold through small outlets, he decided to emigrate, but first he and Smithson decided on more burglaries. After a few nervous sorties that brought little gain, Smithson suggested trying their luck in Scotland. They rode up on the train and burgled a country home whose owners were away attending the wedding of the Duke and Duchess of York. They were arrested on suspicion when exiting a tram in Edinburgh.

They ended up in Calton Gaol, a place they found extreme in climate and food, where they were questioned by English police. By now, a whole list of suspected burglaries had been assembled, including Benham Park and its missing Gainsboroughs. That was it: Smithson rolled over and made a statement detailing much of his and Ingram's work. Police took them to Scotland Yard where, confronted by Smithson's statement, Ingram made one himself.

Detective Inspector Fred Wensley had built a strong case and was in possession of many recovered items, some of which had been found in Smithson's Kensington flat. Smithson had identified a receiver, which brought in a vanload of unsold merchandise. Intense inquiries continued while they were lodged in Brixton Prison. Here they played one of the few cards they had left: they confessed to some of the English burglaries, which meant they would be tried in England and serve any sentence in a less harsh prison environment than they would have suffered in Scotland.

In May 1923, police had an almost complete record of their activities, including Smithson's lone exploits and Ingram's fencing services. The police skilfully manipulated each suspect to get them to provide information on the other. The game was truly up. In spite of their confessions to English burglaries, they were tried first in Edinburgh, where they appeared before Lord Alness, who was Secretary of State for Scotland. Not much shrift was given. Even though both pleaded guilty, Smithson to theft by breaking and entering and Ingram to theft, the nobility of Scotland was not to be tormented by such rascals. Smithson was sentenced to six years' penal servitude and Ingram to four.

On 27 July 1923, they appeared at the Central Criminal Court at the Old Bailey. Three others appeared with them on charges of receiving and, since they had pleaded not guilty, their trial went ahead while Ingram and Smithson, who had pleaded guilty, awaited sentence. One receiver, from Hoxton, identified Ingram as 'the doctor' who had sold him merchandise that he understood to his own property. He had asked him to find a buyer for four paintings, including the Gainsborough portraits. Ingram, who had a fondness for the medical profession, carried phials of potions in his bag and liked people to believe he had received medical training. Police recovered the Gainsboroughs from the receiver's sister, who was 'minding them'. Also recovered was another valuable painting, the Hall of Circassians, stolen from a Shropshire house, that was hidden beneath the backing sheet of another painting.

Ingram and Smithson were brought before Common Sergeant Sir Henry Dickens, son of Charles Dickens. Smithson admitted four burglaries at the homes of Constance Lady Russell of Swallowfield Park, Reading; the Earl of Jersey at Middleton Park House, Bicester; Sir John Leigh at Lilles Hall, Newport, Shropshire; and Henry Cecil Sutton at Benham Park. Ingram pleaded guilty to the Benham Park burglary and to receiving the proceeds of the four burglaries, including the two Gainsboroughs. Police stated that between £50,000 and £60,000 had been stolen by Smithson over the previous year and he had confessed to thirty-six burglaries within that time. His raids had ranged all over the country.

Sir Henry handed down eight years' penal servitude to Smithson, whom he considered a danger to society; to Ingram he handed six years. The sentences were concurrent to the Scottish ones and covered all their English robberies, even those they had forgotten. One of the interesting facets of the trial was how little enmity was held by those who had been robbed. Henry Cecil Sutton had been allowed to meet Smithson in an attempt to find out what had happened to some of his stolen property, and had found him charming. However, Smithson and Ingram were not inclined to offer anything more than apologies. Much of their booty had been thrown away as not being saleable. Items they had sold, they said, could not be recovered. Often Smithson had damaged pieces by crushing them or prising jewels from them.

Smithson confided to Detective Inspector Wensley that he suspected Ingram had been short-changing him: he did not know Ingram's fences and he believed he had been cheated of a fair share. Smithson said Ingram turned against him and threatened to involve his wife unless he alone took the rap for all the burglaries. Wensley put this to Ingram, who admitted he was going to abscond with Smithson's next big hit and told him to search Smithson's flat for firearms: none were found.

The pair arrived at Dartmoor on 30 November 1923. Although they are remembered as consummate cracksmen, it must be noted that from June 1910 to his final known release in 1929, Smithson spent only two years out of captivity; Ingram had slightly more free time. In that period, they burgled over 150 country houses. They were celebrated as the most notorious villains in Britain and were well received by their prison chums. Smithson, however, was indignant that he had twice received a longer sentence than his partner. Ingram, as always, felt that he had been unjustly treated. Their appeals failed.

Within two weeks of their arrival at Dartmoor, Ingram was transferred to Parkhurst Prison; he had complained that the Dartmoor climate was aggravating rheumatism he suffered in a leg injured on one of his raids. While there, Ingram mistakenly believed that Smithson had had two years knocked off his sentence. This was a challenge to the letter-writing, self-aggrandised victim of British justice, and he began a campaign to get his sentence reduced. He had been a well-behaved prisoner, but this ceased when his petition for a reduction in his sentence was refused. Angry letters to Home Secretary William Joynson-Hicks received only bland replies. He went on hunger strike.

Ingram endured two spells of forced feeding, in 1924 and 1925. Both times he struggled violently, doing nothing to earn him any sympathy. Forced feeding is an obscene practice, in which a prisoner's mouth is forced open and gagged: a tube is thrust between his teeth, down his throat and gullet, into his stomach, and liquid food is poured into a funnel attached to the tube. Many suffragettes suffered this indignity. In Ingram's case, and probably also with a number of suffragettes, this was carried out while as many as four warders held the head, arms and legs of the struggling patient. Lost teeth were considered to be the patient's own fault. The practice was carried out twice a day. It must be considered brave of a person to undergo such a practice for more than a few days. Ingram lasted seven months, took a respite of six months, and then had another spell of six months. All this time he was in conflict with prison warders, who were not slow in returning his punches. To give Ingram his due, he seems to have stood up to several at a time. It did him no good at all.

The cost to Ingram of his hunger strike was not only a serious loss of weight, it also cost him a cut in the amount of remission he would have received as a model prisoner. Instead of eighteen months' remission, he received ten and was probably lucky to have that. He was released late in 1928, one year earlier than Smithson, and existed on money stashed away before going inside.

IN OCTOBER 1925, Mike Spellman was jailed for a year for receiving the proceeds of a Hyde Park jewellery burglary. A married father of three living in Bethnal Green, he had previously been an associate of that other notorious receiver, Joseph 'Kemmy' Grizzard. Every time a major jewel robbery took place, Grizzard was suspected of handling the goods. He had a list of buyers ready to take quality merchandise off his hands. Thieves were attracted to him because he paid top prices and 'looked after' those who were caught after leaving their goods with him. He paid for their defence and, if they went to prison, looked out for their families. In this situation, it was unlikely that thieves would inform on him. Information that reached police came through the usual tangled network of informers, always too late for them to do anything more than search his home. He made his headquarters at the Three Nuns Hotel in Aldgate, later a meeting place for the notorious Three Nuns gang of pickpockets. His first sentence was five months for receiving stolen jewellery from Sam Barnett, who lived on his street.

In July 1913, a sealed, registered packet, containing a valuable oriental pearl necklace, was posted in Paris to an address in Hatton Garden, London's jewellery centre. It arrived the next day. Inside was a wooden case that, when opened, contained sugar lumps in place of the sixty-one pink/white matched pearls necklace. Examination showed that the package had been stealthily opened from beneath and re-sealed. Police in both countries traced the route of the packet and believed it had arrived in England unmolested, but the trail then ran cold. A reward of £10,000 was offered for recovery of the necklace, which was valued at £136,000.

Such a huge reward brought immediate information. Police were inundated with leads and spent time eliminating each one, until they were left with the name of Arthur Spain. A chief sorter of foreign mail at Mount Pleasant Sorting Office, Clerkenwell, he sometimes worked shifts on the cross-Channel ferry from France to Dover. Spain was known to police as a member of the Spanish Gang, named for his sons who operated as thieves and confidence tricksters from the Highbury district of north London. The Spanish Gang, naturally thought of as being Iberian in origin, were in fact all English: they were led by Georgie Spain and located at Highbury Corner and the pubs thereat, with a domain from Essex Road to Holloway Road. George was an unlicensed bookmaker, who would take bets on anything. In his later years, he owned a succession of cafés in Shoreditch, Hornsey, Highbury and Ridley Road market in Hackney, where he took bets and sometimes failed to pay up.

Arthur Spain's home in Canonbury was searched without result. However, the Spain brothers were known to shift their valuables through Kemmy Grizzard. Moreover he was most able to dispose of pearls, which, unlike diamonds, were impossible to re-cut or reshape. Surveillance of Grizzard followed and several meetings with visitors from Paris and New York were noted. Police guessed that a sale was being set up. Into their view came Lesir Gutwirth, who also lived in Canonbury, close to the Spain family. Finally, Grizzard came into the picture, when he was observed meeting with Gutwirth and Simon Silverman, who had an office in the same building in Hatton Garden where the package had been delivered. Police suspected that Silverman knew of the consignment, had asked Gutwirth to intercept it and Gutwirth had commissioned Spain to do the intercepting. The package was taken to Gutwirth's home and skilfully opened, then resealed with fake company seals, before being put back into the delivery system.

Police took a chance and pounced on Grizzard, Silverman and Jim Lockett, a burly burglar and hard man, recently released from Pentonville, as they left a lift at the British Museum Underground Station, High Holborn. They did not find the pearls, but found wax samples at the home of Gutwirth that matched the fake seals on the packet. Further enquiries led to the man who had made the seals. The evidence was put together to build a tenuous case. It was then discovered that prospective 'buyers', working for Lloyds insurance company, had been shown three loose pearls as an appetiser and had paid a reward for them.

Shortly after the arrests, a carpenter was strolling through Canonbury when he saw a woman dropping a packet into the gutter. He called after the woman, who was accompanied by a man, but they hopped onto a passing bus without acknowledging him. Inside the packet was a large matchbox containing fifty-eight loose pearls.

No doubt, Kemmy Grizzard deserved the seven-year sentence he received. The evidence was certainly flimsy, but the police wanted to put him away. Gutwirth, who most probably organised the theft and grassed up the others, got away with eighteen months; Silverman received five years and Lockett seven years. Arthur Spain, who police believed had been paid £200 to intercept the packet, was released without charge. As Gutwirth was in custody, it has to be considered that Spain either had a hole in his pocket or had rid himself of the package when he believed he was about to be arrested.

Grizzard took his sentence badly and complained constantly of ill health, which was probably a ploy. Charlie Gordon, who was in Portland Prison with him, wrote in his book *Crooks of the Underworld* that Grizzard spent much of his time in the prison hospital, after being diagnosed as diabetic. He was fed hearty fried breakfasts that were the envy of other prisoners. However, he was ostracised on the say-so of George Smithson, who said that Grizzard co-operated with police, by identifying burglars by their *modus operandi*, to avoid too close an inspection of his own misdeeds. He was released in 1921, six months earlier than normal good behaviour justified, something allowed to prisoners who co-operated in other ways.

Smithson and Ingram became celebrities. Both wrote books. Smithson told how he would ransack a house while the residents were inside and, when it suited him, would go from room to room, forcing desks and cabinets in a reckless manner. They described tense occasions when they were disturbed by servants and people trying doors they had locked from the inside, and the setting off of alarms.

On their final release, as ticket-of-leave men (Ingram in 1928, Smithson in 1929), both saw their books in print. Smithson's *Raffles in Real Life—The Confessions of George Smithson alias 'Gentleman George'* is the more reliable, though it has many gaps. This polished man, with his impish look, given to wearing a top hat and expensive clothes which he exchanged for cloth cap and scarf for work, made no excuses for his life of crime. He seems to have relished it. In his book, he refers to Ingram as Sikes, perhaps envisioning the apparition of Dickens's coarse burglar in his unsophisticated manner.

Papers released by the Home Office in 2006 clear up much of the mystery surrounding Smithson. He is referred to as William Weatherell (or Wetherill) as well as Smithson and Ratcliffe. Described as a native of Barnsley, Yorkshire, he was born in 1890. The clue that confirmed his identity was his arrest in Scotland as William Weatherill. It is difficult to understand why, when police knew his identity, he was allowed to stand trial as George Smithson, and Tragheim as Ingram.

Smithson was born William Weatherill, at Barnsley, Yorkshire. His father was a market gardener and strict Salvationist. At some time, he chose to be known as George Ernest Ratcliffe. This was probably not an official change of name, but it is the one he used when he was married at Kensington Register Office in 1922 to Blanche Hinkes, a domestic servant to whom he had been acquainted only two months. The marriage was witnessed by Alfred Tragheim (Ingram). Throughout his career, Smithson covered his tracks, and those of his family, through a maze of identities. Even on his marriage certificate he names his father as Walter Ratcliffe, not as Alfred Weatherill. At the time of their wedding, Blanche already had three illegitimate children, aged between six and nine years. She was born in St. Pancras and gave her address as Caledonian Road, King's Cross, just around the corner from where Italian gangster, Darby Sabini lived.

Smithson's Kensington flat, from where he launched his forays into the British countryside, has always been a mystery. Newspapers and police never revealed its address, although they did say that he was living at a rate of £20 a week, a prodigious amount in 1922. His marriage certificate gave his home as Ilchester Mansions, Abingdon Road, a turning off Kensington High Street. In 2010, a three-bedroom apartment might rent for around £900 per week and sell for a tad under £1,000,000.

In 1925, Smithson wrote letters from Dartmoor Prison demanding the return of valuables that had been taken from his Kensington flat. The response was a refusal and condemnation for his remarkable impudence. A later request was successful in having some unclaimed valuables returned to his wife.

When Smithson was released in 1929, he went to live with

Blanche in Guildford, Surrey. The last known of him is a letter from there in December 1929, signed G. Ratcliffe, in which he tells the Home Office that he is 'out of employment'. A note by the office states nothing unfavourable has been reported. Smithson died as George Ernest Ratcliffe in 1976, and his wife, Blanche Ratcliffe, in 1980, both in West Sussex.

George Smithson is often described as the senior partner in the slippery duo's exploits. However, Ingram also has a claim here. He may have been a less skilled burglar, but he was an adept manipulator: a lying rogue who was as cavalier with the truth as he was with other people's property and Smithson's trust. He used his alias, George Ingram, to co-write, with journalist DeWitt Mackenzie, *Hell's Kitchen* in 1930, a fairly sanitised version of his life and, in places, close to fantasy. He followed it with five novels of his own, all long out of print, but well received in their time. He used his prison experiences to good effect and received some excellent critical comment:

Stir (1933) is a novel about prison life that provides an insight into English prisons, even to the point of warders stealing prisoners' food supplies to sell. Ingram notes that 'unlike them, the burglar takes his chances'. He foresaw the two Dartmoor riots. *Stir Train* (1935) is an interesting story of detainees on a train, travelling across the United States to Ellis Island to be deported. Some are simply illegal entrants; others are criminals of one sort or another, including Mafia mobsters. *Cockney Cavalcade* followed in 1935. This novel centres on the MacDonald boys growing up in Hoxton and captures the flavour of the times: I felt a certain *déjà vu* in reading this tale. Jack MacDonald is a hard nut fiddling his way through life in London's East End. His younger brother, 'Mac', follows in his footsteps, to provide the drama of a boy going wrong who might yet be saved. His opening recalls the 'Battle of the Nile', when the Sabini Boys (Satani in the book) raid the Titanic gang in Hoxton and get a bloody nose. There are characters that can be identified with Eddie Emanuel, Dodger Mullins and others. Ingram comments on Jewish settlers in the East End and his book contains the earliest use of the word 'Yid' in British literature.

The Muffled Man (1936) is autobiographical in many ways. One can see George Smithson in Charlie Friend and Ingram in Sonny, the leading character. He manages to have Friend bumped off, which may be Freudian wish fulfilment, as the two no longer got on. The story concerns country house burglars working out of Notting Hill. *Welded Lives* (1939) does for Borstal what *Stir* did for English prisons. Ingram flags up Borstals as training grounds for future villainy. The institutions were intended as a means of reforming offenders aged between sixteen and twenty-one. Thye had tough physical fitness regimes, educational classes and long hours of work. Discipline was stern and small infringements were punished by time being added to sentences, or informally by strokes of the cane across a bare bottom. Birching was the only official form of corporal punishment and was used for the most serious offences, usually violence, and carried out in front of assembled inmates. It did have a deterrent effect, although it was customary for the toughest young men not to show fear.

Alfred Ernest Tragheim, *aka* George Ingram, died on 25 January 1976, in hospital in North Kensington following a heart attack. His home address in nearby Finstock Road was just a short walk from Wormwood Scrubs. His occupation was given as 'retired engineer'.

2

GANGS AND GANGSTERS

In These Mean Streets

Street Gangs

STREET GANGS BECAME a national concern in the United Kingdom from around 1870 onwards. Newspapers began to carry reports of their fights and they became known generally as 'scuttlers' in Manchester, 'sloggers' and later 'peaky blinders' in Birmingham, and 'cornermen' in Liverpool. Their principle pastime was fighting territorial battles against their neighbours, armed with buckled belts, sticks, stones, knives and even guns. Many of the gangs were identified simply by the streets where they lived, but others adopted colourful names: the Bengal Tigers in Ancoats, Manchester, Buffalo Bill's Gang in Salford, the High Rip in Liverpool and the Ten Arches in Aston, Birmingham. London too became plagued by street gangs in the same period, especially in the poor, overcrowded areas of east and south London. Hence some London gangs have long pedigrees: the Elephant and Castle gang began in the 1700s and did not run out of steam until the 1960s, while Clerkenwell gangs began in the 1880s and ran right through to the 1990s and the break-up of the notorious Adams gang.

In the early part of the nineteenth century, criminals infested London's rookeries, rundown areas of dense housing. The most notorious was a stinking slum surrounded by festering ditches at Jacob's Island, on the Bermondsey side of the Thames. This served for Dickens's description of Fagin's den of thieves in Oliver Twist and where his villain, Bill Sikes, comes to grief. Another, at Clerkenwell, straddled the area between Farringdon Road, Clerkenwell Green and St. John's Street. A short distance away, running south from Old Street, was the notorious St. Luke's rookery, and close to that was the St. Giles rookery, covering the area where Tottenham Court Road tube station now stands. These rookeries bred and attracted thieves, who targeted the better off parts of London: Highbury, Hampstead, the West End and the City. In east and southeast London, targets included docks and cargo ships. The ghettos had high incidences of murder and provided the hangmen with hundreds of clients. They contained 'flash houses' that served as training places for young thieves and meeting places for established thieves to plan robberies and sell or exchange their plunder. The narrow streets were crammed with dilapidated dwellings and underground escape routes weaved their way through the slums, makeing-police raids unproductive and hazardous. When the rookeries were cleared in the mid-1800s, the crooks remained and simply operated from better premises. A series of incidents give a flavour of the underworld at the turn of the Nineteenth Century into the Twentieth, much of it involving teenagers.

One of the most notable of the early gangs was the Green Gate, named after the Green Gate public house in City Road, Hoxton, east London. Once a wealthy area, Hoxton had been abandoned by its middle classes, who were lured out to the space and fresh air of the new suburbs. Their place was taken by poor workers, serving the heavy industries that boomed after the completion of the Regents Canal in 1820, and soon the area became one of the most densely populated in Europe. Conditions were ideal for the rise of gangs.

On 18 December 1881, twenty to thirty of the Green Gate set out to 'pay', or beat up, the rival Lambeth Boys, based south of the river. They made a foray down to the Thames Embankment, between Waterloo and Blackfriars, in search of their quarry, and two of them split off to confront two young men, Arthur Thompson and Frederick Willmore. The two Green Gates pretended to be from Lambeth.

'Do you know anyone from the City Road?' asked James Casey.

'No,' said Willmore.

'We come from Lambeth; we hold with Lambeth, do you?' lied Casey.

'Yes,' said Willmore, foolishly.

'We want to pay the City Road Boys if we can catch them. You say you come from Lambeth; what do you use when you fight?'

'We use our fists,' said Willmore.

'Do you use any of these?' said the Green Gate lad, and showed his belt, which bore a large, square, brass buckle: a customary weapon.

Willmore said, 'No,' and lifted up his own waistcoat to show he wasn't wearing one.

'You say you come from Lambeth,' said Casey. 'We don't, we come from the City Road, and we are going to pay the Lambeth chaps.' With that, he called to the rest of his mob. 'Here are two of the Lambeth lads. Thrash them!'

Arthur Thompson later took up the story before a court:

> Then the one that was by the side of the one who had had all the conversation struck Willmore on the nose with his fist; the gang then came up and started thrashing us with their belts. I think there were about twenty in the gang. [James] Casey is one of the two who first came up to us, and the one who had all the conversation, but not the one who struck the blow. The gang started thrashing me with their belts and pulled off my hat. All that I could see had belts, except the one that struck Willmore on the nose. I was knocked down, but I got up again. My head was cut at the back, and I was bruised down the back. I saw Willmore struck and knocked down; he was struck with the fist; nothing else that I saw. I saw the others make for him with their belts, but I could not see whether they hit him or not; the best part of them made for him. I saw him on the ground, and I ran into the road and called out for help.

A gentleman came across the road to me. He went to
the side of Willmore, who was bleeding from the head:
blood was running down on to the pavement.

As Willmore lay mortally wounded, he said, 'Please God, I get
over this I will give the City Road fellows the severest hiding
as ever they had.' A hansom cab took him to Charing Cross
Hospital but he died, on 14 January 1882.

Thomas Galliers and James Casey, both aged twenty, were
charged with murder. Casey said he had been standing on
a street corner when about a dozen of the City Road Boys
asked if he would go down the Embankment. He declined,
but later went there with some friends and saw a young man
lying on the pavement. He helped two of the gang to pick him
up and put him in a hansom cab, to be taken to Charing Cross
Hospital. He then added to police that he heard that Patrick
Kennedy had knocked the man down with a file and that
Joe Plenty and Joe Raynor had got stuck in with their boots.
Kennedy was one of a gang of teenagers currently on trial
for an unrelated assault. Galliers, who was blamed for throwing the first punch to Willmore's face, tried to blame another
gang: the Fann Street Boys. Neither story worked. Kennedy
lived several miles away in the upper reaches of Hackney,
while the Fann Street Boys were located in Shoreditch, and
neither had had any part in the affray. Galliers was found guilty
and sentenced to ten years penal servitude. The jury could not
agree on Casey and he was discharged.

The affair that did involve Patrick 'Patsy' Kennedy, and that
was being tried at the same time, had interrupted Christmas
celebrations in Hackney in 1881. On Christmas Eve, a gang
came down Ottaway Street in Lower Clapton, known as 'Tiger
Bay', and picked a quarrel with Charles 'Ginger' Eaton outside
his home at number nine. The attackers were the Dove Row
gang from Haggerston. Eaton fought back. He explained in
court, 'I went into them the same as they did to me, and took

my own defence.' The nineteen-year-old Eaton handled himself well enough for the gang to run off, pursued by Eaton's father waving a poker. They shouted back that they would remember Eaton when they came again.

Late on New Year's Day, the trouble shifted to the Rendlesham Arms in Stillman Street, Clapton, when about twenty of the Dove Row gang went looking for Eaton. When they failed to find him, they started a general rumpus that quickly got out of hand. Three pub dwellers were stabbed in the face, one of whom nearly died from a severed artery. Police rounded up seven Dove Row boys: William Hubbard, David Jennings, Henry Kirby, Frederick Ball, Patrick Kennedy, David Williams, and John Collins. They were charged with riot and wounding. Kennedy was aged twenty; the rest were in their late teens. Others were charged with occasioning actual bodily harm. John Collins denied being there but did admit once belonging to the street fighting gang in the days when Old Nichol Street, in Bethnal Green, fought Dove Row. He had given it up after his head was split in three places. The Central Criminal Court did not believe him. He, Hubbard and Kirby were jailed for twelve months, while Jennings, Ball, Kennedy and Williams got eighteen months, all with hard labour (compulsory physical work imposed in addition to imprisonment).

The Green Gate gang made the news again on 21 February 1882, when Samuel Wallers was attacked by George Collins on Shaftesbury Street, close to City Road. The argument had been about the merits of teetotallers, who Collins had little regard for. When his offer of a drink from a flask was refused, he informed Wallers that he was a pugilist: 'pu', he said, meant hit, 'gi' meant hard, and 'list' meant bloody hard. He then knocked Wallers down. The fifty-one-year-old Collins' belief in his pugilistic ability came unstuck when Wallers got up and knocked him down. Collins regained his feet and pulled a pistol from his pocket, only for Wallers to brush it aside and knock him down again. At this, the gun went off. Two policemen heard the shot and came and arrested Collins, taking two guns from him.

Collins stated that Wallers was one of the Green Gate gang, something Wallers denied. It may be that, because the gang had recently been in the news, Collins had sought to enlist their name to tar his opponent and so support his own defence. A doctor who examined Collins said he had two black eyes, a bite on his arm, a wound from a kick on his shin, a bruise on each hip, and a swollen throat where he had been gripped. A judge at the Central Criminal Court, who had some sympathy for him, gave him only eight days and a fine of twenty shillings, even though he had two loaded guns in his possession.

Guns seem to have been a more serious problem among the London street gangs than in Manchester and Liverpool. On 31 May 1885, William Brown, aged sixteen, Harry Foxcroft, eighteen, and a man named Mason shot James Page in Upper Street, Islington, in return for a previous attack on some of their pals. They then threatened John 'Bunny' Ayres, a resident of White Lion Street, one of the most violent locations in London, with similar treatment.

'We have just shot a fellow in Upper Street,' he was told, 'and we have got a bullet left for you.'

Mason pulled a knife from his sleeve and Ayres ran for his life. A few days later, they approached him again.

'We are only waiting for you to get round a quiet turning,' said Brown ominously. 'We mean to do for you coming down and paying our lads.'

Ayres escaped again, but they caught up with him a third time in Chapel Street, where Foxcroft and six others accused him of fighting one of their lads. Witnesses heard one say, 'What are we going to do, lads?'

'Do as we said,' replied another.

Ayres was hit across the arm with a belt as Brown and others came up on a whistled signal. Brown punched him in the face and Ayres ran to a coalshed to escape, but the door was locked. Foxcroft pulled a long-bladed knife and stabbed him in the arm.

Brown, who admitted wounding Page and firing a shot at Harry Hobbs, received five years' penal servitude, Foxcroft, who resided at Easton Street, Clerkenwell, which was another notorious north London location, got eighteen months with hard labour.

WEST LONDON TOO was gripped by street warfare. In 1888, a long-running series of fights were staged between the Fitzroy Place Boys, from the back of Tottenham Court Road, and the Lisson Grove gang, from Marylebone. Matters came to a head in May, when Frank Cole of the Fitzroy crowd was found with his girlfriend, Cissy Chapman, in rival territory outside Madame Tussaud's Waxworks on Marylebone Road. Cole was challenged by two Lisson Grove Boys.

'Do you know any of the Fitzroy Place lads?' one asked.

'Yes, and glad to know them too,' came Cole's not-too-clever reply.

Twenty more lads were whistled up to help punch and kick Cole to the ground, giving Cissy a black eye when she asked why it took so many of them.

The following evening, Cole gathered together seven or eight friends and went looking for revenge. They met at 'the Fair', a disused ground between Tottenham Court Road and Whitfield Street, where they were joined by a half-dozen others. Soon, they spotted a Lisson lad in nearby Howland Street: David Cleary and George Galletly knocked him down and kicked him. Then they set off to search the Green Man public house on Euston Road and, finding nothing, moved on to Regent's Park, a collecting point for the Lisson Grove gang.

It was there that Joe Rumbold and a girl passed some of the gang, who jostled him. A brief row followed and Galletly pulled a knife and stabbed Rumbold twice in the back and neck. He staggered a few hundred yards before collapsing, later dying in a cab taking him to hospital.

Police arrested eight youths, including George Alexander Galletly, who was aged seventeen, and charged them with murder. Galletly was turned in by David Cleary and Thomas Brown, two of the lads who had been with him and had taken part in previous fights. They saw a newspaper notice offering a pardon in exchange for evidence. Both denied being members of the Fitzroy Place gang and the Decker Gang (a misnaming by police of the Dials gang, from Seven Dials). Evidence suggests they were more involved than they admitted, and saw a chance to put everything on Galletly, who appears to have been avenging Cissy Chapman's black eye rather than Frank Cole's cuts and bruises. He was sentenced to death, later commuted to life imprisonment due to his age. Cole and others were sentenced to short terms with hard labour.

IN THE 1890s, clashes between the Somers Town Boys, located just north of King's Cross, and the Clerkenwell Boys, from south of Pentonville Road, led to several shootings and stabbings. Police described the gang members as being employed in their spare time in faction fighting. Gangs were able to buy firearms from pawnbrokers for around ten shillings apiece and it was not unusual for twenty or more youths to wander the streets looking for rivals to shoot at.

On 17 October 1891, the gangs clashed inside Sadler's Wells Theatre in Islington, a music hall at the time. They went at it with some relish until the outnumbered Clerkenwell Boys, led by sixteen-year-old Harry Hobbs, had to be rescued by a group of navvies. A number of youths were evicted from the theatre. Amongst them was James Bassett, who waited outside for Somers Town boys John Moore and James Sessions. In a flash of frenzy, he stabbed Moore in the head and various other parts of his body, and Sessions in the back. Sixteen-year–old Bassett was sentenced to six months with hard labour for unlawful wounding: this, however, failed to cure him. In February 1897, he went back inside for three years' penal servitude for robbery with violence – and would be heard from again.

John Carey, nineteen, and John Roach, twenty, were sentenced in December 1895 to terms with hard labour, for robbery with violence on Henry Daniels in Ann Street, close to Commercial Road, Whitechapel. This brought into focus the existence of an East End gang calling themselves the Forty Thieves. Carey was stated to be the leader, and Roach a member, and both had previous convictions for robbery. On this occasion, a constable saw them kneeling over their victim and rifling through his pockets. He gave chase and three other constables were on hand to join in. Carey was brought down by PC Walter Rickery and Roach was arrested at a nearby lodging house.

A number of gangs went by the name Forty Thieves, the most famous being one in 1820s New York and another later on in south London. Carey remained a member of the east London version and was jailed again in 1896, with three others, for burglary. Police described them as members of a dangerous gang. In 1906, Carey was sentenced to five years penal servitude, with Jeremiah Barry and Samuel Bromley, for robbery with violence. On this occasion they were said to be some of the most desperate men in east London.

On 7 March 1897, fifty to sixty Bethnal Green Boys, forerunners of Dodger Mullins' gang, went hunting for Hackney's Broadway Boys, a street mob that located at Haggerston: they fired shots at any they came across. Terrified residents ducked bullets whizzing overhead, ricocheting off buildings and smacking into shops. A shower of bottles and bricks accompanied the pistol shots. Charles Luton was shot in the knee and lamed. Joseph Norton, who dodged six bullets, hid and watched the gang run by. He then followed and grabbed

Joseph Fitzpatrick and held him for the police. Frederick Millard had five shots fired at him and, in the harsh employment
environment of the time, lost his job for attending police court
on four occasions. George Morgan had a revolver pointed in
his face and was asked if he was one of the Broadway fellows,
to which he was pleased to reply that he was not. He watched
them fire shots at a young man and into an ice-cream shop.
Six youths, aged sixteen to nineteen, were arrested after witnesses reported seeing them dumping revolvers into Regent's
canal. Six months with hard labour was the reward for Bethnal
Green's Tommy Curtis and Joe Fitzpatrick. Police spoke of
scores of youths wandering the streets, most armed with sticks,
but recently with guns that could be bought in Hackney cattle
market for as little as £1.

On 23 June 1897, Hoxton's Charlie Pinchion and Robert
'Hobnail' Rodway were messing about, as young men do
when they are out for a bit of mischief. They pushed a man off
his bike, who got up and gave one of them a good hiding, so
they ran to Fanshaw Street, near Hoxton Square, where they
took their spleen out on Robert West. Pinchion, eighteen,
stabbed him close to his heart and nearly killed him, although
West managed to follow Pinchion and take the knife from
him. Pinchion was described by police as the leader of a gang
of roughs who were in conflict with a gang called Bishop's
Boys, named for one Henry Bishop. The result of their night's
mischief was hard labour, fifteen months for Pinchion and
eight for Rodway.

On the subject of mischief, Halloween worked its magic
on 31 October 1897 in Islington, when the Pentonville Boys
challenged the Grosvenor Street Boys to a fight, as part of
an ongoing war. These particular Grosvenors were schoolboys,
who considered the offer then declined it. No matter: Billy
Bond shot Alfred Webb in the leg. Bond had declared his
intention of shooting someone that night and it appears he
believed Webb had shown some inclination to fight. Bond's

act brought him fourteen days' imprisonment and three years in a Reformatory. Police Inspector Morgan told the court that, within a twenty-mile area of the attack, about twenty youths under the age of twenty had been charged with possessing firearms and, in some cases, inflicting injury.

James Bassett, when released from his three years prison sentence in 1900, was soon at it again. This time it was over money owed for the pawning of a pair of trousers. Bassett and 'Nobby' Carroll broke into Alfred Worms' house, in search of retribution. When they failed to find him, they went to Baldwin's Gardens, Clerkenwell, and found Worms in conversation with Bassett's sister, Catherine. Bassett rushed at Worms and struck him in the mouth with a knife. Only the intervention of Catherine prevented further damage.

Police tracked Bassett to Gray's Inn Road, where their first attempt to arrest him resulted in PC John Bissell being shoved through the plate glass window of a shop. Two officers chased and caught Bassett, who continued to struggle all the way to the police station. In court, Catherine remembered whose side she was supposed to be on and stated that it was Worms who had attacked her brother with a knife. However, it did not prevent Bassett going down for twelve months. The Worms family were well known in Clerkenwell as receivers of stolen goods. Later, they married into the infamous Sabini family.

The name Sabini came up at the Central Criminal Court in June 1898, when Augustus, of Eyre Hill Street in the heart of Clerkenwell Sabini territory, was shot at by a crowd of about thirty boys. It appears on this occasion that a Sabini was an innocent victim, who had declined to have a fight. One youth, sixteen-year-old Alfred Smith, had the indignity of being given one days' imprisonment.

Better-off neighbourhoods had no immunity to gang warfare. In 1900, Chelsea's Bay Boys and Sands End Boys received a note from their near neighbours, the Manor Street Boys, to come and fight, a follow-up to a previous skirmish outside

Lewis's Club in King's Road. They met in Oakham Street (now Oakley Street), once the home of explorer Robert Falcon Scott and close to the residences of writers and the professional classes: here they battled with studded belts with large buckles. Blood splattered the pavement as gangs of teenagers went at it. Evidence suggests the two gangs had been warring for some time, mostly with their heavy-buckled belts, a popular weapon at the time, as they could be worn legitimately but could cause considerable damage. Sentences of six and nine months with hard labour were the only positive results.

The year 1902 saw the emergence of one of east London's more formidable villains, when John McCarthy was jailed for wounding Whitechapel street bookie Meyer Edgar, from whom he had frequently demanded money. This was a classic example of the danger of being an unlicensed bookie in the East End. Four men – Johnny McCarthy, alias Bonn, said by his victim to be the leader of a gang of 'twelve murderers', Harry Sharper, James Brooks and Jimmy Edwards – rushed into the Black Bull public house in Whitechapel. Sharper punched Edgar, poked him in the eye with a billiard cue and then broke it over his head. Brooks stepped forward with a dagger to finish the job, but was pushed away by McCarthy, who took out a hammer and cracked poor Edgar's nut three or four times, before smashing a water jug over it. Edgar lay unconscious for ninety minutes before staggering to a police station to make a complaint.

Edgar owned a billiards hall that formed part of the Black Bull, where he put on unlicensed boxing matches and organised illegal gambling. Fights often featured West Indian pugilist Frank 'Kid' McCoy, who travelled with boxing shows and worked as a bodyguard to Mabel Priestly, a notorious Bethnal Green madam. In 1911, McCoy was jailed for twelve months for assauting two men and a woman, who had objected to Mabel living with a coloured man. Edgar, who suffered constant demands for protection money, claimed everyone was scared of McCarthy and his gang, who carried firearms. The gang, sometimes called the Watney Streeters, extracted money from a host of illegal gambling dens, squashed into the alleyways of Whitechapel and Bethnal Green. They were being investigated over a fire in a spieler in Saint Thomas's Street, where a woman and two children suffered burns. Sharper, McCarthy and Brooks were sentenced to five years penal servitude and Edwards to four.

In October 1902, Russian Jews belonging to the Bessarabian Society were in conflict with Polish Jews belonging to the Odessa Society. The quarrel, which stemmed from racial differences in their home country, was continued in Whitechapel. On top of this, both were deeply into squeezing money and favours from immigrant tradespeople, who could not go to the police for fear of arrest for their own illicit occupations. The 'Bessas', who had the strongest grip on the protection business, were challenged by envious Odessas. A series of fights culminated in a good old barney in the York Minster pub in Philpot Street, squashed into the area in which Jack Spot and the Kray twins would later blossom. Lots of cuttings and shootings led to one death and several prison sentences for the Bessa Arabs. Their leader was thirty-year-old ex-professional boxer Kid McCoy (not related to Frank 'Kid' McCoy), real name Max Moses.[1] He received ten years. His second-in-command, Sam Oreman, had stabbed Henry Bordovitz to death and was lucky to receive only five years for manslaughter. This flurry of activity ended both gangs' existence.

AT THE TURN of the century, London became a focal point for criminal gangs. Mass immigration had seen a wave of Irish,

---

1 Any boxer using the surname McCoy was inevitably nicknamed 'Kid', after the colourful American middleweight Kid McCoy, real name Norman Selby.

Scots, Jews and Italians arriving, plus a homegrown influx from the English countryside and cities. Unemployment became a major problem, to the point where many Britons sought refuge in the United States, bringing some respite to provincial cities. Soldiers returning from the Boer War swelled the number of unemployed. Other major cities, especially Manchester, saw a decline in gang activity, which was often attributed to the success of the new Lads' Club movement and the growth in popularity of sports such as football, which diverted youthful energies from violence. However, the capital saw, if anything, a movement toward more serious forms of gangsterism. While some old street and neighbourhood rivalries persisted, the heavier street thugs graduated to organised or semi-organised villainy.

Joblessness inevitably leads to an increase in gambling, prostitution and petty and organised crime. All sections of the city's vast working class communities now turned their hand to making a living by any means, only relenting for a spell at the onset of World War One. With the stretching of police resources, to deal with an increasingly militant women's suffrage movement, the scene was set for a new chapter in the story of London's gangland.

The Trampling Herd

THE ELEPHANT AND Castle gang were the premier mob in south London. They were usually referred to as the Elephant Gang or the Elephant Boys, the latter alluding to their younger element. Detective Inspector George W. Cornish described them as being better dressed and more intelligent than other gangs that targeted the city's lucrative West End. The Elephant Gang was in its prime between the world wars, although it had already existed for over 100 years by that time; it was named in newspapers as early as 1873, when sixteen-year-old Charles Bishop was charged with highway robbery. Its activities covered a broad range of villainy, from petty crime to large-scale organised activity and gang warfare.

The gang was a sprawling army of smash-and-grab artists, burglars, receivers, hard men, crafty villains, with an adjunct of female shoplifters known as the Forty Thieves. It was centred on the southeast London district of the Elephant and Castle, at the junction of the boroughs of Southwark and Lambeth. It gave protection to individual crooks, such as pickpocket Camberwell Sam Moss and prolific warehouse breaker Georgie Wilson, who operated strictly in south London and used the gang for fencing. Wilson was a habitual criminal with convictions dating back to 1889. He got his comeuppance in 1910, when sentenced to three years penal servitude, followed by five years preventive detention, for stealing from the railway. Police described him as a one-man crimewave.

The Elephant and Castle gang would control much of London right up to the 1950s, through successive leaders Albert Gorman, George Moss, Wag McDonald, Tommy Benneworth,

Wal McDonald, Billy Howard and Johnny Carter, and their alliances with the Camden Town gang and Jack Spot's East-enders. They were in fact many gangs within a gang. Among the early leaders were: the Gorman brothers; Billy Endelson, who had more brains than brawn; George Hatfield, known as the 'chief welsher', who had the run of the racing men; Charlie and Frank Pitts, credited with the original organi-sation of shoplifting sprees; and George 'Mad Mossy' Moss, their 'top man' and one of the ubiquitous pests that infested racecourses.

Albert and James Gorman were born in Kennington, in 1863 and 1868 respectively, to parents William and Mary. By the time of the 1881 census, the family resided at Upper Marsh, Lambeth, where it was headed by Mary: William had died in 1877. The boys were constantly before the courts for every type of racing scam, often with the use of violence. In one trial, Police Sergeant John Gillan described them as part of a dangerous gang of thieves who terrorised bookmakers and punters through blackmail and welshing. One trick was to hand in a betting slip with hidden writing in invisible ink, which later became visible, enabling a claim to be made for a race they already knew the result of.

In 1889, Albert Gorman married Minnie Ralph in Lambeth. Married life failed to tame him and, in June 1891, he, George Lester and Jim Davis were charged with highway robbery in Kennington Road, Lambeth. A man had been knocked down, kicked in the head and had his pockets rifled. The case col-lapsed when the victim admitted to being drunk and hav-ing previously engaged in betting activities with two of the accused, on one occasion betting one cigar against two on the result of the Derby. The incident was regarded as a scrap between racing men.

Four months later, Albert Gorman and Davis were found not guilty of fraud, after they were accused of handing a bet-ting slip to a north London street bookie, on which wording gradually appeared with the name of a winning horse in an earlier race. On the same day, Albert and James, together with Richard Price, were acquitted of fraud for offering a betting slip with invisible writing to a Camden Town bookie. They were next cleared again of a similar charge, but on a third charge, on the same day, Albert was convicted and given twelve months with hard labour. In 1896, Albert, John Nolan and John Wheeler were arrested for affray. Albert was acquitted, Nolan and Wheeler jailed and Wheeler given twenty strokes of the 'cat'. Police said tradesmen were afraid to come forward and give evidence against this violent gang, who made their living though blackmail.

In 1906, Albert handed a betting slip to bookmaker Harry Cavanagh, who watched in amazement as words began to appear, showing winners from a previous race. Two years with hard labour was Albert's reward. It was his fifth offence, one of which had brought him three years. In 1908, his brother James, aged thirty-seven, died after a brawl in the Borough: no one seems to have been blamed.

Leadership of the Elephant and Castle gang passed to George Moss and Charlie Guerin, who formed an early alliance with the Birmingham gang. This combination of south Londoners and 'Brummagems' would terrorise bookmakers across the country (see Part Three), though the gang's more outlandish activities were restrained with the arrival of the McDonald brothers and Billy Kimber.

PROTECTION GANGSTERS ALSO plagued small businesses in the East End of London. Chief among them was John 'Jack' Marks, a vicious thug born in Bethnal Green in 1871. In 1891, he received seven years plus twenty strokes of the 'cat' for highway robbery with violence; he then served four years for brawling and a further twenty months for assault. In 1902, he and his sister Ellen, known as Dolly, were jailed for robbery with violence: John got four years and Ellen, who had ten previous convictions, three years. By 1906, John had picked up nine convictions, mostly for violence.

Others were by then contesting his authority, and he came under attack from the Bethnal Green gang of Arthur Harding and William Emms (also known as Ed Spencer). Marks demanded money and free drinks in the King's Arms in Sclater Street, Shoreditch, while Harding's gang were lounging in the snug. When his demands were refused, Marks knocked down two men, but then came up against Emms, who he had inflicted battle scars on in previous fights. This time Emms smashed a glass in his face and Harding's gang gave Marks a pasting. Emms was charged with wounding.

In court, various witnesses, including Harding, said it was Marks's fault and that Emms had been forced into the fight. Emms was acquitted, mostly due to Marks admitting his past criminal record during cross-examination.

IN 1906, JAMES BASSETT was back. With four of the Clerkenwell Boys, he robbed Martin Julian of his drinking money. Julian had treated them to a drink and, to show their gratitude, they followed him home, bashed him over the head and rifled through his pockets. Julian was brought round by people washing his face. Police arrested Bassett, James Granville and William Davis and charged them with robbery with violence. Police Sergeant John Bissell, no doubt remembering his passage through the plate glass window, informed the court that he overheard Bassett say to Davis, 'You keep quiet; I will get you out of it. I know Julian. If he prosecutes me I will do him properly.' His plan seems to have worked: they all got off.

On 6 October 1906, around a dozen Donkey Row members descended on The Ship public house at Stepney Green, in search of George Davis, who they had fought with on several occasions.

'Here you are, Bill,' said one of the gang. 'Here is Davis. We'll kill him.'

At that, Bill Wake, aged seventeen, fired two shots at Davis, missing both times. PC William Rose heard the shots and arrested Wake, whom he described in court as a dangerous hooligan and member of the Donkey Row (the local name for Carr Street, Limehouse) gang. Six months with hard labour was the punishment.

Gang fights were punctuated by regular muggings. On 11 December 1906, James Lynch was robbed of cash by two men in Whitechapel. A claim by defendant James Hughes that he was drunk cut no ice with the judge, after he heard that Hughes was the leader of the Brick Lane gang and had a number of previous convictions for theft. He was said to be an associate of the worst thieves. His sentence was three years penal servitude.

IN 1907, GANGSTER Eddie Guerin (no relation to Charlie) became the focus of London's underworld scene. Eddie, often thought to be American, was in fact British. He was born at Robert Street, Hoxton, east London, in 1862, to Irish parents who had married in Chicago. Robert Street was north of present-day Pittfield Street and not far from Nile Street, a notorious breeding ground for pickpockets. Eddie and his parents returned to Chicago in 1867. As a youth, he was arrested there and in Canada for petty crimes. In 1880, he was a labourer living in lodgings in Rochester, New York. By 1887, he was wanted by the Pinkerton Detective Agency for an attempted bank robbery and shooting down a police officer to escape arrest. He fled to England in that year. In January 1901, he married Emily Chapman and became a Soho fixture, taking part in an attempt to rob a Post Office. For this he was sent to Holloway Prison, which still housed male inmates at that time. He was released within two months and deserted

Emily to rekindle an affair with 'Chicago May' Churchill, who he had bumped into at the Horseshoe Hotel in Tottenham Court Road.

In April 1901, he and American pickpocket 'Dutch Lonzo' Henne stepped up a few grades: they robbed the Paris offices of the American Express Company of about $200,000 in cash and cheques by blowing the safe. They were soon arrested and sentenced to terms at the French prison complex on the Îles du Salut in French Guiana. Guerin's sweetheart, Chicago May, received five years for being an accomplice, although she served less due to her co-operation with French police.

Chicago May was born Mary Ann Duignan in Dublin, in about 1871. She ran away to New York after stealing money from her father. At fifteen, she married Albert 'Dal' Churchill, a bank robber from Rock Bluffs, Nebraska, who claimed to have ridden with the Dalton gang. He was in fact one of a minor band of store robbers, who graduated to higher things in 1891 when they robbed a train in Arizona. They were captured by a disgruntled posse who curtailed their ambition by hanging them from telegraph poles. May moved to New York, married conman Jim Sharpe, and took to prostitution and extortion through the badger game of luring clients to rooms where they were robbed. She appears to have met Guerin in 1901.

In 1905, Guerin escaped with the help of friends who smuggled him money to bribe guards. Others escaped with him, but only he was rescued by a British ship that found him adrift in a small boat. This gave rise to the legend that he had eaten his partners; just what others were doing while he was consuming one of them is never suggested. Guerin revelled in his daring 'escape from Devil's Island', even though he had escaped from the mainland, the notorious island prison having closed before his confinement.

In 1906, Eddie returned to his wife, now known as Emily Skinner. This upset Chicago May, who tried to force him to return to her by threatening to notify French authorities where he was hiding. When Guerin returned her threats, she grassed him to Scotland Yard and he was arrested in London. Whilst held in Brixton Prison, Eddie met an American who was another old sweetheart of May, Charlie Cubine, also known by the names Cubby Jackson and Charlie Smith. Guerin sought to persuade him to throw acid in May's face. However, Cubine was acquitted of the charge of burglary for which he was being held and then told May what was in store for her. She rewarded him with a passionate affair. Guerin avoided extradition to France by claiming he was still British and was released in 1907. The following year he was arrested as a suspicious person after being observed entering banks and making notes. He was acquitted after explaining that he was researching a book and needed up-to-date information on bank security systems.

When Guerin was released, May was terrified at the thought of the acid attack and decided to get in first. On 15 June 1907, with Cubine, she tracked him and Emily to their love nest in Marchmont Street, Bloomsbury. Cubine jumped out of a hansom cab and fired five shots; only one hit Guerin, in the foot. Cubine also aimed his revolver at two constables and squeezed the trigger several times, but was out of bullets. He was grabbed by the constables and some passing civilians, who wrested the gun from him. When May tried to intervene, Emily pointed her out to a constable who had run to investigate what the fuss was about. May was arrested and both were charged with attempted murder.

At the Old Bailey, Guerin reluctantly gave evidence and received some choice words from the dock. The pair treated their trial as a joke – until they were found guilty and severely sentenced by Mr Justice Darling, a most erratic judge. Cubine got life and May fifteen years. Feeling less than jocular, they exploded with rage. May had to be carried from court; Cubine ranted and raved as he was bustled down the steps of the dock.

CARR STREET WAS the scene of another incident when, on 25 August 1907, Donkey Row gang member Alfred Potter fired a gunshot at a schoolboy. Potter, himself only sixteen, had been showing off with a revolver given to him by a mate: his victim suffered a slight wound to his armpit. Potter admitted previously belonging to the 'Forties', the shortened name of the Forty Thieves, another Stepney street gang. He was found guilty of common assault and placed in the care of a boys' home.

October 1907 saw an eruption of violence at King's Cross, when the Clerkenwell Boys and their allies, the White Lion Street gang, clashed with the Bemerton Boys. The action took place around Caledonian Road and Copenhagen Street. On 13 October, the Clerkenwell Boys confronted William Churchwood in the Swan pub in Caledonian Road and demanded to know where he was from. When he said he was from Bemerton Street, and proud of it, he was punched and kicked by those that could get at him. He managed to crash out of the pub and ran into Charlotte Street, where John Harmond fired two shots at him. He ducked into the nearby Rothbury pub just as three bullets whizzed his way. Friends of Churchwood came up and attacked Harmond; fourteen-year-old Frank Lewis did his bit for the Bemertons by pointing out to a policeman that Harmond had put a revolver in his pocket. PC James Syred arrested Harmond. Describing the incident in court, Syred said that thirty to forty youths were running about terrorising the neighbourhood.

William Churchwood denied he was a member of the Bemerton Boys and claimed he was an innocent victim. Harmond was found guilty of shooting at Churchwood with intent to do him bodily harm. Although only seventeen, he had previous convictions for disorderly behaviour and had been disowned by his father. He was given three months with hard labour to consider the way life was leading him.

Four days later, on 17 October, the White Lion Street gang took up the cudgels on behalf of the Clerkenwell Boys. They arrived in Copenhagen Street to avenge John Harmond. This time the Bemertons were ready for them and were armed with shooters themselves. A running fight developed, with shots being fired by both sides. Police arrived in time to witness some of the gunplay: they arrested Henry Hunter after seeing him send shots after the fleeing William Churchwood. Others said that Churchwood also had a gun and was seen to fire at Hunter. Churchwood went into the police pot and others from both sides were rounded up.

At the Central Criminal Court, Hunter admitted being one of the Clerkenwell Boys, but said he had picked up the gun in the street. Arthur Francis, a Bemerton Boy, was seen to fire a derringer. Thomas Streetin, of the White Lions, was accused of shooting at Churchwood, and Churchwood was accused of shooting at Streetin. Police said there had been a long-running gang war that brought terror to the neighbourhood. Despite this, and the clear threat to life, the sentences handed down were very short: Henry Hunter, aged nineteen, Frederick Dyson, seventeen, William Churchwood, nineteen, Arthur Francis, nineteen, and Thomas Streetin, nineteen, all received two months in prison; three others received just a month.

In Bermondsey, in April 1908, Elephant and Castle gang member Edward Connell inflicted grievous injuries on publican Thomas Causer, who had given evidence against Reuben Vaughan for defrauding him of £10. Vaughan, who had a bad record, had been given a six-year prison sentence. Connell was described as a member of a dangerous gang of racecourse thieves and was given eighteen months with hard labour.

The Forty Thieves were heard from again in April 1908. Their leader, George Johnson, headed up a gang of thirty or forty youths seeking Alfred Fox, who had upset them in some way. They knocked on his door and called him into the street, where they surrounded him and called on Johnson to 'fire' with his gun. His first shot went into the ground and two more narrowly missed Fox as he ran to his home. Johnson, who was arrested at Carr Street (Donkey Row), was described as the leader of a gang that terrorised the neighbourhood of Limehouse and went about armed with belts, sticks and revolvers, using them indiscriminately. He was jailed for three months with hard labour.

In June 1908, two members of the Forties fell out, in what may have been a contest to find a successor to George Johnson. Roger Hellen went to George White's place of work and invited him to fight. White said he would fight him in the evening: Hellen thought for a moment, then pulled a knife from his sleeve and stabbed White in the chest. White's employer detained Hellen for the police. Doubt as to just what had been going on resulted in the eighteen-year-old Herren being bound over.

On 29 April 1908, there was a falling out between the Globe and Duckett Street gangs and the Bow Boys that resulted in two bystanders being being hit in the leg by ricocheting bullets. About twenty-five youths were involved in the scrimmage. Seventeen-year-old George Askew, of the Globe gang, panicked when he saw the opposing side heading towards him. He pulled a revolver from his trouser pocket and fired two shots into the ground, with the effect of wounding the two lads. In court, Askew was said to be living in very bad surroundings and to be going around with a rough gang. He said he had bought the gun for three shillings. He had recently been cautioned for disorderly conduct and, on this occasion, was sent for Borstal training.

The Silver Hatchet gang occupied a manor from Hoxton's City Road to Highbury Corner, until one group split off to become the Canonbury Boys. In the longstanding tradition of gang lore, this was an affront to those who felt deserted. On 10 June 1908, the gangs, both between fifteen and thirty strong, battled in Essex Road, Islington, where the Silver Hatchets managed to shoot one of their own in the leg. The leader of the Hatchets, seventeen-year-old George Price, paid the price of poor shooting with twelve months with hard labour. The leaderless Hatchets subsequently merged with the Hoxton Boys, while the Canonbury Boys became the Spanish gang.

The was more careless shooting on 26 June 1908, when Harry Jarvis, nineteen, of the Somers Town gang, took aim at Annie Pateman in Caledonian Road, King's Cross. Annie had asked him not to point the gun at her and to shoot at stones instead. Having the welfare of the stones in mind, Askew complained that they would fly up in the air, then asked Annie if she wanted a shot through her. He turned the gun and fired, missed Annie and hit Sarah Dodd, who was walking hand-in-hand with her young son. The bullet struck her in the arm. The Recorder at the Central Criminal Court bemoaned the fact that guns were sold to young lads. Nine months with hard labour seems a light sentence, bearing in mind he tried to murder Annie.

CHARLIE GUERIN demonstrated the difference in class between street hooligans and elite criminals. On Sunday 22 August 1909, Detective Inspector Robert Lyon and Detective John Shuard spotted two suspicious persons lurking in the vicinity of Mappin and Webb's jewellery shop in Poultry, in the City of London. Guerin was leaning on a railing opposite the shop, reading a newspaper and occasionally peering over the top of it. He was joined by Charles Knight, who was wheeling a bicycle and stooping down to examine it, as though it was in need of repair.

Lyon went off to gather reinforcements while Shuard observed Guerin and Knight shifting their positions, sometimes moving close to the doorway of the shop. Guerin was seen to be nudged by a third man, prompting him to cross the road and examine the doorway of the shop. As police kept watch, John Taylor, William Russell and George Taylor came out of the shop door and fastened it behind them. They were immediately arrested and offered no resistance. Guerin and Knight were arrested close by.

A police officer heard a rattling noise from within the shop and entered it with a set of keys taken from the prisoners. The noise had come from watchman William Henry Smith, who was in state of collapse from three serious head wounds. Inside the shop police found a scene of great disorder. A bag of jewellery valued at £1,700 lay on the floor, close to two jemmies and two broken padlocks. In a corner of the shop they found a pool of congealed blood, Smith's uniform jacket, pieces of rope and brown paper, all saturated with blood. The gang had broken the padlocks on the outside grill and used a set of duplicate keys to open the inside door. The watchman had been cooking his dinner on a gas stove when he heard the noise of cabinets being forced open. He saw two men, one masked with a hood with eye-holes cut into it, the other unmasked, and heard a third man close by. When he approached the men they clubbed him down with jemmies, tied him up and carried him semi-conscious to a corner of the shop, where they gagged him.

After the gang left the shop, Smith used his teeth to untie the ropes binding him and stumbled to the door, which he rattled with a hook used to open the outside grill. Jewellery valued at £29,000 was found on George Taylor and £10,500 on John Taylor. An assortment of jemmies, chisels and gloves were also found on the prisoners. Guerin denied knowing the others, but police reported seeing him with Russell on Waterloo Road two days before the raid, while returning from Sandown Races.

Knight was found not guilty. Russell, a northerner with a dreadful criminal record dating from 1899, George Taylor, also from the North with a similar record of offences and prison terms, and John Taylor, an Elephant and Castle man, not related to George but said by Inspector Thomas Divall to be an associate of thieves and a pickpocket almost from the time he could walk, were sentenced to terms of ten years penal servitude.

Guerin was described as the leader and brains of a very dangerous gang of thieves infesting Waterloo and Elephant and Castle. He had been seen on numerous occasions travelling with thieves to race meetings, he never worked and was a habitual criminal. He was suspected of being part of a gang of thieves who had narrowly escaped arrest a year earlier, when they stole some valuable silver. His sentence was only eight years, as he could not have taken part in the wounding of Smith.

Another interesting member of the Elephant and Castle gang was burglar Charlie Gordon, born in Plumstead, south London, in 1887. He committed his first burglary at the age of sixteen, after being estranged from his family and becoming domiciled in Lambeth Workhouse. His venture brought him a Borstal sentence, after which, using his alias Henry Barrett, he became a dedicated criminal, spending more than twelve years in prison. His most celebrated crime was not a burglary but a mugging. In 1913, with three others, he waylaid wages clerk Eugene Seyfang at the gates of a subway entrance to Blackfriars Railway Goods Station in Holland Road, on the south side of the Thames. The victim was held fast while one of the villains clamped a sheet of brown paper coated with treacle over his face. He was then punched unconscious before the gang made off with his bag, containing £51 in change. The four were arrested at Penton Place, Islington, and tried for the 'Treacle Plaster Outrage'. Charlie was sentenced to seven years penal servitude. For many years afterwards, he proclaimed his innocence, although his brother worked as a clerk at Sennett Brothers, whose payroll they stole.

His pals were a bad bunch whom police were delighted to put away, guilty or not: Danny Harris, a Liverpudlian who had settled in Whitechapel, received a seven-year sentence; Harry Willis, who was the son of a jailbird and lived in Clerkenwell; and Harry Hickson, were each sentenced to five years, plus an extra five for being habitual criminals. Acquitted was William Blake, who had confessed to the robbery under some duress, probably from Gordon and the others. Mr Justice Avory grudgingly decided against ordering a flogging, as they had not inflicted serious injuries on their victim.

On his release in August 1918, Charlie Gordon was denied entry into the Army because he was a habitual criminal. Desiring to go straight, he sought employment by presenting the *Daily Express* with the following advertisement:

> Ex-convict, burglar, confidence man, well-educated, exceptional abilities, smart appearance, tired of crime, desires to become respectable citizen. Would devote himself entirely to service of employer. What offers?

Sadly, his tongue-in-cheek cheek was not tested; the newspaper returned his ad. He did write a book, *Crooks of the Underworld*, published in 1929, catalogued by the British Library as being written under a pseudonym; however, Charlie had only dropped his first name of George.

East End Vendetta

ARTHUR HARDING CAME out of 'The Nichol', a notorious slum located between Shoreditch High Street, Hackney
Road, Brick Lane and Bethnal Green Road. Police regarded
him as a leading East End villain from about 1905 up to 1921.
He never was a great thief, more a violent hooligan, existing
on petty theft and handouts of cash and food from small businesses, particularly market stalls. He entered into crime at an
early age when he ran errands for 'One-eyed Charlie' Woolgar,
before graduating to robbing Jewish spielers at gunpoint. He
acquired a number of convictions for assault and many more
acquittals due to a study of the law that served him well in
police courts.

Harding was born in 1887 to unwed parents Henry Tresadern and Mary Ann Milligan. Henry, a dissolute rogue known
as 'Flash Harry', was already married, to Eliza Clayton. At nine
years of age, when The Nichol was being bulldozed to make
way for the Boundary Estate, Arthur was placed in Dr Bar-
nado's Home in Stepney Causeway, because his mother could
no longer cope. His early arrests were: 1901, aged fourteen, for
being a suspected person, case dismissed; 1902, stealing from
a van, which brought him twelve months with hard labour;
1903, pocket-picking, discharged; 1905, pocket-picking, again
discharged. He frequently complained of being picked on and
being accused of things he had not done.

By 1905, he was leading a gang that fired a fusillade of shots
at the home of Joe and Jack Bailey in Ducal Street, Bethnal
Green, hitting Jack in the leg. Several of Harding's men were
arrested and police described the incident as one of gang war-

fare. On this occasion, his gang was referred to as the Brick Lane Boys. One of them, Charlie Callaghan, was jailed for six months by the Central Criminal Court for shooting with intent to cause grievous bodily harm; another, Bill Newman, was acquitted. Two year's later, Callaghan, this time with Steve Cooper, Tom Venables, Fred Knight and Dick Ayrton – all known members of Harding's gang – were given terms with hard labour for violent theft. When Harding later wrote his memoirs, he put himself across as a serious villain, disdaining pickpockets and pimps. The truth is that his gang was into every type of criminal activity, from petty theft, through hooliganism, to attempted murder.

Harding's team took a shock in 1909, when Morris and Mark Reuben were hanged for beating to death drunken sailor William Sproull in Rupert Street, Whitechapel. Hanging was the ultimate sanction for violent villains, and its protocol was well-known to them. The condemned would be awakened at about 6 a.m., washed and dressed in their own clothing and given breakfast, after which the prison chaplain would visit. Just before 8 a.m., the chaplain would leave to put on his official robes. He would then join the governor, senior prison staff, warders, medical officer and press reporters to escort the prisoner to the condemned cell. Early executions were carried out in an execution shed, which meant the condemned person had a long walk: this was later changed to an execution room adjacent to the condemned cell. The chaplain would begin his prayer and the chapel bell would toll. In the execution room, the hangman was waiting. Quickly, he pinioned the prisoner's arms and adjusted the clothing around his neck. The prisoner was quickly stood on the trap, his legs pinioned, a hood pulled over his head and the noose placed around his neck. A cotter pin was then pulled from a lever, which was immediately operated to drop the prisoner about eight feet. The jerk broke the prisoner's neck. The body was left hanging for an hour or more and was then buried, after a cursory inquest, within the prison precincts. For double hangings, prisoners were brought from adjacent cells and stood on the gallows together.

One-eyed Charlie, Harding's mentor, was a dangerous man who flirted with the gallows, despite his impaired vision. On 3 April 1911, he was at the centre of a gunfight that shattered the peace of Hackney: thirteen men opened fire on another group in Gascoigne Place. It was an example of how police on the beat can react quickly to quell violent incidents; they came running from all directions to round up fleeing gangsters. Charles Goddard, twenty-two, and Harry Goldsworthy, twenty, said they were responding to an attack on Goldsworthy by the gang of Charlie Woolgar. Goldsworthy had been in a fight with Woolgar and Johnny O'Brien in Hoxton the previous week, and had been stabbed under the right eye and in the back of the head. He felt it was sensible to buy a gun for his own protection. Both accused had a string of previous convictions from childhood. Police considered them to be rogues and vagabonds who had never done a day's work. The Common Serjeant at the Central Criminal Court fixed that by giving each of them nine months with hard labour.

THE EAST END Vendetta was a short-lived, confusing gang war in the dives around Brick Lane: it was fought between a gang at the Whitechapel end of the lane and another from the Bethnal Green end. It seems to have been a case of street gangs testing each other's protection rights and was yet another example of warfare between 'manors'. Whitechapel's Isaac 'Ikey' Bogard, born in Spitalfields in 1888, was a dark-skinned Jew known as 'Darky the Coon'. He took over the manor of Whitechapel by hammering the local terrors led by Jack Marks, a villain with a reputation for drunken brawls and vicious wounding. Marks had beaten up Alex Johnson in the Wheatsheaf in Commercial Road, after failing to squeeze money out of him. Small businessmen turned to Darky for protection, leading to a two-year feud between the gangs. In July 1909, more than twenty men waving guns and knives chased Marks's gang. Marks, John Scales and Mickey and Jesse Tyam escaped, but were hunted to their hangouts. Bogard, Lennie Osborne, Jack Millard and Phil Silverman came upon Marks in Collingwood Street and set about him with iron bars, while the others were attacked at their homes. Marks complained to police but then failed to show up as a witness, allowing his attackers to go free.

Bogard had a string of convictions for assault, several of them on police officers, and living off immoral earnings In 1911, he turned his attention to Harding's Bethnal Green Boys. Harding appears to have been regarded as their leader, in tandem with Timmy Hayes, but Hayes was in prison at the time of the vendetta; Dodger Mullins later succeeded to the East End domain. Battle commenced that August and Bogard won the first round by kicking Tommy Taylor around Brick Lane after Taylor had sworn at his wife. A gunfight followed, in which Bogard man Georgie King, a thief and extortionist, shot William Spencer in the mouth; Taylor shot Bogard's right-hand man, Phil Shonck, and Harding came up and fired several shots after a fleeing King. Police found Spencer bleeding profusely from his mouth and Schonk lying unconscious in the road.

That September, 'Darky' was hunted to the Blue Coat Boy pub in Bishopsgate, by Harding, Taylor and several other heavies. He saw them walk in, and offered them a drink, but the tension was palpable.

'Do you know what we are going to do to you?' taunted Harding.

Then Taylor tapped Bogard on the shoulder to make him turn and slashed his throat with a knife. The rest then smashed their beer glasses and plunged them into Bogard's face and hands. Someone hit him with an iron bar and two of his pals who tried to help him received similar treatment

'That's for Taylor, you fucking bastard,' shouted one of Harding's mob as as they ran out.

The pub manager blew a whistle and police arrived, but Bogard, who was now soaked in blood, refused make a statement and headed off towards Shoreditch. He later attended London Hospital to have his wounds stitched.

Eight days later, police were called to a mini-riot in Bethnal Green. They arrived to see Steve Cooper, another of Harding's gang, pull a revolver from his pocket and take aim at Georgie King, who was getting the best of a fight with Bob Wheeler. A quick-thinking constable grabbed Cooper by his gun arm and the two fell to the floor; another man grabbed the gun and ran off with it. Cooper was dragged off to the cells. Despite the contrary evidence of at least two policemen, it was never proven that a shot had actually discharged, although Cooper would later serve three years for his actions.

Astonishingly, Darky was soon on his feet and able to inflict battle scars on gang rivals in Walthamstow market. The inevitable comeback followed and Darky needed to be rescued by police. To remain out of harm's way, he and Georgie King 'coughed' to some minor misdeeds and came up at Old Street Police Court. Harding and a small army blockaded the court and threatened Detective Fred Wensley and other officers as they escorted Darky and King away after sentencing. Fingers drawn across throats and the brandishing of shooters reinforced threats. A few stabbings and occasional shootings followed, ultimately bringing Harding his fifteenth conviction and a prison sentence to think over his future. Other members of his gang, all with previous convictions for violence, received sentences of up to three years:

Harding was described as the captain of a band of young desperadoes, a terror to the police and inhabitants of Bethnal Green. He and William Spencer (Edward Emms) received twenty-one months with hard labour, plus three years penal servitude; Steve Cooper, three years (included the previous shooting); Tommy Taylor, Charlie Callaghan, two years; Bob Wheeler, Bill Newman, Bill Andrews, fifteen months. It was not illegal to carry a firearm in 1911, which accounts for the light sentencing. Bogard, when giving evidence at their trial, was asked if he was 'the terror of the district' and caused people to go about in fear of their lives. He denied it.

Darky now took advantage of Harding's absence to become the 'guv'nor' of East End street markets. He rented out stall pitches and collected premiums for protection against other gangs' demands, until he joined the London Regiment in 1914. During the war, he earned a good record and is said to have been decorated with the Military Medal, after which he became a bookmaker.

Harding's team was associated with the Watney Streeters, some of whom came unstuck after a shooting outside the Empire Music Hall in Shoreditch in 1912. They wounded Harry Silvester, of the rival Abbey Street Boys, another violent bunch from Bethnal Green who were always looking for trouble, without any profit in it. Detective John 'Jew Jack' Stevens saw a bunch of youths engaged in a street fight: one man was surrounded by about twenty lads who were trying to get at him. Stevens heard five revolver shots and saw Silvester fall and the gang run off. He summoned help and four youths were arrested. Police charged teenagers John Jenkins, James Bennett, Charlie Tompkins and Henry Barker with riot, and Bennett with shooting at Silvester with the intention of causing him grievous bodily harm. Bennett, said to be the leader of the gang, was sent to Borstal for two years. Jenkins was conditionally discharged and the two others found not guilty. Chief Inspector Wensley said that, during the past nine months ,there had been five cases of the use of revolvers in his district. He added that police had the greatest difficulty in obtaining evidence, as various gangs of lads had become a terror to the neighbourhood.

In 1916, Harding was jailed for five years for receiving stolen banknotes. The job had been done by Ed Spencer of the Titanic gang, who had picked the pocket of a railway executive at King's Cross Station. Harding had given some of the money to his sister to hide in a Christmas Club and she had taken it to a bank, where the notes were identified as stolen.

Harding's last serious conviction came in December 1921, when his early release license was revoked. He was returned to Dartmoor for assault on a plain-clothes police constable, whose jaw had been broken when he queried what a group of men were doing breaking into a taxi. Benny Hall struck the blow, but a witness said Harding had taken a kick at the fallen officer. Hall received three months. Shortly after his release, Harding married, and when he got into a brawl in 1926, his wife laid their marriage on the line. After that he went tame.

Harding's story was told by Raphael Samuel in *East End Underworld*, published in 1981. It is an interesting read and Raphael reports it pretty much as Harding recalled events, even to the point of repetition. Watch out, however, for errors such as Saul for Sewell, Rubin for Reuben, Marx for Marks and Walker for Woolgar.

HYMAN EISENBERG WAS an immigrant from Eastern Europe, born about 1884. He was feared in the Whitechapel district by citizens, police and other crooks alike, mainly because of his unpredictable nature and vicious streak. He was known to fire off a pistol at random targets just to get a reaction, shooting at policemen with particular relish.

His activities were pocket-picking, garrotting, burglary and extorting shopkeepers and publicans. Garrotting was a crime prevalent in the East End, whereby a strong man would come up behind a victim in a dark street, grip his neck and squeeze, until the frantically struggling soul passed out and was then robbed. It was much sensationalised by the newpapers of the day. The trick was to avoid killing the victim. In May 1905,

Hymie was acquitted of mugging commercial traveller William Wilcox, who he tapped on the shoulder and, when he turned round, punched him in the stomach before snatching at his pocket watch; all he got was the gold chain. When Wilcox gave chase, half a dozen others impeded him. He picked Hymie out from an identity parade, but Hymie's girlfriend, Polly George, swore he was with her at Forrester's Music Hall when the robbery took place.

In February 1906, a row occurred outside a pub in Vallance Road, Bethnal Green, when Arthur Harding and four of his 'boys' picked a fight with a group of workers who were leaving after a quiet drink. The workers ran off and shots were fired after them. One of the group became separated and, when his friends returned to find him, a gunman placed a pistol close to the face of Dan Corby and fired. The terrified man took off, but returned when he saw two constables arrive. Corby pointed out Harding as the man who had fired the shot near his face and, after a chase, the constables captured him. Harding was charged under his true name, Arthur Tresadern, of riot and wounding Corby and a young woman who had suffered splinter wounds from a ricocheting bullet. His defence was simple: 'It wasn't me, it was Hymie Eisenberg.' Witness Annie George, who had replaced her sister Polly as the live-in lover of Hymie and was the mother of his son, Hyman junior, said Harding had fired the shot. However, Harding must have been believed, for he was found not guilty. Hymie was put away for ten months in June for robbing an old soldier of his cash and medals.

In October 1910, Hymie, with the equally fearsome and unstable Tommy Hoy and five or six others, travelled from Whitechapel to Poplar, searching for a man who had threatened the wife of one of the gang. They did not find the man they were looking for but, bent on bringing terror to the local populace, they shot and wounded William McLoughlin and fired four shots at Freddie Smith: both of them had wandered into the street after hearing a commotion outside a pub. The gang went to ground until January the following year, when a constable spotted Hoy in Stepney. Hoy and his dog attacked the constable, who still managed to arrest him. In court, Hoy was said to be a member of a dangerous gang. He had seven previous convictions for violent behaviour, including beating a man with a hammer, and had been dismissed by the Army for being worthless and incorrigible. His sentence was seven years.

It was a burglary in Enfield, north London, that led to Long Hymie's downfall. He was caught in the act by a constable, who took a terrible beating in the process and spent several weeks convalescing, before picking out Hymie from an identification parade. Hymie was jailed and deported to South America, which he claimed was his place of birth, eventually entering the United States. He is rumoured to have been one of Hymie Weiss's wiseguys in Chicago at the time of his war with Al Capone, but no evidence has come to light. He left Annie and young Hymie behind when he was deported.

The Titanic

THE TITANIC ARE generally placed in Nile Street, often referred to as 'The Nile', in the Shoreditch-Hoxton-Hackney districts of east London. They were mostly pickpockets, although they had the muscle too. In his memoirs, Detective Fred 'Nutty' Sharpe described them as being violent when cornered. They plagued Petticoat Lane market and operated further afield, at racing and other sporting venues and the trains travelling to and from them.

Their leadership has never been fully ascertained: George Measures was an enforcer who was tamed by the Elephant's Wal McDonald in a fist fight in the 1910s, while Arthur Phillips was a notorious longstanding member. East End gangster Arthur Harding, in his memoirs, names Billy Chandler, from Hoxton, Charlie 'Cossor' Gilbert, born in Islington, and Edward Spencer, from Hackney; he also said the leader became the owner of a dog track but unfortunately he does not say which one. Billy Chandler's sister, Lizzie, and Arthur Phillips's wife, Annie, were members on the distaff side.

Edward Spencer (referred to as William Spencer during the East End Vendetta trial) was born in Bethnal Green as Edward Emms, in 1882. He belonged to a class of people known as the 'terrors of Brick Lane', which included Harding and Charlie Callaghan. His convictions dated back to 1899 when, at age eighteen, he was one of a trio who robbed a man of his watch in Shoreditch. In 1908, he received four years for picking pockets at White City during the Olympic Games.

Harding recollects seeing some of the Titanic when he was on remand in 1902, which brings up the question of how they came by their name. The famous liner sank in April 1912. Was it a talking point in 1902, or was Harding mistaken in his recollection? As the idea of the Titanic and its two sister ships only came about in 1907, and construction began in 1908-9, it is likely they adopted the name around 1907, to complement their size, stylish dress and belief in their invulnerability.

The gang certainly originated in the Hoxton-Shoreditch district and comprised a large team of pickpockets that infested public transport systems at the dawning of the twentieth century. In 1898, John Ryan was hanged at Newgate for stabbing to death PC James Baldwin, who had tried to break up a large group of pickpockets in Wilmer Gardens, Hoxton. This murder prompted calls for arming police with revolvers. In 1906, Henry Field, John Abrahams, Tommy Jones, Tommy Harrison, Billy Johnson and Edward Day were arrested at Waterloo tram terminus by a police surveillance team, after they were observed targeting passengers. On the same day, Patrick Baker, Clement Beaumont, Alf Clark and Fred Jones were arrested while picking pockets at Hammersmith Bridge during the University Boat Race. Most of the accused lived in Shoreditch, with just one member hailing from south of the Thames.

Between 1908 and 1921, the Titanic were known throughout London's underworld as a gang of pickpockets, numbering around fifty. In their team were many individuals, well known to police, who considered themselves too crafty to be brought to book. This included eighty-seven-year-old Mary Brunton who, in October 1922, was given a conditional discharge even though she had twenty-three previous convictions. Barefist fighter Harry Bargery, born in 1884 and known as 'Bargee', was reputed to be their toughest fighter. His record included three months at Liverpool Police Court for being a suspected person, loitering to pick pockets, followed by twelve months in 1921 as an incorrigible rogue. The gang worked in groups of from three to ten to target one area, which might be a crowded Underground railway platform, a packed music hall, a section of a football stadium, or anywhere a dense crowd collected. The Boat Race and the Lord Mayor's Show were among annual favourites.

Detective Inspector Bob Higgins gave an insight into the method by which three men went to work. One overtook the 'mark' and walked slowly in front of him while the other two came up, one behind and one to the side, usually with a wall on the other side. The victim was jostled and the outside man went through his pockets or lifted his watch and chain: if he was detected, his confederates helped overpower the victim. Higgins described the gang's members as ugly and exceedingly rough with their victims. An example of how a cell operated was uncovered in September 1921, when Shoreditch-born George Measures was arrested with Dominic Mack, Alf MacLennan, Dick Canter and Jim Parrott, at Euston Square Underground Station. Canter went from coach to coach obstructing doors by gripping the handrails on either side, thus preventing passengers from getting on, while the others set about dipping into their pockets and bags.

It is impossible to say when London's pickpockets first organised themselves into bands to target countryside fairs. As early as July 1805, some of Bob Barney's gang from south London were arrested in the course of raiding Suffolk fairs. One operative, named Bullet, carried a constable's staff with the intention of taking charge of any of the gang who was detected: he would offer to take them before a magistrate, but instead allowed them to escape. In February 1824, police identified a gang of north London pickpockets who dressed in fashionable attire. This gang sat through a sermon in St. John's Church, Clerkenwell, before going about their business of 'dipping' for booty among the crowded congregation as they left the church. An alert clerk sent for constables who managed to arrest one old gent, James Mortimer from

Whitechapel, who they described as belonging to the higher class of pickpocket.

Police gave periodic public warnings, particularly at holiday times, which highlighted pickpockets' tactics, including:

> *The shove up — when one operative causes congestion by blocking the entrance to a public vehicle, to allow other operatives to push up and rifle pockets.*

> *Diversion — where a woman faints in order to draw people around her, who stoop down to expose their hip pockets and watches on chains, and loosen their grip on handbags; also by using a baby to distract vehicle passengers by touching them, gaining friendly attention ,while operatives go to work on the unsuspecting victim who is enjoying a pleasant exchange with the child or its mother.*

> *Cover — a raincoat hanging loosely over an arm while the operative goes to work with fingers, or scissors to cut handbag straps or coat pockets, also performed by holding up a large newspaper.*

> *Crushing — three or more operatives crowd a passenger on an omnibus, and one roughly removes a wallet or purse and runs off. He jumps from the bus and the others make a show of pursuing him, but impede anyone trying to stop him. Stolen articles are quickly passed to another party so that, if apprehension follows, no incriminating evidence is found.*

Elephant and Castle gang member Jim McDonald spoke of Alf White as being the Titanic's early leader. He was born Alfred Henry White on 3 August 1887 in Copenhagen Street, close to Caledonian Road, Islington. His father, also Alfred, had spent his early years in Boston Street, Hackney, which also housed the Titanic's Edward Spencer, before joining the

Merchant Navy. In 1881, Alf senior was living in Islington. In 1885, he married the daughter of a commercial traveller. By this time, he had left the Merchant Service and become a nightclub proprietor.

In 1906-7, young Alf participated in the protracted warfare between the Bemerton Street Boys of King's Cross and a combination of their neighbours, the White Lion Street gang from the Angel and the Clerkenwell Boys from the other side of Pentonville Road (see pages 80-1). Residents of Caledonian Road and Copenhagen Street in King's Cross complained of large gangs of boys battling in the streets, without any effective police action. Fights between north London gangs have a long history. Often, police constables, patrolling on foot in known difficult areas, were alerted by the use of whistles and came running from many directions.

In 1908, Alf married Caroline Wooder, a flower hawker born into a notorious Clerkenwell family headed by George and Julia (nee Kiddy), who both had convictions for violence. The Wooders were something of criminal dynasty, while the Kiddy family was a violent bunch from Warren Street, Islington. Julia's brother William had convictions as a member of the Clerkenwell Boys. Alf and his bride later lived at Farringdon Road, Finsbury, where they carried on a business as florists. It meant the White family were now established in the Farringdon district around Clerkenwell Green and adjacent to Sabini family dwellings. As the Sabinis were enemies of the Titanic, and Alf White became a leading light in the Sabini gang, his leadership of the Titanic seems unlikely, until a closer look is taken.

Charlie and Freddie Wooder were certainly among the Titanic's leaders, and were in-laws of Alf White and also lived in the Farringdon area. On 14 June 1913, Alf White, Charlie Wooder, Levi Fetterman from Stepney Green and Harry Leonard from Walworth Road, south London, were arrested at Crewe railway station. A farmer had complained that he had been hustled and his pocket picked of £7 on the West Coast Corridor Express travelling from Carlisle. Alf White was jailed for three months, the three others for six months each. The fact that they were operating a great distance from London confirms the calculated, deliberate nature of the Titanic and their organised pocket-picking binges. In April 1914, Freddie Wooder was acquitted of robbing a rent man with violence in Back Hill, Clerkenwell. Another Titanic, Larry Ford, who had obstructed pursuit, was jailed.In his later years, Alf was associated in some way with Hackney Greyhound Racing Stadium. This may be what Arthur Harding was alluding to, although it is doubtful he was the owner. The likelihood is that Alf, who would have been twenty-two in 1908, sat uncomfortably astride a fence with the Sabinis on one side and East Enders on the other.

The Titanic were involved in the first 'Battle of the Nile', in January 1908, when they repelled an attack by a rival gang and wounded some of them in a shootout. This may have been an attack by the Sabinis. If so, it would have been led by Fred and Darby Sabini, who would have been aged about twenty-seven and twenty respectively, and the only likely leaders of the Italians at that time. Among those arrested and bound over to keep the peace was Annie Phillips, mother of future Finsbury tearaways John and Arthur.

In 1910, there was a territorial dispute over protection rights in the West End between Alf White's King's Cross gang, who were at the core of the Titanic, and the Elephant and Castle gang, led by Wag McDonald. This led to a brawl in Shaftesbury Avenue, in which the north Londoners were given a bloody nose and a stern warning to stay out of Soho. A fistfight between Elephant enforcer Wal McDonald and his opposite number in the Titanic, George Measures, followed soon after, confirming that the King's Cross Boys and the Titanic were at the time intertwined.

According to the notorious country house burglar George

Ingram, who fenced much of his loot in Hoxton, the Titanic headquartered at the Duke of Portagus public house in Nile Street.

THE PERIOD FROM 1908 to 1914 saw numerous battles between four major gang manors – King's Cross/Clerkenwell, Elephant and Castle, Hoxton/Finsbury and Hackney/Bethnal Green – for control of the West End and the rich pickings that went with it. The conflict recommenced after World War One, and included a second Battle of the Nile, in which the Titanic repelled an attack by the Sabinis and captured an unconscious organ grinder, Paola Boffa. The Titanic women generously shielded him from police officers who arrived from the station around the corner in Shepherdess Walk. Boffa was returned to pals and three women were arrested.

This was followed by the Titanic suffering a severe mauling from the Elephant and Castle gang in 1919, after which they sank as soundly as their namesake. They continued their depredations under the banner of the Finsbury Boys, sometimes still referred to as the Titanic, until their final fling in December 1920. They were the object of a major police operation after they had dumped Police Sergeant Tommy Tongue onto the railway line at King's Cross Station, when he enquired about their day at Alexandra Park races. A tip-off enabled police to ambush the gang on a Baker Street Underground Railway platform, where they arrested some of them after a fierce struggle. Similar raids occurred at other stations. One of these developed into a nine-mile car chase across north London, with the police driving their newly equipped, souped up Crossley Tenders, followed by many more arrests. Sentencing was three and six months terms with hard labour.

George Measures was jailed again in August 1924, for practising his trade at Charing Cross Underground Station. He had been observed opening up a newspaper in front of a passenger and feeling for his wallet. His record revealed thirteen previous convictions, commencing in 1907, all for pocket picking. Police described him as one of the notorious Titanic, living at Westmoreland Place, City Road, adjacent to the Nile.

The Finsbury Boys continued under the leadership of Freddie Gilbert and John Phillips, as an alliance of the Elephant and Castle and Camden Town gangs, under the general influence of Wal McDonald and George Sage. They also associated themselves with Dodger Mullins and became violently hostile to the King's Cross gang led by Alf White, who was by then firmly in the camp of the Sabini and Jewish gangs.

Although the Titanic gang centred on east London, their catchment area included King's Cross, Islington, Hackney, Shoreditch, Bethnal Green and, to a much lesser extent, Bermondsey, Southwark and Lambeth. Their strength at any given time was about fifty, older members being replaced by younger family members. Before taking on the title of Titanic, they referred to themselves as the Swell Mob, as distinct from Bill Patterson's Flash Mob that operated out of Bethnal Green. No doubt, many rogues had dual memberships.

The following list identifies some leading members through the years, with the age they would have been in 1920 (if still alive) and where they were born. Their ages indicate the generations of pocket artistes who became the Titanic. Having many previous convictions did not deter them. Sentences were usually three months with hard labour, rising to twelve months only after many previous convictions. Police must have suffered considerable frustration when, after arresting known long-term pickpockets, magistrates let them off lightly. A point to consider is that, in times of high unemployment, some were inclined to take the desperate route, again and again.

Alf White, thirty-three, Islington; Frank Gilbert, fifty-nine, Kentish Town; Fred Gilbert, twenty-eight, Kentish Town;

John Gilbert, twenty-nine, Finsbury; Arthur Phillips, Snr, forty-eight, Birmingham; John Phillips, twenty-one, Hackney; Arthur Phillips, Jnr, eighteen, Hackney; Charlie Wooder, thirty-three, Clerkenwell; Fred Wooder, forty, Clerkenwell; George Wooder, forty-three, St. Luke's; Henry Wooder, forty-one, St. Luke's; Charlie 'Cossor' Gilbert, St. Luke's; George Measures, thirty-eight, Shoreditch; Billy Chandler, forty-five, Hoxton; Tommy Scott, Islington; Edward Spencer, thirty-six, Hackney; Annie Phillips, forty-five, City of London; Lizzie Bargery, thirty-two, Hackney.

'Soldiers' of the gang included:

Maud Price: A professional pickpocket, called the 'Mystery Woman of Sidcup' after she was traced to London's Kent suburbs and found to be hoarding much plunder. She had a string of convictions.

Jim Clarke, John Brown and Charlie Smith: Arrested as a cell of a dangerous gang in 1904 and typical of those who became the Titanic. Clarke, from Shoredith, had many convictions and was sentenced to five years.

Eddie Guerin: A celebrated international bank robber who hit the skids. He was associated with the Titanic in his later years.

Arthur Mitchell: From Hackney, Mitchell had multiple convictions, including one in 1912 for assaulting the Lord Mayor of London during an attempted robbery.

Charlie Andrews: Prolific Hoxton pickpocket and named by police as one of the leaders of the Titanic.

Joe Harris: A well-travelled pickpocket with convictions in Australia, Belgium, France and America.

Charlie Wilmott: A newspaper dipper with a record going back to 1902, he was captured in 1925 after being chased over railway lines. Police said he was member of a notorious gang.

Charlie Taylor: Arrested on a Chelsea omnibus while lifting the wallet of Sir Reginald McLeod.

Arthur Brown: Hackney betting commission agent with many convictions.

Frank Wigg: Known for the 'shove up' method and amassed numerous convictions, some for violence.

William Boniface: Arrested as part of a team working Charing Cross Underground Station. His victim was crushed by a half-dozen men, had his wallet stolen, and was badly kicked about after he chased and caught Boniface.

Harry Bargery: A Shoreditch bareknuckle fighter who also lifted wallets. He married Lizzie Chandler.

James Bryan, Charles Hendy, Jim Edwards, John Lyons, John Lampey, George James, John Driscoll and Joe Harrow: Arrested as a group (with George Measures) in a police raid on a bus in Bethnal Green, after they were seen targeting dock labourers with pay packets on their way home. Police 'arrested the bus' and took it to Bethnal Green Police Station. All had many convictions.

John Byron, Harry Watson, Fred Johnson, Jnr, Bill Patterson: Career criminals arrested as a group after a violent struggle in a police sting at Waterloo Railway Station.

Eddie Westfall: A habitual criminal from Bethnal Green.

Michael Gold: An expert 'whizzer' with a dreadful record.

Billy Ford: Had convictions as a leader of the Swell Mob, forerunner of the Titanic, and was said to be an expert pickpocket who carried a knife and considered himself chief of the City.

Fred Orrell: A Shoreditch crook with many arrests, including one by a female victim at Horseguard's Parade.

Rueben Fisher: A prolific, violent offender.

Bill Gardner: An Islington 'newspaper' specialist who hid

behind a broadsheet paper, holding one end in his teeth, while his free hand went to work.

Jimmy Ward: A versatile Finsbury thief who also worked with the Spanish Gang.

John Casson: A notorious Shoreditch pickpocket and walk-in thief.

Pat Baker, Clem Beaumont, Arthur Clarke, Fred Jones: Arrested as a group for picking pockets at the University Boat Race.

Harry Penley: Named as one of a notorious gang.

Charlie Wilson: A bookmaker's clerk with a bad record.

Bill Carter: A Finsbury tearaway with a habit of assaulting police.

Harry Hawkins: Tommy Benneworth's grandfather-in-law, who had a dreadful record.

Charlie Harrington: He racked up many convictions and police considered him one of the leaders of the Titanic.

Henry Grant: Pulled a gun to escape after a victim seized him at Piccadilly Underground Station, but was captured in the tunnel. He amassed eighteen convictions in twenty-nine years and the magistrate took pity on him when told his first offence had resulted in ten years for wounding his girlfriend, which he thought was excessive and had set him on the path of crime. He refused to sentence him as a habitual criminal, but gave him five years anyway.

Henry Phillips: An incorrigible rogue from Bethnal Green and relative of the Phillips brothers.

Levi Fetterman, Harry Leonard: Arrested with gang leaders Alf White and Charlie Wooder. Both had many convictions.

Dominic Mack, Alf MacLennan, Dick Canter and Jimmy Parrott: Arrested with George Measures while raiding Tube trains and named by police as incorrigible rogues.

John Abrahams, Tommy Jones, Tommy Harrison, Bill Johnson, Ed Day: Arrested together for targeting Waterloo and Blackfriars railway termini. They were well-known to police.

Edward Graham, Frank Martin, Charlie Harrigan: A Hoxton trio arrested with Charlie Wooder and all core members of Titanic. 'Fat Charlie' Harrigan was adept at obstructing entrances.

George Windred: Originally from Manchester, as a twelve-year-old he was an inmate of the Industrial School ship Formidable at Bristol, an early form of Approved School for abandoned or destitute children. His nautical training somehow turned him into a Holborn bookmaker and member of the Titanic, with a record of arrests in Leicester, Australia, Johannesburg and London, for keeping disorderly gambling houses and general bad behaviour. One conviction in 1912 was for picking a packet of diamonds from the pocket of a Hatton Garden diamond merchant by the 'crushing' method. He got four years on that occasion.

BEFORE LEAVING THE pre-First World War period, it is important to mention that there is no single reason why a gang comes together. Over the years mutual protection, territorial rivalry, criminal enterprise and political unrest have resulted in the formation of groups ranging from small cliques to large assemblies, intent on pursuing their own interests. This account looks mostly at criminal gangs. However, although political gangs have been rare in Britain, they have still existed. The most notorious of past political gangs was a group of Russian Federation dissidents, who had fled their homeland after the 1905 uprising in the Baltic State of Latvia, to plot action from the UK to overthrow the Russian Tsar. Some of these men had been imprisoned and tortured before fleeing to other countries. They were anarchists, owing allegiance to Lenin, and were sought by Russian secret police. To fund arms, ammunition and propaganda, they resorted to burglary, mostly in the East End. They had settled there among a sizeable Eastern European immigrant population, including Tsarist supporters, who made inviting targets.

What newspapers described as The Tottenham Outrage occurred on 23 January 1909. It began outside Schnurmann's Rubber Factory on the corner of Tottenham High Road and Chesnut Road, when two Latvian dissidents ambushed two payroll clerks. The clerks fought back and a passer-by, George Smith, joined in, bringing one of the men down. The second gangster shot Smith and they took off with a money satchel containing £80. Three constables and a number of civilians joined a modern day 'hue and cry' pursuit.

In Mitchly Road, the gunman turned and fired at his pursuers, instead hitting and killing ten-year-old Ralph John Joscelyne. PC Ernest Newman was wounded and PC William Tyler was killed: other civilians and police officers suffered wounds as they arrived on the scene. In Chingford Road, an elderly man was shot as the fugitives boarded a tram, only to find themselves pursued by armed police on a second tram. Shots were exchanged in a wild shootout, forcing the gunmen to abandon the tram and hijack a milk wagon, shooting the milkman in the chest. When the wagon crashed, they jumped onto a horse-drawn greengrocer's van and galloped off at a furious pace until the horse collapsed. More people and police joined the chase and the killers were finally cornered, causing Paul Hefeld to shoot himself and Jacob Lapidus, who tried to hide in a cottage, to do the same.

Reflecting public outrage, the newspapers demanded government action on foreign dissidents. However, members of the same dissident group carried out more robberies. The exact number of thefts is not known, but is believed to run into dozens: they targeted moneylenders, jewellery outlets and business premises. The gang had successive leaders, as others took over after arrests or deaths. It was under the leadership of George Gardstein that they embarked on a burglary that would have terrible consequences.

In December 1910, two houses in Exchange Buildings, Houndsditch, were rented by the gang. They planned to burrow through the back wall of number eleven into Harris's jewellery shop, which they believed held £7,000-worth of jewellery belonging to a Tsarist. They thought it would be just for the Tsar's supporters to pay for the revolt against him.

The team would work in shifts, using number ten as rest quarters. On the night of 16 December, people in neighbouring houses called the police to investigate noises coming from the back of the jeweller's. Police Constable Piper attended and decided to make enquiries at number eleven. George Gardstein answered the door and pretended to struggle with his English language. PC Piper feigned satisfaction, but summoned help, and nine officers took up positions outside the building. PC Robert Bentley next knocked on the door and, not being satisfied by Gardstein's mumbling, forced his way in, closely followed by PC Bryant. PC Bentley was shot twice, the second bullet hitting him in the neck and killing him; PC Bryant was wounded, as was PC Ernest, who was close behind them. The gang fired on police outside the building, killing Sergeant Charles Tucker, before rushing out into the street: PC Walter Choat grappled with Gardstein, who shot him in the leg. One of Gardstein's confederates shot PC Choat in the back, killing him and accidentally wounding Gardstein. The gang disappeared into the darkness, carrying their wounded comrade and leaving behind three dead and two wounded, unarmed, constables.

The discovery of Gardstein's body at his home in Grove Street the following morning led to a round-up of suspects. The gang re-formed under the leadership of Peter Piatkow, known as 'Peter the Painter' due to his cover as a painter and decorator, and went to ground. On 3 January 1911, police learned that three suspects were hiding in a top-floor flat in a three-storey tenement in Sidney Street, Stepney. This time the response was by armed police – but poorly armed. People were cleared from adjacent flats, including a mistress of one of the gang, without alarming the occupants on the floor above. Police called on the gang to surrender by banging on the door, throwing stones through windows and yelling for them to come out. The response was a fusillade of shots, one of which felled Detective Sergeant Lecson, causing serious injury: three other policemen were slightly wounded. It has to be said that the gang made a fight of it: they were better armed and seemed resigned to death rather than surrender, no doubt fearing death or torture at the hands of police, as they would have expected in their home country.

Because the police were poorly armed, Home Secretary Winston Churchill authorised the callout of a platoon of Scots Guards from the Tower of London. This triggered controversy for apparently besmirching the efficiency and bravery of the police, even though it was clearly a sensible thing to do. The Army shot the building to pieces, causing a fire to break out on the top floor, which forced the gang to descend floor by floor as the flames spread. William Joseph, also called Sokoloff, tried to leave through the street door and was blasted back in. Fritz Svaars continued the fight, firing automatic pistols from each hand, until he was overcome by smoke and died from suffocation. A firefighter was also fatally injured when a wall collapsed on him. If Peter the Painter had been in the house he somehow escaped, returning to Russia where he became a secret policeman.

3

THE RACECOURSE WARS

Razors, Guns and Knuckledusters

Billy Kimber and the Brummagems

THE BRUMMIES WERE so closely connected to London gangs that they must feature here. Many of them operated at racecourses in and around London, as allies of gangs from Elephant and Castle, Camden Town and Hoxton: some transferred their homes to the capital. Their leader, Billy Kimber, also became a major player in Soho's clubland.

It cannot be escaped just how much trouble was attributed to 'racing gangs', nor can it be said that racing enterprises began in the 1910s when Billy Kimber came on the scene. Riots at racecourses had been commonplace in the eighteenth and nineteenth centuries, on courses so badly policed that they attracted ruffians in great numbers. There are instances of bands of roughs attacking turnstile offices and making off with the day's takings. These toughs had frequented meetings from the beginnings of horse and dog racing, when they began as fairground pursuits. In any open meeting place where revelling is the main occupation and where money and drink freely flow, there is always temptation that leads to some criminal activity.

By the Nineteenth Century, riots were a familiar scene to racegoers feeling the effects of a depletion of wealth due to a day's poor judgement at the track, followed by further deprivation of funds in the beer tent. In one example, at Brighton in August 1822, as was reported in *The Times*, punters lingered after the racing was over. As the beer flowed so did insults, followed by fists, followed by general public alarm. Policing was in the hands of beadles, familiar to most people now only as the mercenary guardians of Oliver

115

Twist. The beadles tried to come between rival groups but, as would become common in later years, both sides turned on them. They beat the beadles unmercifully. Word was sent to Chief Beadle Sir David Scott beseeching him to call out the military. He responded by getting on his horse to see what the fuss was about. With one assistant he galloped to the fray, where he was surprised to see the extent of the disturbance and even more surprised when a barrage of stones, bottles and anything else that came to hand met his pleas for calm. Both men were badly wounded and fell from their horses to lie beside their prostrate beadles. The rioters then decided it was time to go home.

Robbery and intimidation were the lines of work for rogues who plagued, not only fairgrounds, but also city alleys, where they would be called footpads, or hid behind trees or mounds waiting for a coach to pass, where they would be called highwaymen. London's fairs, such as Southwark, Barnet and Mayfair, were infested with ruffians, as was Vauxhall Gardens. All of them closed when they became so notorious the public no longer felt safe: those who had opposed their original foundation for the purposes of pleasure, were able to lobby for their closure.

In the countryside, horse fairs developed into race meetings that not only attracted, but also became inviting to, the crafty brigade, who knew hundreds of ways of separating gullible punters from their money. Scams ranged from 'find the lady', the three-card trick, 'crown and anchor' a dice-based game of chance that much favoured the banker, to race-fixing through agreement with owners and sometimes the substituting of horses. When rascals were caught cheating or robbing, they came together as a gang for protection.

Betting adds to the enjoyment of a race. It also adds book-makers. Bookies have their share of rogues, and attached to them are the confidence tricksters who specialise in fiddling punters. In early days, racecourses were unregulated, entry was free, and a bookmaker was anyone who hung a satchel from a fencepost and offered to increase a punter's wealth. On a bad day, and often on a good one, they simply refused to pay out. Punters had their receipts snatched as they sought payment, or had genuine claims denied. Bookies' minders set upon those who persisted in demanding their winnings. If that did not work, the bookies took off before racing was over. Welshing became the term for such practices and it was an art form in itself. One gang specialised in offering incredible odds on all the day's races, bringing in wads of betting money, then folding their stand to steal away before racing started. Anyone who tried to stop them was 'done over'. Brawling soon became part of the festive activities. Added to this was pocket picking on a grand scale, a skill hatched in public gatherings and practised with astonishing skill at fairgrounds.

Gangs formed among the coarsest type of foul-mouthed ruffians. They occupied the best pitches and were strong enough to drive smaller outfits from the more profitable areas. Some of the worst fights were over the boundaries of a pitch and its location in the line; first and last pitches had a higher footfall than those in the middle and, inevitably, someone thought of charging bookies a fee for a trading positions. This led to gangs visiting bookies' stands to demand a few quid. They also took up collections for 'distressed relatives' and sold draw tickets at five or ten shillings a go for this same charitable purpose. Failure to pay meant a stand was demolished and likely the bookie with it. The cut-throat razor became the favoured weapon of intimidation. Bookies were often required to pay more than one gang: this became intolerable, to the point where bookies failed to make a living and threatened to shut up business. Larger, more organised gangs then offered protection for payment to them alone. Warfare ensued.

THE FIRST OF the organised racecourse gangs seem to have arisen in the Northeast and Midlands, primarily Newcastle and Birmingham. There was also a Welsh gang operating out of Cardiff, that gave its name to 'welshing' on bets. Around 1910, when race meetings became stewarded and conditions became tougher for the gangs, a compromise was reached between race organisers and rogues. If they regulated themselves, they would be recognised and allowed to operate their enterprises unchecked. They needed a leader and, as Birmingham had the strongest racing gang, it fell to Billy Kimber. Although still in his twenties, he had a reputation for brains and brawn, that desirable combination that produced many a gang boss. Many of the Birmingham toughs who associated with Kimber were drawn from the dark and dangerous streets of the Aston district, in the northeast of the city.

Kimber led the Brummagem mob in partnership with George 'Brummy' Sage, who had introduced him to racecourse enterprise. However, he was so closely associated with the Elephant and Castle gang that he was generally thought to have been from south London. The fact that he lived at addresses in Manor Road, Walworth, and York Road, Lambeth, both under the protection of the McDonald family, led me down this path in my earlier book *Elephant Boys*.

William 'Billy' Kimber was born on 7 February 1882, to William, a brass founder, and his wife, Catherine, at Court 55, House 6, Summer Lane, in Aston. William senior's parents were both Brummies, while Catherine's parents came from Ireland, something common in that area of the city. She had a brother, also William, who was no stranger to the inside of Birmingham's Winson Green Prison. The Kimber household was close to the renowned Gun Quarter, where much of Britain's munitions were made, and to the Royal George, Stag's Head, Bull's Head and Barrel Inn public houses. When Billy was shot and wounded in 1921, a newspaper reported that he belonged to a family well known in the Summer Lane district, including his brothers Harry and George. Although Billy by then gave his address as Hospital Street, a turning off Summer Lane, he was not there at the time of the shooting. He had moved in with his girlfriend, Florence Brooks, at Warren Street (now Grant Street), in Clerkenwell, London, not far from Darby Sabini's home in Collier Street.

Hospital Street was in the Aston district, which also housed Kimber associate Joe Gandley. In his teens Kimber would live in Warner Street, close to the Bordesley district; the only old part remaining is the Adam and Eve pub, and no doubt a number of Kimbers supped there. Nearby is Garrison Lane, where Billy knew all of the participants in a long-standing local feud. He grew up in a community where families took sides in disputes and would have been a natural gang member.

Birmingham had its share of teenage gangs, known colloquially as 'peaky blinders' for the caps they wore, and Billy joined up with the local 'boys'. At the age of eighteen, he was convicted of assault and served a term in Winson Green. By 1905, he was a leader and caught the eye of George Sage, five years older than Billy, who was associated with the Birmingham underworld during what would become known as the Garrison Lane Vendetta. In 1909, Billy's best mate, Joe Witton, received a four-year sentence and fifteen lashes of the 'cat' for a violent attack on rival gang member John Bagby. With the assistance of Isi Jacobs, he had bludgeoned, robbed, and then bludgeoned the unfortunate Bagby a bit more, just for the fun of it. The fact that Bagby was robbed obscures this event from recognition as an early incident in the vendetta.

Flogging was a punishment in regular use with military and naval services. It was also in use roughly from 1862 to 1962, as a corporal punishment for civil prisoners who broke prison regulations and as part of a court's sentence, although they lost their power to order it in 1948. It took two forms. The birch was a bundle of tough birch twigs bound together at one end with wire to make a handle. It was administered across the bare buttocks of a prisoner, who was laid across a cushioned 'horse' and had his legs and arms strapped down. A maximum of twenty-five strokes for under-eighteens and fifty strokes for older offenders was allowed. Birching was usually given for offences considered to be in need of discouragement, in addition to a custodial sentence. It was meant to hurt and was administered with relish. Offences punished by strokes of the birch included indecency such as importuning, living off immoral earnings and engaging in homosexual acts. It was originally introduced to discourage the abominable practice of white slaving. It was also used to discourage begging, sleeping rough and for being an incorrigible rogue, that catch-all for persistent offenders. In modern times it was given for crimes where serious violence had not been used; sometimes first offenders that had used violence were given the birch instead of the 'cat'.

The cat o' nine tails was a whip made up of nine knotted strands of rope and administered across the bare shoulders and back of an offender, who was strapped to a frame with his head covered so he could not see who was giving the punishment. There was a maximum of fifty strokes for over-eighteens. The 'cat' was given for robbery or assault with intent to rob by a person armed with an offensive weapon, on their own or in company with others. It was also ordered for violence leading up to a robbery or following it. It was meant to be a deterrent and was laid on with great force. Sometimes the birch was ordered for violent crime instead of the 'cat'. Older offenders more often were given the 'cat' than the birch, it being considered that birching, or the threat of it, at a younger age had not deterred their violent behaviour.

BILLY KIMBER MADE the step up from being just another tough when he went into partnership with Andrew Towey. Andrew was born in Nottingham in late 1888 but his parents moved their family to Cardigan Street, Birmingham. They teamed up to produce dot-and-dash cards that identified the form of racehorses and were sold to punters and book-makers. The cards were a useful addition to race cards but not altogether necessary. It is likely that Towey made them and Billy provided sales support, with the assistance of his racecourse acquaintances. Bookies were obliged to buy them at five shillings a time, then the sellers would 'prick' them with dots, dashes and other symbols to identify favourites and their closest challengers. Often they revised their opinion of form and updated the cards, for an extra five bob, of course. It was prudent for customers to purchase the cards for a quiet life. Those who declined found their pitches hemmed in by George Sage's men, who proceeded to jostle bookies and their customers, making business impossible. Kimber later described himself as a bookmaker, but his early occupation appears to have been a supplier to, and blackmailer of, bookies.

Handsome, well-built and charismatic, Kimber became overlord of the racing underworld. He used his Birmingham connections to organise the allocation of pitches at tracks all over the country, taking a donation or percentage as an administration fee. Without payment to Kimber, bookies and a range of conmen and welshers could not operate; there was also a scale of fees for the most favourable pitches. He did not allow everyone to benefit from his organisation. He preferred to drive off the small gangs of thugs and pickpockets who waylaid punters and robbed them at the edge of an open razor or with a clump on the head from a cosh, as they brought unwelcome attention to racecourse illegality. Jewish gangsters, who had held early dominance on racecourses, generally refused to pay Kimber. Their reward was to be evicted amid a series of punitive beatings and full-blooded gang fights. Course authorities and police mostly turned a blind eye, no doubt pleased that the Brummagem gang had ousted the lowlife who had made life uncomfortable from the north to the south of England.

Business success brought about Kimber's relocation to York Road, Lambeth, the street in which the tough McDonald brothers resided. It may be that Billy lived with them at number 116, the home of Grandma Mac, the mother of the McDonalds. Jim McDonald described the four-storey house and basement as 'a cottage'. The family occupied two top floors, landlord Max Frank had the second floor, and the downstairs was occupied by Florrie Dellow, a prostitute who allowed Stinie Morrison to move in to protect her, at the time he was sought for a murder on Clapham Common. Max Frank, who had jewellery shops in Southwark Bridge Road and Walworth Road, did time for receiving stolen goods. Kimber's purpose was the expansion of his business to southern courses, part-controlled by the brothers and to some extent by the burgeoning Sabini gang. This would become a major cause of conflict with the Sabinis.

THOMAS MACDONALD (my great-grandfather) was born in Exeter, Devon, of a Scottish military family. In 1831, cholera came to southern England, courtesy of Germany, and spread rapidly to all cities with poor sewerage systems. Thomas married Susanna Chapple in October 1834 and the following year they joined the exodus from Exeter to escape the epidemic. They went to London and left the train at Waterloo Station, settling in nearby Oakley Street (now Baylis Road), Lambeth. Had Thomas arrived directly from Scotland he would have alighted at King's Cross and settled in that district, in which case he would have sired north London gangsters instead of giving south London his grandchildren: Wag, Wal, Jim, Bert and Tom McDonald. The change in spelling of the surname came about at the birth of William, one of Thomas's three children. Registration of births altered William's surname and it remained with him and his own thirteen children, who became the 'fighting McDonalds'.

Thomas and Susanna's transfer to London was not without risk. Cholera struck all around the Lambeth area, killing thousands of people crammed into the streets and alleys of Lambeth Marsh. The only decent outcome was an eventual cleansing of rivers of filth and construction of improved sewage systems in major cities. Ironically, Susanna died from tuberculosis contracted in the squalid tenements of Lambeth.

Charles 'Wag' McDonald was born on 5 February 1877 at Valentine Place, Southwark, to Thomas's son William and his wife Phoebe. The nickname 'Wag' became attached to the name Charles through the mischievous adventures of 'Charley Wag the Boy Burglar' that appeared in penny dreadfuls from 1860. One edition, *Wild Boys of London*, so alarmed police that they had it banned, in the year of Wag's birth. He enlisted in the 1st Mounted Infantry, fought in the Boer War, and was present at the Boer surrender at Vereeniging in 1902. When demobbed, and in search of a trade, he developed widespread illegal street bookmaking operations, from his headquarters at Elephant and Castle. He became a major south London gang leader, with a significant presence in the West End, where he was an early nightclub protector. By 1909, his younger brothers Walter (Wal), Arthur James (Jim), Albert (Bert) and Tom (alias Tom King) had joined him. He was never an official bookmaker: instead he made his living from small punters who patronised local street bookies, and on racecourses where he hired himself out as a bodyguard and indulged in obtaining 'favours' from bookmakers who sought a quiet life.

Billy Kimber made an alliance with the brothers after learning they had gone nose-to-nose with the King's Cross Boys. Kimber needed London support to maintain his control over the racecourses, a grip that loosened when the McDonalds did their bit in the 1914-18 war. Tom was lost at sea and another brother, George, died on the first day of the Battle of the Somme. Following the war, sisters Ada and Annie contributed to the gang's organisation. Although bookmaking was central to their operations, the control of a network of shoplifters and receivers was their greatest accomplishment.

Wal, born on 1 January 1883, in Lambeth, led the Elephant and Castle gang during Wag's absence and is remembered as a tough street fighter. He was a bookmaker who also had many business interests in the West End. His greatest coup was the snatching of the Pari-mutuel takings at Longchamps, Paris, while the grandstand, which had mysteriously caught fire, was commanding the attention of its custodians.

Annie McDonald, born 20 March 1875 at Valentine Place, married Billy Burnup in 1899. They had business interests in Calcutta, India, where they dealt in expensive silks and made many trips between there and their Brixton home. They supplied England's black market with tax-evaded silks. Billy later became accountant to swindler Jake Factor. When the deals went sour, Billy tied a bootlace round his neck and rolled himself off his bed. Annie died on 4 July 1957.

Ada McDonald, born 31 January 1879 at Valentine Place, dealt in clothing and jewellery from her Walworth home. She purchased goods legitimately, from the giant Houndsditch Warehouse in the East End, and sold them to private customers and through various markets. She is said to have been at the head of a network of receivers of illicit goods and the controller of fencing outlets, although she was never convicted of any crime. Married to Elephant gang member Dan Johnston, she died in 1967.

Jim, born 13 September 1887 at Princes Buildings, Lambeth, backed up his brothers but was not comfortable with gang warfare. He was a good friend of Alf White, who was on the opposing side. Jim worked as a bodyguard and bouncer in Soho. Bert, born 5 March 1889 at Princes Buildings, was a quick-tempered fighter and close friend of Billy Kimber: he ran street bookie pitches in south London and was the chief organiser of a huge ring of shoplifters and receivers. Thomas (Tom King), born 10 September 1891 at Princes Buildings, was a dealer in stolen goods who had a number of stalls in East Street market.

THE WEST END gang was particularly spirited in defiance of the McDonald brothers and their new partner, Billy Kimber. They were led by Matt and Mike McCausland, both born in the Seven Dials district, just a spitting distance from Soho. Their parents had arrived from Dublin at King's Cross Station, looked around and found the area did not quite come up to their expectations; prudently, they settled in the more salubrious environs of Soho. However, their eldest son, Matt, soon moved himself back to King's Cross, where he teamed up with the King's Cross Boys under Alf White, in order to stand up to the south London's McDonalds. In later years, he formed an affiliation with the Sabini brothers. To complicate matters, Mike McCausland moved to Dodson Street, Waterloo: this was a bottle's throw from Elephant and Castle, where the McDonald brothers ruled, dishing out beneficence and punishment as suited them. Perhaps he fancied a takeover.

The earliest recorded clash between the Kings Cross–West End alliance and the Kimber–McDonald alliance came in Denmark Street, Soho, on 2 August 1909. Two of McDonald's boys, John Henry Dyer and Antonio Brizzie, attacked Fred Fisher and Charlie Milman, both King's Cross bookies who had extended their street pitches into the West End. Dyer opened hostilities by demanding a piece of silver from Fisher, a well-known invitation to pay up or receive a cut. Fisher declined and was knocked down by Dyer, then knocked down again by Brizzie when he got up; he was then given a good few kicks in the face. Dyer and Brizzie then turned on Milman and beat him to the ground, where Brizzie gave him a hefty kick in the groin.

Late the following day, in nearby Stacey Street, commission agent Jim Carey was struck by a piece of gas piping held by Brizzie, and was punched and kicked by Henry Byfield and Dyer, for a similar intrusion into McDonald territory. Brizzie and Dyer then attacked two police constables who tried to arrest them, Brizzie pulling a carving knife from his sleeve

125

and threatening to kill one of the constables. He was arrested after a considerable struggle. In court, he was given twelve months and recommended for deportation to his native Italy. Dyer was acquitted. It is clear from evidence given that these were revenge attacks for a fight on August Bank Holiday. Brizzie, Dyer and Byfield ran pitches in Soho for Wag McDonald. Byfield, the brother-in-law of Charlie Guerin, was once a leader of the Donkey Row gang of tearaways out of Carr Street, Limehouse.

Sometime in the early summer of 1910, Mike McCausland was holding forth in the Duke of Wellington public house, in the Waterloo Road, on his brother Matt's disdain for Kimber and the McDonalds. He was confronted by Bert McDonald, the youngest of the brothers, and urged to 'leave it out or step outside'. Mike, who was only twenty, decided that Bert, who was twenty-one, was not so advanced in years that he should be giving such admonitions. They fell to blows and Mike ended up in St Thomas's Hospital. There he was visited by his brother Matt, who was nine years older. The elder sibling then went in search of Bert, who also had older brothers. Before Bert could be 'sorted', Wag McDonald visited the King's Cross haunts of Big Matt, tracking him to his home in Osnaburgh Street. With him was Billy Kimber, who had added his strength to the McDonald camp. He was looking to move in on the McCausland's West End business of extorting money from low dives to let them operate in and around Soho. Wag and Billy, accompanied by a contingent of the boys, called on Matt: when he did not answer his knocker, they battered down the door, to find his mother trying to barricade herself into a bedroom. They left a message for Matt in the form of wrecked furniture.

Matt McCausland, however, was not afraid of this new combination. Moreover, he knew where Kimber lived. In July, he led a raid on his Lambeth home but Kimber was out. Two days later, Matt and Mike McCausland, accompanied by Sid Berman and others, raided the White Bear pub in Berwick Street. It was in the heart of Soho, an economic zone contested by the gangs. Again they found nothing. But as they left the pub at midday, they almost walked into Kimber, Henry Byfield, John Dyer and Henry's cousin Sue. Before fists could fly, Mike McCausland hauled out a heavy revolver and fired, prematurely. A bullet kicked up the tarmac in front of the four, who did the sensible thing and took off in all directions – Kimber, Dyer and Sue back the way they came, Byfield into Tyler's Court and on into Wardour Street, where Matt McCausland caught up with him and hit him with an iron bar. Byfield, who was as prepared as any Boy Scout ever was, pulled a life preserver[1] and a dagger and smashed Matt over the head with the former. Matt staggered around a bit, and then took off for Piccadilly Circus with Byfield in pursuit.

Mike McCausland, who had not been able to keep up with the nimbler Kimber, followed his brother's exodus to the Circus, where he came up behind Byfield, fired again – and missed again. Byfield stabbed him in the hand, causing him to drop the revolver. By now police had arrived and they grabbed Matt, who was bleeding heavily, and then Mike, leaving Byfield free to stab Matt several times in the neck and face while a policeman obligingly held him. The policeman let Matt slide to the pavement to grab Byfield, who was still striking at Matt as he wobbled his way to the ground.

At the Central Criminal Court, Byfield said he was only defending himself. After knocking Matt down, he had intended to stab him in the heart, in response to being struck with an iron bar. It was revealed that no guns had been found on the

---

1 The life preserver had many forms. In one police account, it is described as a piece of cord with metallic threads or binding, capable of dealing a dangerous blow. Tommy Benneworth carried a rubber truncheon bound with copper tubing. In American films, gangsters use a sap, a rubber cosh designed to knock a victim unconscious without killing him, hence the name life preserver.

McCauslands; strangely though, one was found on Byfield, who said a boy had picked it up and handed it to him. Police stated that a form of tribal warfare existed between two gangs in Soho, who took it upon themselves to beat, stab and shoot each other. Surprisingly, such battles did not make headline news. At the time, the papers were filling their columns with the saga of Dr Harvey Hawley Crippen and his young mistress, who were being sought after the remains of Crippen's wife were found under the cellar of their Camden Town home.

Henry Byfield, a twenty-eight-year-old denizen of Soho, was found guilty of attempting to murder Matt McCausland. Mr Justice Hamilton remarked that Byfield had been extremely candid in the witness box and was possessed of good intelligence for a primitive ruffian, then sentenced him to five years. Mike McCausland received eighteen months with hard labour, the judge being satisfied he was the ringleader. Matt, who had no previous convictions, got twelve months. He would be heard from again.

Charges against Sid Berman were dropped; he was a Bermondsey Boy, the forebear of a family of villains who would infest south and east London and the West End in the 1920s and '30s (in fact as late as 1970, a descendent of Sid Berman was blasted with a shotgun from a speeding car outside a Bermondsey shop, part of long-firm gang warfare in southeast London). Within a month, Sid was shot and wounded by McDonald man Bert Conway, who got three years for the deed. Billy Kimber made himself scarce by returning to live with relatives in Birmingham – and probably Salford, near Manchester, for a while – before coming back to London in 1911 to live in Clerkenwell, north of the river. To understand the world in which Billy Kimber matured, it is worth describing incidents he was involved in, and villains he associated with, around Birmingham's dark and deadly streets at the onset of the Twentieth Century.

The Garrison Lane Vendetta

GARRISON LANE SNAKES eastwards from the Birmingham district of Great Barr towards Bordesley Green. In the 1910s, it was a drab mixture of small shops, public houses and a sprawling brick works that sprinkled its red dust over the landscape. The Bristol-to-Birmingham Midland Railway crossed the lane for trains to curl their way to the main station at New Street. The lane lent its name to a feud between two families that became known as the Garrison Lane Vendetta.

The vendetta had started around 1908 and its principals were the Sheldon and Beach families, who fought a four-year war. Anyone aspiring to villainy, and who lived in the Great Barr district southeast of Birmingham's city centre, had to choose a side. After his hasty departure from London due to the McCausland-Byfield affair, the twenty-seven-year-old Billy Kimber affiliated himself with the Sheldon faction. Kimber had moved in with relatives in Warner Street. The area around Great Barr Street, where much of the fighting took place, housed many senior Brummagem Boys, including: Frank Simmonds, a music hall entertainer and acrobat, Joe Witton and Tommy Ingram, amply supported by hard men Joe Gandley, Alf Bradbury, Billy Draper, Eddie Ashdown and Jack Allard.

The Beach group was located around the Garrison Lane area, where they headquartered at the Royal George pub. The original cause of the dispute concerned William Beach beating up a Sheldon after an evening's drinking. Both protagonists had large families and many friends spread throughout the city. The final throes came in 1912, when Samuel Sheldon of

Barr Street, Tommy Ingram of Heathermill Lane, and Edward Tomkin of Floodgate Street, were summonsed for causing grievous bodily harm to William Beach. The three cross-summonsed Beach for assault. Sheldon and Ingram also assaulted Charles Franklin, who had threatened them with a revolver. Sheldon took the gun from him and Ingram cut Franklin on the cheek. In court, it was stated that a notorious vendetta between the Beach and Sheldon parties had developed into a long-standing feud, in which both parties were knocked about. Each gang had previously been prosecuted. Beach had since announced his intention of emigrating to Canada. After a month's adjournment, for police to find further witnesses, the trial was put back until later in the year.

This was overtaken by a fresh incident that resulted in some of the main protagonists being arrested. In court, it was stated that Sheldon's brothers were in prison for an earlier attack on Beach, who was the leader of Franklin's faction. Beach had since left the country in April or May 1912 to go to Canada. The feud was now said to be wider than just the Beach and Sheldon families.

In the late evening of Saturday, 12 October 1912, Sam Sheldon and Tommy Ingram sat in the bar of the King's Arms, Great Barr Street, at the end of a day's tour of their local pubs. Soon after 9 p.m. Ingram departed, leaving Sheldon alone. Ingram was fortunate in that he narrowly avoided four men who had heard he and Sheldon were doing the rounds and had come looking for them.

Charlie Connor entered first, followed closely by Charlie Franklin, Sammy Morris and Albert Broome, who closed the door behind him and leant his back against it. Connor went up to a man named Birkett, who he was friendly with, and advised him to clear out, as it was 'going to be on'. Then he turned to Sheldon and said, 'Hello Bossy, we've got you now.'

'You haven't come here for a row, have you?' asked Sheldon.

Connor, who was now short of words, struck Sheldon a blow with a life preserver and Morris and Franklin pulled revolvers from their coat pockets. As Sheldon toppled forwards across the bar, Franklin put his revolver over Morris's shoulder and fired two shots. One went through Sheldon's hat into the wall behind the bar; the other hit him in the side of the head, cutting a furrow across his scalp. The four men ran out. Sheldon shook his head, downed his drink, and collapsed on the floor. In hospital, he recovered sufficiently to be discharged the same day.

The four assailants were soon rounded up and, because the Recorder at the magistrates' court had warned previously that he did not have sufficient powers to deal with the feud, the prisoners appeared at Birmingham Assizes. Connor produced an alibi, saying all four of them had been drinking in the Royal George in Garrison Lane and when they left, he had gone home. Other witnesses placed him in the Sailor's Return in Great Barr Street shortly after the shooting. Evidence was given of shots being heard on the Friday evening before Saturday's shooting. Witnesses described the area as a place of war.

Morris denied that he had a revolver and gave evidence that Sheldon had approached Franklin and went to attack him with something he pulled from his pocket. Someone fired shots over his shoulder. He suggested a witness, Birkett, had not been present. Franklin admitted he fired the shots. He said Sheldon was about to attack him and that Morris got between them, so he fired twice in the air. The jury found Franklin, Morris and Broome guilty of attempted murder and Connor guilty of causing grievous bodily harm. Detective Sergeant Collins stated that, for the past four-and-a-half years, there had been periodic outbreaks between two gangs in the neighbourhood. No matter how badly members of either side were injured, they would not give information to the police.

His Lordship, Mr Justice Scrutton, asked if that meant they

preferred to 'fight it out'. Collins replied, 'That is so my lord, in this case I had the greatest difficulty in getting evidence, members of the public are terrified when called as witnesses and will frequently say what is not true.' His Lordship then asked Inspector Bennett if each side recruited members. Bennett replied, to laughter within the court, 'They have never let me into that secret.'

That was enough for the judge. He made it clear that a bitter feud existed between brotherhoods, who took it upon themselves to settle their arguments outside the law. He added that 'for a man to go into a public house with a revolver in his pocket, in order to look for a man who had taken part in a previous quarrel, was a state of things which it was undesirable should exist in any civilised city'. He sentenced Franklin to ten years, commenting that it was fortunate that he and the friends engaged in this silly war were such bad shots. There was an outcry and much weeping in the crowded gallery. Morris, who had a previous conviction for assault, received four years. Broome, who was Franklin's brother-in-law, received three years. Connor was sentenced to five years for striking Sheldon and acting in concert with Franklin's shooting of the victim.

Justice Scrutton rounded off the proceedings with a warning that penal servitude for life would be the next sentence if this state of affairs continued. He commended Inspector Bennett and Detective Sergeant Collins and recommended them for favourable consideration of their superiors. Connor's sentence was later reduced to three years on appeal. Thus ended the Garrison Lane Vendetta.

THE TROUBLES intermingled with racecourse business. When Charles Cutler, a thirty-three-year-old Birmingham bookmaker's assistant who had taken sides with the Beach faction, was asked to contribute to George Sage's pension, he told George it was virtuous to live in penury – or something like that. Cutler, who had been in some trouble with the law, fancied himself as a fighting man. Sage, who could not allow himself to be treated with such frivolous disdain, summoned his pal Jack Allard, a forty-two-year year-old racing man recently released from prison, to help him settle the matter with Cutler. A scuffle broke out, bringing reinforcements for both sides until a shaky armistice was agreed.

Later, in the Royal George pub on the corner of Garrison Lane and Tilton Road, Allard sought out Cutler and threatened to 'bodge his eyes out'. Patrons who warned Cutler of the risk he was taking separated the men. Cutler was not to be put off and made it plain he was not afraid of taking on the Sage outfit. When he saw Allard and Alf Bradbury in Stratford Road, he went straight up to them and offered to fight them one at a time. On his hand flashed a large knuckleduster. Both declined the invitation. Detective Sergeant Farrington, who had been posted to Kimber territory to watch out for such goings on, had seen Allard and Bradbury leave Kimber's residence in Warner Street. He had followed them into Stratford Road, where he saw Cutler approach them. He sensed trouble and headed towards it just as Allard and Bradbury turned away. He heard Bradbury say, 'If you want a fight, fight fair.' Cutler went to his mother's house in Larches Street, where he told her of the incident and said Allard had again threatened to 'bodge' his eyes out.

Late in the evening of 29 February 1912, the row between Cutler and Allard came to a head. Cutler had spent the evening with his girlfriend, Beatrice Bannister, at a leap-year dance at the Hippodrome Amusement Park. Afterwards, Cutler had seen Beatrice to her home in Larches Street, where he dallied until 11 p.m., before leaving for his home just around the corner in Marshall Street. When he reached the corner, Allard stepped out of the darkness and hit him several blows with his fist. Cutler staggered and fell into the gutter, where Allard bent over him and punched him some more. He then picked up his umbrella, stood astride the prostrate man, lined up the steel ferrule at the tip of his brolly; with surgical adroitness, he speared it through his victim's right eye socket into his brain, fracturing his skull in the process. Witnesses restrained Allard as he tried to walk away, and summoned the police. Constable Alden arrived to find Allard struggling with John Malins, a young master baker who had been waiting for his girlfriend. On seeing Allard break free from two men and a woman who were trying to hold him, Malins had gone after him. All the while, Allard was threatening to take out a revolver and blow out Malins' brains. Constable Alden was threatened with the same fate: with considerable difficulty, and the assistance of others, he managed to get handcuffs on the prisoner.

At the police station, a search found that Allard did not have a revolver on him. Obligingly, he said that he had been waiting for Cutler all day so he 'could do for him, if he did have his revolver with him he would have done for him by blowing his brains out'. As it happened, the revolver was not needed. Later the next day, Cutler died from his terrible wound.

Charged with murder, Allard said that he had stepped out to confront Cutler, who then swung at him with a knuckleduster. He had held his umbrella out in an attempt to keep Cutler off and the other man must have impaled himself upon the tip. Witnesses for Allard said that Cutler was a very quarrelsome fellow who had threatened Allard, a thoroughly decent chap, on numerous occasions. It nearly worked. A sympathetic jury convicted Allard of manslaughter with a recommendation for mercy. Then, however, his record of petty crime as a youth, leading to housebreaking and assaults on racing people and police in his maturity, was read out in court. He was sentenced to seven years penal servitude, the judge remarking 'that what might be possible in a mining camp on the frontiers of civilisation was absolutely impossible in the streets of Birmingham'. In 1912, thoughts of the quality of frontier life in South Africa and Australia would not have seemed strange. Further afield in Bolivia it had not been long since the demise of Butch Cassidy and the Sundance Kid. The wild frontier was not yet dead: even, it would appear, in Birmingham.

Frank Simmonds was a music hall contortionist, acrobat and sleight-of-hand practitioner, the latter of which skills had brought him a prison sentence for lifting wallets and watches from a less appreciative public when he was with the Camden Town gang. He became associated with Sage tyro Billy Kimber after performing at Birmingham's Hippodrome. He was arrested and jailed as one of Kimber's racecourse pests, a term frequently applied by police who resented the forbearance racing authorities gave to blackmailers and pickpockets. In 1912, Simmonds failed to fulfil a condition of reporting to his local police station, after the granting of a ticket-of-leave. Neither did he wait for the police to call for him at Kimber's parents' home. He took off for Newport, Wales, where he met up with his eighteen-year-old girlfriend, Pearl Lazar, who had sneaked out of her Cardiff home without telling her husband, George, she was leaving. The two set up home in a flat in Newport.

The Birmingham police, who could not find Frank, picked up a lead on Pearl. Acting on this tip, Cardiff police visited her home, where they learned from her husband that she had been visiting Newport recently and that, after challenging her over a suspected lover, he was convinced she was meeting someone there. The police had no lead on where the couple were staying, until Frank Simmonds obligingly fell out with his landlord, Francis Hobbs, and knocked him down the stairs. Hobbs, who did not consider this a reasonable exchange for the rent, called the police. He did not name Simmonds, who was using an alias; what he did say was that his assailant was sharing an apartment with an unruly woman called Pearl.

Detective Inspector Tanner and Inspector Cox swiftly departed Newport Police Station and arrived before Frank and

Pearl could complete their midday flit. They entered through the already opened street door. As they approached the kitchen, Simmonds pulled a loaded revolver from his trouser pocket. Tanner leapt at him and gripped his hand, and they crashed about the kitchen in a desperate struggle. Simmonds got off a shot that went into the fire grate. Tanner managed to jam his finger between the trigger and trigger-guard, thereby saving himself, as Simmonds pressed the revolver against his stomach and tried to get off another shot. The struggle continued. Cox tried desperately to pull the gun away from Tanner's stomach. Landlord Hobbs joined in: Pearl was not happy with that, and jumped on Hobbs's back. He felt something sharp stick in his neck and twisted away as Pearl jabbed him again and again with a handful of hatpins. Meanwhile, Cox succeeded in getting the gun from Simmonds, much to Tanner's relief: his finger was skinned down to the bone.

Simmonds was exhausted. 'You ought to go down on your knees and thank God you are not in eternity,' he gasped to Tanner. 'Tonight my intention was murder. If I had seen you come in I would have shot you both dead. I am a good shot but will not give you any trouble now.' Simmonds was jailed for shooting with intent to murder. Pearl Shibko was cautioned for causing grievous bodily harm.

THE ONSET OF World War One brought a temporary end to large-scale racing, which was almost entirely banned for fear of Zeppelin attacks. It was too late, however, to prevent Tooting bookie George Morton being coshed with an iron bar and stabbed seventeen times after a dispute at Gatwick Races: he was then thrown from a train onto railway lines at Clapham Junction by Elephant and Castle men Jim O'Neill and Alf Catlin. He was held sufficiently responsible for his own death for charges to be reduced from murder to manslaughter.

Some gangsters did their bit by going off to fight Germans instead of each other. Kimber joined up in 1915. In 1916, he was back in Birmingham with a medical discharge. In 1919, when racing made a spectacular recovery from its hiatus, rival organisations began to encroach on Kimber's operations. Gangs took on a fresh boldness. It was not easy to obtain work and the more shiftless variety of ex-servicemen, and those who had not enlisted at all, travelled by train and taxi to race meetings for an opportunity to swindle and steal. Gangs of pickpockets swarmed over courses, where they became such a menace that peaceable racegoers refrained from taking an enjoyable day out. There were incidents of gangs grabbing men, stripping them of their clothes and valuables, even their railway tickets, all witnessed by racegoers too scared to intervene.

Boxing matches, too, were a regular target for the race gangs. Boxing was hugely popular before the war and London venues such as The Ring at Blackfriars and Premierland and Wonderland in Stepney hosted regular contests. According to the account related by Patsy Hagate, a well-known master of ceremonies in the boxing ring:

> It was quite a common thing for promoters of box-
> ing shows to pay what is sometimes called "protection
> money" to gangs who otherwise would have made
> themselves decidedly unpleasant. This money would
> occasionally be paid before the show started, a sum
> previously agreed upon being passed over, but often
> enough the organizer of the programme would merely
> be confronted by a number of men in his office as he
> was in the act of couting his receipts and receive a
> demand for a specified sum. Generally the money was
> handed over without any argument ...[1]

1 Gerald Walter, *White Ties and Fisticuffs*, Hutchinson's Library of Sports and Pastimes, 1951.

Interestingly, the gangsters would not make their demands too often, as this might kill the goose that laid the golden egg.

From time to time, a well-organised mob would stage a mass raid on a crowd, relying on speed, ferocity and overwhelming numbers to grab cash and valuables in the minimum time for the maximum return. Perhaps the worst such raid was in November 1908, on the night the hard-hitting Canning Town lightweight Johnny Summers took on American Jimmy Britt, at the Memorial Grounds in Canning Town. Summers won a famous victory before a sellout crowd, but the night was marred by the scenes that occurred immediately afterwards. They were recorded by James Butler, one of a number of ring-side reporters forced to climb through the ropes for safety.

> From the outskirts of the large crowd an organised bunch of thugs advances, planned with the skill of a modern Commando raid. There must be two to three hundred of the boys, robbing spectators with lightning speed. Watch-chains are ripped from waist-coats of indignant men. Race-glasses are snapped from straps by one swish of a razor and wallets are snatched from the surprised crowd mostly too afraid to protest. Even gold spectacles are grabbed from their owners' noses.
>
> To resist is asking for trouble. One big fellow protests, but is immediately silenced by a cosh and as he rests there is given a most scientific and speedy going over. The little fellow with the rat-like face and ferret eyes who has slugged him even relieves his unconscious victim of his dental plate. This, after all, is a gold rush.[2]

The mob didn't have things all their own way. One old knuckle fighter, Alf Mitchell, dropped several of 'the boys'

2 James and Frank Butler, *The Fight Game*, The World's Work: Kingswood, 1954.

like skittles. Future world champion Freddy Welsh, then a top lightweight contender, was left unmolested at ringside, with his hands on his hips and his straw boater pushed back on his head, looking on bemused as the battle raged around him.

Gangs that Billy Kimber had ousted from the tracks sought to re-establish the old practices of blackmail and pocket picking. Dodger Mullins and Alf White were the toughest of Kimber's rivals and, for a while, it looked as though these east London and north London toughs would combine to form a rival organisation big enough to take control. Both gangs plagued trains travelling to and from racecourses, where they stole from wallets that were loaded for betting or snug with winnings, and ran crooked card games and every type of scam. White's gang had members all around the Hoxton and King's Cross districts and were sometimes referred to as the Titanic. Dodger Mullins's gang was located in Bethnal Green and was sometimes referred to as the Flash Mob.

At Brighton and Hurst Park races, in the summer of 1920, police and magistrates took a firm stance against racecourse pests by jailing many with hard labour. Among those arrested at Hurst Park, near West Molesey in Surrey, were members of both the Mullins and White gangs: Bobby Jacobs and brothers Wally, Belcher and Ed Lee, all hailing from east and north London, who had got together to come up with a unique money-making wheeze. Police observed them crossing a river at Hurst Park by ferry after demanding pound notes from punters who arrived on the free racecourse. The idea was that they would be allowed unmolested views of racing only if they forked out a quid. When police pounced, the four jumped into their boat and began rowing furiously against the current, only to find the constables rowing towards them. They were arrested while scrambling up the riverbank.

But the Mullins–White partnership soon fractured. A major brawl followed on the Brighton course between White's King's Cross Boys and Mullins's Bethnal Green gang, who had fallen out after White invited Darby and Harry Sabini to his home to discuss joining the alliance. Harry Sabini set up a stand at Brighton on a site usually occupied by Mullins man George Sewell, who called for reinforcements. Over thirty men battered and chopped each other and police, armed with truncheons, broke a few heads before hauling miscreants before magistrates. Among the arrested was Mullins, who received three months to brood over White's treachery.

There were calls for a force of specialist police to be set up that could recognise and deter ruffians. Police exerted pressure on the worst of the gangsters and on those operating in a semi-legitimate style. When racecourse authorities realised they could not deal with the problem with police alone, they looked again to Kimber. To thwart Mullins and Alf White, Kimber rekindled his alliance with the Elephant and Castle gang, led by the McDonald brothers. They had fought with Mullins for pickings from East End and south and west London drinking clubs, pubs and gambling spielers, and were increasing their interest in racecourses. Together they expelled Mullins's gang from the courses and Kimber used his new alliance to move into the London underworld.

The Elephant and Castle gang became a by-word for criminal organisation and enterprise. Proceeds from shoplifting on a grand scale provided funds for moving in on the West End, where they battled with Matt and Mike McCausland's West End Boys for control of protection rackets and money soaked from illegal gambling dens. They received kickbacks from other gangs' profits and were hard on those who did not 'kick in'. Their partnership with Kimber and George Sage made them dominant on racecourses throughout England and in the West End, where they paid for little and enjoyed much.

The gang is fabled for its massive shoplifting raids on the West End and other city centres. Stolen goods were fenced by the gang, who fiercely protected the female hoisters and boosters. Because of their expertise in thievery, their propensity for violence is often overlooked. However, they were tough enough to push around other gangs from north, west, central and east London, whom they fought for control of other business enterprises such as protection and the lucrative allocation and control of turfside bookmaking pitches.

Perhaps at their most notorious in the 1920s and '30s, the gang was the focus of the newly created Police Flying Squadron (soon truncated to Squad) that marked them for extermination and engaged them in a number of battles. The Flying Squad was formed by Chief Inspector Wensley in 1919, to combat the growth of motor car gangs. It comprised of handpicked, burly officers, with a reputation for stretching the rules of engagement, equipped with fast Lea Francis cars, surveillance vans, and two-way radios. They were ordered to stake-out gangs and ambush them. Perhaps their most famous clash with the Elephant was a major Saturday night brawl, after some of the gang were followed from Old Kent Road to Pimlico, where they were interrupted while trying to break into a furriers. A wild chase ended in Westminster, when their motor car was brought to a stop and a fierce fight ensued: seven villains against ten coppers, jemmies against truncheons. Both sides suffered injuries before the seven were arrested. There was much singing of Albert Chevalier's 'Knocked 'Em in the Old Kent Road' in south London pubs that night.

Seven men were subsequently jailed, including George Smith, William Woods and Arthur Williams for eight years, plus six years for being habitual criminals. Smith was also convicted of attacking a police constable who tried to arrest him whilst he was burgling a Brixton factory. Smith's weapon was a can of condensed milk, filled with lead and attached to a rope, which he swung with great ferocity, knocking the constable unconscious. Four men received lesser sentences: Frederick Cole, six years; Henry Jackson, three years; John Morbin and Thomas Burfield, twelve months.

AT ABOUT THIS time, a new player entered the game. Eddie Emanuel was an East End Jew who had made money from the clothing trade and from fraud. He could afford to move to more pleasant surroundings in northwest London and had new ideas to offer, including race sheets, which he printed for pennies and sold at exorbitant prices to bookies at racecourses. He charged for chalk and sponge services for board wiping, which had to be paid for by dropping half crowns into a bucket, and proposed to take royalties from food vendors as well as bookies, as a 'tax' on their pitches. He and his ilk ensured bookies bought services they could have supplied themselves at little cost. The printing of racing lists was a good earner. Kimber and Andrew Towey supplied dot-and-dash cards (sometimes called card pricking), but Emanuel bettered this by printing detailed race cards which bookies were persuaded they needed: the dot-dashes were not as helpful as printed lists. In both cases, it was prudent to buy them, but as the bookies were already paying Billy Kimber, the scene was set for trouble.[3]

Emanuel could handle himself. He had graduated from the dark streets of Jacob's Island Rookery in Bermondsey, in southeast London. His parents came from Spitalfields, where the famous East End fruit and vegetable market stood, and his father had a greengrocer's shop. Edward was one of six children, including brothers Alfred, Philip and Isaac. The family surname is correctly spelled with one 'm', although it crops up in numerous books and newspaper reports with a double consonant.

As young men, Eddie and Philip crossed the Thames by Tower Subway and later, by way of the new Tower Bridge, to

---

3 Towey gave up his dots and dashes in the 1940s after Kimber had transferred his interests to other areas, and at a time when Emanuel's services had become a legitimate business and achieved universal acceptance at courses across the country. Andrew Towey continued as a heavy backer of racehorses and is rumoured to have been badly roughed up in the 1940s by newcomer Jack Spot.

work as fish porters at Billingsgate market. They also mixed with gangs misbehaving around Aldgate Pump, particularly 'the Forties', a Stepney street crew of teenage tearaways at war with their neighbours, the Wapping Boys. They then moved on and became associated for a time with the East End's premier tearaway, Arthur Harding, and his tribe of petty dock thieves and pickpockets. They also met Bethnal Green hardnut Hyman 'Long Hymie' Eisenberg, who tutored them in the dark arts of terrorising shopkeepers and stallholders for a share of their income. Eddie and Philip later worked as porters at Spitalfields market before opening their own fruiterer's businesses.

Arthur Harding considered Emanuel to be the guv'nor of the Jewish underworld:

> He was the Jewish Al Capone – everything was grist to his mill … He used to fix boxing fights and all – there was a fight between Cockney Cohen and Young Joseph of Aldgate. Well there were thousands on the match: two Jewish chaps fighting each other and thousands of Jewish people betting. Cockney Cohen was the favourite; he was regarded as the top man of the two. Emmanuel wanted Cohen to lay down: they tried to pay him to take the drop, but Cohen refused. Somebody stuck a knife in him.[4]

In 1904, Eddie was cautioned for threatening David Masters, the owner of a market stall behind the Angel, Islington, with a revolver. Apparently, Masters had not paid a £22 bill for his victuals and Eddie thought a lead slug was a fair response. Police, who found a loaded gun on Emanuel when they arrested him, described him as a very dangerous man. He got off on a promise to behave in future. The same year he was

---

4 Raphael Samuel, *East End Underworld*, Routledge & Kegan Paul, 1981.

fined for running a gaming house in Whitechapel. The club owner got off, but fifty-seven punters were fined.

By 1907, Eddie had moved permanently across the Thames and married Elizabeth Pruden, from Stepney Green. He was living at the time at Stoney Lane, in the City of London. Elizabeth was twenty-one, Eddie twenty-six. They would have two daughters.

In September 1908, John McCarthy, a twenty-seven-year-old contractor and leader of Stepney's Watney Streeters, was sentenced to three months at the Central Criminal Court for unlawfully wounding Emanuel by shooting him. The incident centred on Spitalfields market, where Emanuel carried on his business as a fruit supplier. McCarthy had beaten up Henry Ivey, who called on Emanuel to sort it out. Emanuel summoned McCarthy to the Nelson pub, near Watney Street, where he questioned him and, not being satisfied by assurances he would leave Ivey alone, bolted the door and set about him. The landlord quickly unbolted the door and the fight spilled into Nelson Street, where Emanuel gripped McCarthy by the throat and tried to strangle him over a barrow. McCarthy broke free, pulled a revolver from his belt, and squeezed the trigger three times: the first two brought only clicks, but the third put a bullet through Emanuel's chest, leaving a gaping exit wound. Even so, he chased after McCarthy before collapsing. Police arrested McCarthy at his home off Watney Street. Emanuel spent five days in hospital and made a full recovery. His doctor, in evidence, described him as a powerfully built man.

In 1909, Emanuel appeared as a witness in a deception trial concerning monies not paid for market goods: in this, he seems to have been the guilty party but managed to blame someone else. In 1912, he was fined for keeping a gaming house and in September 1917, police mounted a late-night raid on a house in Whitechapel where, amid pandemonium, they arrested 101 men for gaming. The property was a disused tailor's workshop converted into a gambling hall, with card tables, faro, incandescent lighting, a bar, refreshment counter and extra room in the loft for overspill. Emanuel, described as a gaming house keeper and bookmaker of Globe Road, Bethnal Green (where Dodger Mullins lived as a child), paid the rent and charged per game. Although it was suspected someone else had responsibility for the club, Emanuel took the blame and paid a fine of £300. Police said they were checking details of men of military age and would charge some with being absentees. Of the 101 prisoners, only twenty-eight were British subjects. Many were tailors. None of them had joined the war effort by becoming munitions workers and indeed Emanuel himself would not see service in World War One.

Emanuel also had connections with the clothing trade and was a clever, though nasty, organiser of money-making scams, including fixed boxing matches. It is known he set up a club to which crooks subscribed a weekly ten shillings to provide for defence and for bail, in order to enable an opportunity to set up an alibi. If that failed, the fund would provide £3 a week family subsistence. At this time, the practice of demanding money from tradespeople to pay fines, or prop up the families of jailed villains, had been developed into a business. In October 1922, Emanuel would forfeit bail he had put up for Harry Sabini for the Paddington Railway Station disturbance (see page 174).

But it was his involvement in the racing world that brought him into conflict with the formidable Billy Kimber and his allies. Emanuel had acquired some knowledge of printing and used his skills to print the race sheets that he now sold to bookmakers and punters. He had no intention of backing off from this lucrative racket and set up a meeting at his home at Elm Corner in Finchley Road, Hendon, issuing a summons to Kimber and Wag McDonald to attend. They declined, feeling they were in a position of strength and had the troops to win any fight with this interloper. By doing so, they threw down the gauntlet to Emanuel.

Emanuel knew that his old protector, Arthur Harding, was not robust enough to stand up to the Brummagems and their south London allies. For his fighting partner he instead enlisted Alf Solomon, a truly bad man from central London with solid connections to the east London Jewish community. Solomon often crops up in the history of British crime: always he fails to be treated with the notoriety he deserves. This man was a major criminal. Wag McDonald said he was the worst man he ever knew and he knew many, both in Britain and the United States. It is typical that Alf should later be the man who shot Billy Kimber.

Abraham Alfred Solomon was born on 15 February 1892 at Long Acre, Strand, central London. Like Emanuel, his parents sold fruit and the family lived close by the Covent Garden fruit, vegetable and flower market, which Alf haunted between prison spells and terrorising race goers. He never strayed far from this patch. He had seven brothers and two sisters and all attended Covent Garden School. His five elder brothers later operated a respectable bookmaking business under the name of Charles Lewis, a combination of two of their Christian names. Other members of the Solomon clan riddled Covent Garden market. His Uncle Alfred and Aunt Virginia ran a fruiterers' business and were known for being quarrelsome, so much so that they were eventually kicked out of the market and turned to operating a rifle range in Fulham. In the summer of 1919, Alf married twenty-one-year-old Esther Shaps.

Solomon and his gang had been at war with Dodger Mullins's Bethnal Green mob. He lived uncomfortably in the Covent Garden district, with the East Enders on one side and the unpredictable Italian gang from Clerkenwell and King's Cross on the other. With a master stroke, Solomon teamed up with the Italians, led by Charles 'Darby' Sabini and his King's Cross allies, to create a truly powerful force.

Emanuel provided the Sabinis, Alf White and Alf Solomon with the means to make money. In 1921, his new combination set up the Racecourse Bookmakers and Backers Protection Association, an organisation headed by Walter Beresford and managed by Eddie's brother Philip. Among stewards appointed were White, and Darby and Joe Sabini. Freddie Gilbert also claimed to have been employed by the association. By 1922, it had shed its sinister staff in order to establish a decent reputation.

Emanuel's new friendships did not endear him to Harding neophytes such as Dodger Mullins, George Dido and Bobby Nark, whose crude blackmailing of bookmakers was not in tune with Emanuel's business plan. On other occasions, Emanuel was shot at by Freddie Gilbert and shaken up by Jim McDonald, proving he was not loved any greater in Camden Town, Finsbury and Elephant and Castle. In the 1920s, the Elephant and Castle and the Birmingham gang teamed up with London's Camden Town and Finsbury gangs, to do battle with the these north, east and central London gangs led by White, Solomon and the Sabini brothers, with the latter providing the real muscle. The stage was now set for the biggest gang war Britain had ever seen.

Arrivederci Roma

TRADITION HAS IT that the Sabini were a tribe in ancient Italy with lands close to Rome. In legend, followers of Romulus, who had founded Rome and needed women to increase its population, carried off the Sabine women. The Sabini besieged Rome until peace was made.

Their English incarnation were no less formidable. The first sign of them was in southeast London: Charles H. Sabini was born in Elephant and Castle in 1835. In 1881, he owned a tobacconist and newsagents shop in Walworth with his wife Charlotte, who was born in Kent. Another Sabini, born in London but removed to the United States, was Henry: a bookkeeper born in 1838. He had two sons, Harry and Willie, born in Detroit, Michigan. Harry is a name that runs through the extended Sabini family. In September 1842, John Sabini (using the name Henry), of Kennington, was convicted of fraud.

The central north London Sabini family appears to have arrived some time in late 1881. In crime mythology, they sometimes appear as Sicilians, even to the point of importing Sicilian knifemen to strengthen their team. Census returns show they were in fact from Borgotaro, near Parma, in the Emilia Romagna region north of Rome: a district more famous for its mushrooms than its knifemen. The elders seem to have been peaceful enough; it was some of their children, particularly those born to Anglo-Italian unions, who became villains. The reason for this is the settlement of the modern Sabinis into an area seething with criminals: Clerkenwell is bordered by King's Cross, Holborn, Hoxton and Finsbury. Close by are Camden Town, Islington, Shoreditch, Bethnal

Green and, across the Thames, Lambeth, Southwark and Bermondsey. Each of these districts provided allies or enemies, or both. Sometimes all of the gangs battled in nearby Soho, in the heart of the West End.

The adult Sabini immigrants were artisans, such as bootmakers and farriers. The dozens of children they produced spread around the back streets and alleys of the Clerkenwell district that came to be called Little Italy. The 1891 census shows Italians, Irish and English packed into hovels within narrow streets. Also there was the House of Correction for adult male offenders, at Coldbath Fields. The prison was for short-term prisoners serving between seven days and two years. Prisoners were subjected to deliberately irksome hard labour. This was a different regime to convict prisons such as Pentonville and Brixton, which were for penal servitude and those awaiting transportation. All inmates worked to contribute to their own support and keep them occupied, and some were taught trades.

The acknowledged leader of the Sabini brothers, Darby, was born Otavio Handley in Holborn, in 1888. His father, Otavio Sabini, but known as Joseph, was born in Italy, while his mother was Eliza Handley. Marriage registrations show that Eliza did not marry Otavio until 1898. In 1890, Otavio senior, of Little Bath Street, Clerkenwell, appeared as a witness in the murder trial of Marzieli Valli. He had stabbed Ugo Melandri to death after a row in the Anglo-Italian Club in Great Bath Street. In 1894, as an ice-cream vendor of Clerkenwell, Otavio was wounded in a fight with a sixty-year-old pimp, Thomasso Casella. In court, Otavio needed an interpreter, but one witness said he had heard him shouting in English. Darby's uncle and aunt, Guiseppe and Domenica Sabini, lived near the Elephant.

Darby grew to about five foot eight inches tall, with a barrel chest. He was immensely strong, with a punch that could break a jaw, especially when reinforced with his favourite knuckleduster. In conversation with James Morton, author of many authoritative books on Britain's gangland, Darby claimed to have fought forty-seven bouts as a welterweight out of Clerkenwell, from 1909 to 1917, under the name of Fred Handley. In late 1913, as Ottavio, he married Annie Potter, from Hackney. They lived in St Helena Street, Clerkenwell, a tiny alley tucked away behind Amwell Street and just a short stroll from Farringdon Road.

Joseph Sabini, brother of Darby, was born in 1893, on Baker's Row, which still runs off Farringdon Road right into the heart of Clerkenwell's Italian community. The extended Sabini family still occupied many dwellings in the narrow streets behind Clerkenwell Green, adjacent to the White family's residences that lay slightly more northwards towards King's Cross. Brother George was born in 1895 and Harry, the only one born in wedlock, in 1900.

The mother of the Sabini children, Eliza Handley, who could not write her name, was English. She met Otavio Sabini when he visited her family's home at Easton Place, Clerkenwell. Her children were born with, or adopted, names identical to her own three brothers: Frederick, Charles and Joseph. It has been suggested that Darby's sister was a driving force behind the criminal Sabinis; if so, this would be Mary, who was born in 1890. Otavio senior died in Clerkenwell in 1902, aged forty-nine, while Eliza died in 1919, aged fifty-four.

The lesser known of the criminal Sabinis is Frederick, born in 1881. In 1917, he was cited as co-respondent in the divorce of Mark and Mignonette Goldstein. In May 1921, he married Mary Austin. He gave his age as thirty-six, knocking off a couple of years; Mary, who may have been one of the Forty Thieves, was twenty-one. Fred, a turf commission agent, was living in a charming three-storey house in West Square, at Elephant and Castle, not far from Charles and Charlotte Sabini's Walworth shop: perhaps this is how the Sabinis once were friends of the McDonalds. Some believe Fred was actually the worst of the bunch, but that he managed to keep out of the spotlight.

The Sabinis' entry into racecourse hostilities came at the request of Eddie Emanuel and Jewish bookmakers, who were being severely roughed up by East End toughs such as Dodger Mullins, by the Birmingham gang led by Billy Kimber, and by the Camden Town gang led by Freddie Gilbert and George Sage, who charged for pitches and services, backed by an open razor. When the Jewish bookies turned to the Sabinis and their allies, the King's Cross gang led by Big Alf White, Kimber strengthened his alliances with the Elephant and Castle and Finsbury gangs. The result would be years of warfare until the pivotal year of 1925, when some sort of accommodation was reached. Even then, there were sporadic outbursts of violence up to the so-called 'Battle of Lewes' in 1936.

At the same time as the fighting between the Bethnal Green and King's Cross gangs, another major clash happened at Brighton races in 1920. A section of the Italian gang, led by Joe Sabini, younger brother of the more celebrated Darby, went around the free side of the course with a bucket: they compelled bookies, vendors, grafters and punters to throw in half-crowns for 'services', evicting those who declined, and cutting one argumentative bookie with a cut-throat razor. They also chased off Kimber's token force. The next day they tried it again: it was a mistake. Bookies had made contact with Kimber and a large force, led by Wal McDonald, was on its way. Sabini and his gang were frisked, had their collection money confiscated, and were given a kicking as a disincentive to be so cheeky in future. When police arrived, all that was available for arrest was a gang of local pickpockets and other sideliners: fourteen small fry in all. But Joe Sabini, had been humiliated.

According to Tom Divall, a former detective and later race-course security adviser, in his book *Scoundrels and Scallywags*, the trigger for intervention by the Sabinis when racecourses reopened after World War One was this:

Three low blackguards, always more or less full of liquor, visited the cheap ring at various meetings and terrified and blackmailed a number of small East End bookmakers working there. If the latter did not shell out, they were cruelly assaulted and badly damaged. This sort of thing went on for a while until it became unbearable, and the Sabinis took up the cudgels in defence of the bookies.

These three have mistakenly been cited as northerners or Brummies. In fact, they were south Londoners who were part of the unwholesome alliance between the Elephant and the Brummagems.

George Moss was born in 1880 at Orb Street, Southwark. The street feeds directly into East Street market, which runs down to Walworth Road, which winds its way to Elephant and Castle, the hub of south London's gangland. Moss went round racecourses demanding payment for unwanted services. Usually he stood sideways-on to bookies, so they could see the hammer nestling in his half-opened coat. He had a criminal record dating back to before the war and was in Pentonville Prison in 1911. His last fling came on Easter Monday, April 1921, while practising his unsubtle menacing of bookmakers. He was arrested with John Carpenter, from Walworth Road, and Barney Cook, a Bermondsey Boy and close friend of protection gangster Joe Jackson, after they were seen going from bookmaker to bookmaker at Kempton Park Racecourse, demanding money. All three were heavily built and had hammers protruding from their coats. Cook shook a hammer in the face of one bookie who was slow to cough up and Moss threatened another with a beer bottle.

Although the bookies handed over money, none of them would appear as witnesses for fear of retaliation. Even so, magistrates jailed Moss, known as 'Mad Mossy', for twelve months and Cook and Carpenter for three months, all with hard labour. The three described themselves as number callers legitimately collecting their wages. Number calling was a crude means of intimidation. Villains would shout to bookmakers the numbers of horses and the jockeys riding them, even though the information was displayed on boards hoisted high enough for all to see. The chaps would then approach to collect their 'wages' and would be extremely unpleasant if they were denied. It was simply a means to obtain money by bullying and blackmail.

It is probable that the Sabinis had identified the trio to police. One story tells that they rubbed chalk on the palm of a hand and slapped a villain on the back in friendly fashion, leaving a telltale handprint for police to know whom to observe.

Another account of the escalation of violence in 1921 comes from former boxing referee Moss Deyong, who knew many of the thugs. He suggested the trouble originated at Sandown Park in Surrey, when a mobster tried to force a Jewish bookmaker named Lewis, real name Solomons, to pay out on a bet he had not accepted. Lewis refused.

> Suddenly the mobster swung his race-glasses, heavy and solid, into the bookmaker's face. Down went Lewis, and the assailant promptly stepped on his unprotected face as he lay on the ground, immediately afterwards slipping away into the crowd. Lewis was picked up, his face a bloody mass and with several teeth missing. From that moment the gang wars between the North and South opened up in earnest.[1]

Lewis was an alias of Alf Solomon and the story is supported by Detective Ted Greeno, who refers to the victim as 'Bernie', a name he applies to Alf Solomon in other incidents:

---

1 Moss Deyong, *Everybody Boo*, Stanley Paul, 1951.

A bookmaker I'll call Bernie was a friend of Sabini, so when the Birmingham boys asked him for £25 at Sandown Park he refused. The boys knocked him down and kicked in his teeth.[2]

A short-lived foray into blackmail by the Jones brothers, Alex, Fred and Owen, from Shepherd's Bush, west London, ended in the same way when the Sabinis ensured their conviction for demanding money with menaces at Hurst Park.

By this time, leadership of the Elephant and Castle gang had been taken over by Wag McDonald, who lived in Walworth, close to Mad Mossy, and Wal McDonald. Both McDonalds would have been pleased to see the back of Moss and company. Membership now had a more subtle leadership, although plenty of brawn existed in Johnny and Larry Tobin, Tommy 'Monkey' Benneworth, Bert McDonald, Len Winter, Ed and Charlie Marchant and John and Joe Jackson.

In 1921, Jewish bookmakers refused to pay their tribute to Kimber. On 12 March, at Sandown Park's Military Race Meeting, these refusals led to a brawl: Birmingham's Tommy Armstrong killed fifty-two-year-old Whitechapel bookie Philip Jacobs, also known as Phil Oker, with a blow to the head. A jury later acquitted him of manslaughter. On the same day, Billy and Joe Kimber attacked Mullins gang member Moey Levy and all three were bound over to keep the peace. Also in March, Moses and Harry Margolis welshed on a number of bets, some of them with Camden Town tearaway and Kimber ally Freddie Gilbert, who decided to do something about it. He caught up with Harry Margolis and Alf Solomon's younger brother, Simeon, in the Rising Sun pub, opposite Waterloo Railway Station: they and their cohorts engaged in a free-for-all. Margolis was pinned to the floor by Gilbert, who held a

2 E. Greeno, *War on the Underworld*, John Long, 1960.

razor's edge to his throat until he promised to pay up. Margolis agreed.

Gilbert had made a mistake. Margolis, the thirty-three-year-old son of Russian Jewish immigrants who had settled in Whitechapel, was a close friend of the Solomon brothers. He was also and an associate of Alf White's gang of pickpockets and conmen, who now formed the nucleus of the King's Cross gang. They had previously been humiliated by the Elephant gang and for consolation had made a pact with Darby Sabini and Alf Solomon. It was a time to choose sides carefully. A rift developed between Gilbert's Camden Town gang and the Sabini outfit.

It was Freddie Gilbert who offered the information to Billy Kimber that Darby Sabini would be present at a small trotting track at Greenford Park in the Middlesex suburbs. Kimber passed the news to Brummy Sage's Kentish Town mob and Wag McDonald, who were responsible for his operations in the south of England. On 23 March 1921, Billy's representatives sought out Darby. They found instead Joe Sabini and set about him and his mates with clubs and bottles. Darby arrived armed with a revolver. At his first shot, in the air, the crowd scattered. The second shot struck the ground in front of Wag McDonald's boot after it had slammed into Joe Sabini's jaw. McDonald, Sage and retinue took off. Darby surrendered to police, money changed hands, and a favourable police report brought about an acquittal at Ealing Police Court for shooting at persons unknown. He was, however, fined a tenner for having a firearm without a certificate. Freddie Gilbert and Sandy Rice, part of the gang that attacked the Sabini crowd, had charges of disorderly behaviour dismissed.

Kimber's old enemy, Matt McCausland, who was now forty-two, took matters into his own hands and confronted Kimber in the Lord Nelson in Cleveland Street, Marylebone. Perhaps he thought the Brummie, being from the sticks, was an easy mark. But Kimber made a bloody example of McCausland, who promptly reported him to the police. At about the same time, Wag McDonald fought two Sabini men who tried to force their way into his Walworth home. It may be that they had called to arrange a meeting that got out of control; both were knocked down and dragged to their car as a message to Darby that his overtures were not welcome.

On 26 March, two fights occurred on London Bridge Railway Station platforms: one in the morning when men arrived to board the train for Plumpton Races, in East Sussex; the other in the evening, when Elephant gangster Billy Westbury and Brummagem Bob Harvey were razor-slashed and badly injured by over a dozen unnamed men, while returning home. Police described the two as welshers. The attackers undoubtedly were part of the Sabini-White-Solomon combine.

In a local feud with the so-called Barnsbury Boys, Freddie Gilbert, George Sage, Billy Moore and others cut up, shot up, and otherwise mistreated the three Droy brothers – Georgie, Frankie and Billy – for tuning up Kimber neophyte George Moore. Moore happened to live in Barnsbury Road, Islington, almost next door to the Droys, and had hit one brother with an iron bar. Freddie Gilbert then turned his spleen on two Hoxton bookmakers: brothers Ted and Billy 'Jumbo' Joyce. He did Ted at Brighton and hit Billy on the head with a stool at Alexandra Park. Neither would identify their attacker.

Things were getting out of hand and bookmakers, under the leadership of Walter Beresford, attempted to bring the sides together. It has been hinted that a powerful man was the brains behind Eddie Emamuel's enterprises and Beresford's favourable treatment by the Sabinis suggests he was that person. He was a leading bookmaker of his day, married well and would have had all of the necessary contacts. Bookies conceded they needed to pay for peace, they just wanted to pay once and not to a host of regional gangs. Beresford invited Darby Sabini and others to his West Hampstead home to hear terms put forward by Kimber. The Jewish bookies, represented by Alf Solomon, did not like the deal that limited their numbers to a token few. This caused Beresford to report to the Brummagems that the Sabini alliance laid claim to as many pitches as they wanted, on racecourses wherever they pleased. The Brummagems retaliated by telling Beresford that he and other London bookies would not be allowed anywhere near the Midlands and the North. The Sabini faction responded by escorting Beresford and his friends to Doncaster races, followed by quick retaliation from the Brummies who evicted London bookies from Yarmouth. Business prospects were bleak for all concerned.

Shrewdly, Darby Sabini sought to make peace. It was his idea that he should control the southern, eastern and western racecourses, leaving Kimber with the North and Midlands. This was something Kimber could not agree to. If he did, he would betray his friends at the Elephant and Castle. Kimber's idea was to share interests, excluding the Jews, whom he hated. This offer presented difficulties for Darby, who had gone out of his way to cultivate Alf Solomon and Eddie Emanuel when he needed them. He invited Billy Kimber, Wag McDonald and George Sage to his rented flat, which occupied two upstairs floors in Collier Street, King's Cross, to talk terms.

When they arrived they found they were not alone. Darby had bought in the booze and invited racing men from all over. What was intended to be a meeting turned into a party, a party where differing factions became quarrelsome as liquor loosened their tongues. In the early hours of Sunday, 27 March 1921, Alf Solomon, Jim Ford, Sam Baws and others arrived. Kimber, who was now the worse for drink, shouted insults at Solomon and barged through the partygoers with the intention of taking a swing at him. Wag McDonald grabbed him and pulled him back. As this was happening, Ford, a former lightweight boxer, drew a rubber truncheon and whacked Kimber over the head, cutting his scalp and eye. Sage punched Ford, who fell among the party folk. Solomon reached into his pocket and pulled a revolver just as Kimber recoiled from

Arrivederci Roma

Ford's blow, thinking it had been delivered by Solomon. As Kimber charged his enemy, Solomon fired a shot from just a few feet away, hitting him in the right side: the bullet passed through him and ricocheted around the room, landing in the brim of a bowler hat that sat on the mantelpiece. Kimber rocked backwards, and again tried to lunge at Solomon, but dropped to his knees in agony. Darby Sabini grabbed Solomon and McDonald wrenched the gun from him and threw it through a half-opened sash window into Collier Street. The gun disappeared.

Amid the plume of blue-black smoke and smell of cordite, there was pandemonium. McDonald wrestled Solomon to the floor, where Darby Sabini sat on him. McDonald and Sage then carried Kimber from the house and a taxi was called to take him to his home about a half-mile away. When it arrived, the driver took one look and drove off to fetch a policeman. At first, it was thought Kimber was not badly hurt, but when he was seen to be leaking a lot of blood, an ambulance was called. Before it had arrived, the taxi driver returned with a policeman who took charge of the situation. No one was arrested. McDonald and Sage sloped off to King's Cross Railway Station where they took a taxi to Sage's house in Mornington Place, Camden.

Kimber was taken to the Royal Free Hospital in nearby Gray's Inn Road, where it was discovered the bullet had passed through him without causing much more than heavy bleeding. It may well be that the taxi driver's return had prevented him from bleeding to death. Kimber discharged himself after a few days. He would recover at the home of John Cheesewright in Angel, Islington. Cheesewright had been a member of the White Lion Street gang that waged war with the Bemerton Street Boys and Alf White in 1907/8; his daughter married Georgie Spain, son of north London villain Arthur Spain.

One week later, Solomon walked into King's Cross Police Station to own up to the shooting. He said it was not his gun

159

and that he had taken it from Kimber, who had pulled it on him. The likelihood is that Darby Sabini had told Solomon to give himself up to stem police investigations at his home. Solomon appeared at the Central Criminal Court, where he repeated his story, claiming that Kimber was the leader of a gang of Birmingham terrors and a very quarrelsome fellow. The Sabini household was described as a resort of disreputable people and Mrs Sabini was stated to be in the habit of throwing unruly parties. Kimber, who gave his address as Hospital Street, Birmingham, denied the gun was his but agreed it was an accident. Solomon was found not guilty of unlawful wounding on the direction of the judge for lack of evidence. When the case was dismissed, Mr Justice Darling called Kimber before the court to explain why he had not appeared to answer the charge of assaulting Matt McCausland in the Lord Nelson. The charge had since been withdrawn and Kimber's only excuse was that he thought he did not need to appear. He was fined £5.

Although he comes to prominence with the shooting of Billy Kimber on 27 March 1921, we can be sure this was not Alf Solomon's first venture into violence. In court, he was said to have had many convictions. At the time of the shooting, he was twenty-nine. That he carried a gun to a party says something about him. There have been claims that it was Darby Sabini who did the shooting and persuaded Solomon to take the rap, however Solomon's demeanour shows this to be unlikely.

Wag McDonald, who was there, recalled that Kimber had a hatred for Solomon, who he saw as one of the scum that threatened racecourse bookies at the edge of a razor and whom he had driven from racecourses. Solomon wanted to get back to a lucrative business of skinning bookies, something he continued to do in the East End and central London. Just what Solomon was doing at the party, which had been set up by Darby Sabini to hold peace talks with Kimber's crowd, is not known. He may have been invited; more likely he had word that Kimber was there and had come primed for action.

ON 2 APRIL 1921, hostilities shifted to Alexandra Park racecourse in north London, where George Sage felt he was being denied his rights by the Sabini faction. He attacked them in full view of police, who were on standby to prevent such an incident. A terrific free-for-all, involving Brummagems, Sabinis, police and punters, took place: it resulted in some men being escorted from the course by Tom Divall, with the assistance of boxing referee Moss Deyong. Somehow, Darby and Sage managed to remain. Juices were still flowing when Joe Best arrived in a car to collect Darby. Sage, realising Darby was still in the grounds, rushed to attack him. When Best stepped in to prevent it, Sage knocked him down. All this was seen by Birmingham bookies' minder Antonio 'Tony' Martin, who had lost part of an ear in a previous fracas with the Sabinis and who now joined in. He shot Best as he lay on the ground and was caught by plain-clothes officers as he ran away. Best recovered and did not identify Martin, who walked free from police court. Martin, born in Aston, Birmingham, was unusual in that he was an Anglo-Italian who chose to side with Brummies. He was associated with Clerkenwell's Cortesi gang, which had remained friendly with George Sage and Freddie Gilbert's Camden Town gang, but had dissolved an alliance with the Sabinis.

Wag McDonald, without Kimber, who was recovering from his wound, and in the face of mounting police and newspaper interest, decided to make peace. He had been told that Alf Solomon was not all bad and had only intended to shoot Billy in the leg. But a meeting at Sandown races quickly became heated and McDonald found himself surrounded by hostiles. The reward for his détente was a clump over the head from behind, which he believed was delivered by Jim Ford and which scuppered any chance of peace. The situation festered. At Epsom on 2 June 1921, the day after the Derby, the Brummagems bowed to police presence and left the course early. They did not go far, just a few miles, where they lay in wait for the Sabini crowd to make their way home. Wag McDonald, who would not normally associate with the thicker element of the Birmingham crowd, did so because of that bash on the head. He took charge and set up the ambush.

At 4.30 p.m., a charabanc loaded with well-armed Brummies blocked London Road close to the Brick Kiln beerhouse. When the Sabini lorry appeared it was rammed by a taxi, causing its occupants to scramble over the side. As they did so, they were attacked and battered by thirty to forty Brummagems who swarmed from the charabanc. Witnesses described general mayhem as the injured fell in the road, on grassy verges and in fields where they tried to escape. Split heads, broken bones and shattered teeth resulted from hammers and hatchets in the hands of a furious, boozed-up mob. The victims turned out to be a party of Leeds bookmakers.

The Brummagems boarded their charabanc and headed for further sustenance at the George and Dragon on Kingston Hill. After a drink some of the mob moved on, leaving about thirty men propping up the bar. Police, responding to a reported riot by probable 'Sinn Feiners', headed their way after a constable reported the mob's presence. Twenty-eight were arrested by a large armed force.

Much has been made of this event and it has to be wondered why, on discovering their mistake, the Birmingham crowd did not stop. The reason is that while the Leeds bookmakers, led by a thirty-seven-year-old Russian-born Jew, Lazarus Green, had been tolerated previously by the Brummagems, they had since offered their support to the Sabinis. They paid a heavy price. The aftermath of what police called 'the Epsom hold-up' saw seventeen of Kimber's men jailed – including John Allard and Joe Witton, who had been part of the earlier Garrison

Lane troubles – and greatly reduced the strength of the forces opposing the Sabini gang. William Giles, the taxi driver who had driven his cab head-on into the Leeds lorry, was acquitted, the judge thinking it unlikely he would have willingly placed himself in such danger.

Wag McDonald, whose head was cut by a misplaced hammer blow, made it home, but quickly fled to Canada to escape arrest. He travelled on to Los Angeles, where he became bodyguard to Los Angeles Mafia boss Jack Dragna and ran his own bodyguard and escort service for film stars, including Charlie Chaplin. The attack was part of a violent campaign against not only the Sabinis but also Dodger Mullins's Bethnal Green gang. One of its members, Moey Levy, was arrested for carrying a gun at the same Epsom meeting. He was acquitted when counsel proved police knew a dangerous gang was targeting Mullins's crowd and Levy was in fear of his life.

Despite the mass arrests, the war intensified. On 5 July 1921, the Elephant Boys, led by Wal and Bert McDonald, attacked the East End branch of Alf Solomon's gang, led by Jim Ford, as they made their way to the railway station at Salisbury races. Police intervened and arrested Ford, dragging him aboard an open-top Crossley Tender. When Ford's men boarded the vehicle in an attempt to free him, they were fought by a strange alliance of police and Elephant Boys. This resulted in more arrests and severe injuries to a police constable and a Ford man, who was knocked down by a taxi containing some of McDonald's men. Ford and eight of his team were later jailed, among them Sid Berman's younger brother, Jackie, who later joined up with Dodger Mullins. Ford served two months. On 6 August, four of Alf White's gangsters shot at Camden Town gang member Billy Fowles outside his home; the Camden mob were allies of Kimber. Subsequent charges were dropped through lack of evidence.

Then occurred 'The Battle of Bath'. On 18 August, Alf Solomon was dragged from his car on Lansdown Hill and attacked by Birmingham and Elephant and Castle gangsters, led by Wal McDonald and the now-recovered Billy Kimber. They set up a road block to stop Solomon's car and he was hit with a hammer by Freddie Mason, a twenty-six-year-old Elephant Boy and racing tipster from Walworth, who had more form than his recommendations. Two of Solomon's pals, Charlie Bild and Frank Heath, were also 'sandbagged'. As Solomon staggered about, his younger brother Henry pulled a revolver from his coat pocket, at which the crowd melted. Henry also received a hammer blow to the head and, in his confused state, was still waving his gun about when the police arrived. A number of east London bookmakers were subsequently turned away from Bath races and there were fights on the racecourse.

In court, George Riley, a Brighton bookmaker who had also been rounded up by the police, said he had been threatened with a gun by Henry Solomon: he had since been chased from Waterloo Railway Station by about fifty men who wanted to stop him giving evidence. Henry stood before the bench with a heavily bandaged head. Though he lived in the shadow of Alf, he had just as bad a character. His first court appearance had been in May 1920 when, aged twenty-six, he stabbed Harry Finn in Soho. Finn had been spoken to by a girl, who he told to go away as he was drunk. Solomon and another man caught up with him and slashed his neck and throat before running into Leicester Square Underground Station. After an adjournment, the case was dismissed because the victim could no longer identify his attackers and a witness who had given his name and address to police had not since been seen. On this latest occasion, Henry said he had been attacked by fifty men and only the arrival of police had saved him from death. Victims, however, were in the habit of exaggeration and claims of attacks by fifty or more should be treated with scepticism. Although the magistrate accepted he had acted under provocation, he was jailed for one month with hard labour for possession of a firearm and ammunition.

That same evening, a fight occurred in Freddie Gilbert's Camden Town manor in northwest London. Police Constable Starkey observed several men arguing outside the community room of the Southampton Arms, near Mornington Crescent. Next, he heard breaking glass and gunshots: he had happened upon the final throes of a major punch-up. A Sabini contingent had raided the pub with the intention of retaliating for the earlier attack on Alf and Henry Solomon. Inside, they found a large number of Gilbert's Camden Town gang, now merged with Brummy Sage's mob, who were hosting a party for Billy Kimber.

The constable summoned help and a taxi that fled the scene was stopped by a police car. Sam Baws, the thirty-six-year-old licensee of the Prince of Wales pub in Northdown Road, King's Cross, next to Collier Street where Darby Sabini lived, was arrested with great difficulty. Inside the taxi, police found a loaded revolver. Others who were hiding nearby were rounded up: amongst them were Sabini men Jim Ford, who was back on the streets pending an appeal, and George Kent. Police picked up a stick bomb lying in the road. In court, Baws claimed he had gone to the Southampton Arms to sell a horse and had been chased by forty men and hit on the head. He must have been believed, for charges of disorderly conduct and fighting were dismissed against him and Ford. For some reason Kent was fined £1.

In October, another large-scale fight erupted in the Royal George, on the corner of Summer Lane and William Street, in Birmingham, in which several men were seriously disfigured. The combatants are not known, but as it was the Kimber family's drinking hole it is a fair bet they were involved. The year 1921 ended amid continuing rows and threats.

On it went into 1922. In January, Wal and Jim McDonald were attacked outside a club in Jermyn Street, Piccadilly, by a large crowd of King's Cross Boys. Wal was stabbed in the arm. The brothers ran into a bar where they found 'friendly faces', who prevented them being seriously carved up. On 23 February, two King's Cross bookmakers, Archie Douglas and Michael Sullivan, who police described as part of the 'Birmingham gang', were stabbed in Coventry Street in an attack by Alf White, Harry Mansfield, Jimmy Wooder and Alf and Henry Solomon. The following day, four men were stabbed by George Sage, Freddie Gilbert, Freddie Brett and others, during a revenge attack in Tottenham Court Road. Victims refused to confirm the identity of their attackers and no charges were brought. This was followed by Gilbert, Sage and Brett being arrested for administering a severe kicking to Sabini man Charles Putney in Exmouth Market, Clerkenwell. They gave false names to the police and Mr Putney developed a severe dose of the jitters and withdrew his complaint.

The Feuding Continues

FREDDIE GILBERT WAS particularly hated by the north London alliance. The attack on Joe Sabini by Gilbert, Sage, Wag McDonald and others at Greenford Trotting Track demanded punishment, and Gilbert's affiliation to the Elephant and Castle gang and his role in the attack were seen as treachery. The Sabini brothers felt Gilbert had forsaken his natural friends to side with Birmingham men and, worse still, with the south Londoners: the latter had subdued the Hoxton and King's Cross gangs and backed out of their friendship with the Sabinis, as Wag McDonald would have nothing to do with Alf Solomon and had joined with the Birmingham crowd instead.

Frederick Arthur Gilbert was born on 26 November 1892 at Circus Road, Kentish Town, and was one of twelve children. He is said to have boxed under the name Clancy, but none of the Clancys recorded as boxing around 1910–1920 are him. However, a Fred Gilbert fought more than sixty contests within that period. In 1922, at the time of much gang activity, he was living at Moreland Street, Finsbury. Gilbert was born not far from Alf White and it is likely they belonged to one gang covering the area of King's Cross, Barnsbury, Islington, Camden Town and Highgate. Throughout the 1910s, they were in conflict with south and east London gangs for control of the West End, and were sometimes referred to as the West End Boys. Some time around 1919, they combined with Clerkenwell's Cortesi and Sabini families.

The rift appeared when Darby Sabini allied his Italian gang with Alf Solomon's Jews. This caused the Cortesi family and

Gilbert's Camden Town gang to take sides with Kimber's Brummagems and McDonald's Elephant Boys, in search of the best means of extorting money through racecourse and West End rackets. Through his father, a Hoxton thief and leading light in the Titanic, Gilbert had connections with that infamous pocket-picking gang. He became their leader at the time of their transformation into the Finsbury Boys, when he in turn passed leadership of the Camden Town gang to George 'Brummy' Sage. Gilbert had dreams of becoming the number one racecourse gang leader, a role that had been filled by Billy Kimber up to the early 1920s. He hated Jews and attacked them at every opportunity. Now he extended his hatred to Italians, with whom the Jews had teamed up for protection – though he was prepared to ally with the Cortesis. Gilbert, Sage and the Cortesis formed a counterbalance to the Sabini–White–Solomon alliance in north London.

Gilbert's criminal pedigree seems to have started with seven days' jail in 1919 for leading a drunken riot on a racecourse. This was followed, in 1920, by twenty-eight days for assaulting a policeman. After the Epsom riot all but wiped out the Brummagem's fighting arm, Billy Kimber came to rely heavily on support from the rougher element of the Camden Town gang. Gilbert's relentless, violent nature, expressed via razors and revolvers, terrified bookies and rival gangsters.

ON GOOD FRIDAY, 1922, peace came and settled on the land; well, not all of it. Freddie Gilbert was to pay for his duplicity. He had offended Darby Sabini and he did not have enough back-up to win that sort of argument. Nor was he the sort to be much cared about by Kimber or the McDonalds. Gilbert, with three of his pals, also added to his list of misdemeanours by threatening Alf Solomon's clerk at Sandown Park races and relieving him of his wad.

In the evening, Gilbert left the New Raleigh Club, a haunt

of racing men and illegal gamblers in Haymarket, Piccadilly. He turned into Jermyn Street, where he was ambushed by a bunch of East End Jews including the Solomon brothers. Afforded special treatment, he was slashed with knives, razors and a machete. Newspapers reported that his wounds required sixty-nine stitches: sixty in his leg, five in his face and four in the back of his head. He never walked the same again. This was the most serious of a flurry of cuttings and beatings; even so, Gilbert never split on his attackers.

In June, police made a serious attempt to prevent trouble at the Epsom Derby meeting by rounding up ninety-two people for criminal behaviour, including fourteen for welshing. Most were from the Midlands and North. Welshers generally received a sentence of three months with hard labour. Such police activity, however, did not prevent the beating up of Andrew Towey, by attackers he refused to name. Next, on 24 July 1922, Alf and Henry Solomon, Jim Ford and ex-boxer George Langham (real name for Giovanni Gianicoli) attacked John Phillips at Brighton races. Like Epsom, the Brighton course was too difficult to fence off and so remained unregulated after the organisation of other courses, allowing punters free access. Phillips had taken the stand of Freddie Gilbert and refused to cough up £2 for the pitch; his punishment was a razor cut across his cheek that nearly removed an ear and required twenty stitches, disfiguring him for life.

It is only in opera that when a man is cut he starts to sing about it: John Phillips was a fighting man. Late in the evening of 28 July, just four days after he was so badly wounded, he made his comeback. Accompanied by his brother Arthur, Freddie Gilbert, Bill Edwards, Larry Tobin, Joe Jackson and more, he searched the Yorkshire Grey at the junction of Theobalds Road and Clerkenwell Road, a well-known ecosphere of criminality favoured by the Sabinis and Alf White. They must have picked up a lead, for they immediately moved on to the Red Bull in Holborn, where they rushed through the doors and laid into some Sabini men. Some of the Italian crowd ran from the pub pursued by Phillips and his mob, just as Detective Constable John Rutherford happened along. He saw the attackers flourishing revolvers. Tobin fired a shot at some men and then spotted Rutherford, who he warned to back off. When he did not, Tobin called out: 'There's Rutherford, let him have one.' He then fired at the detective but missed. The brave Rutherford chased Tobin into Portpool Lane, where Edwards and Arthur Phillips both fired at him and again missed. Jackson and Tobin ran into Hatton Garden, pursued by the determined detective.

'Go away or I will do you in,' Jackson warned.

By now, Rutherford must have been fed up with bullets zipping about his ears, even though he could not have been impressed with their marksmanship. As Jackson levelled his revolver, the detective brushed it aside with his left and followed it with a right cross to the jaw. He then took the revolver from the figure sprawled before him. It was discovered afterwards that one bullet had struck a tramcar passing along Gray's Inn Road and lodged within twelve inches of a passenger.

Joe Jackson, Arthur Phillips, Edwards and Tobin were charged with shooting at Rutherford with intent to murder. Tobin, thirty-six, and Jackson, a thirty-four-year-old, pint-sized ruffian, both represented the Elephant and Castle branch of the avengers. They lived at Hickman's Folly, in the heart of Jacob's Island, Bermondsey, and were the terrors of the neighbourhood, demanding money at the edge of their finely honed, blue steel razors. Jackson passed himself off as a dealer in furniture and antiques around Bermondsey's many markets, where most of his dealings were at the expense of honest traders. It may be wondered why little Joe, who could be laid low by a single detective, was so frightening. The reason is that he and his younger brother, John, were two of Tommy Benneworth's branch of the Elephant Boys: they in turn were associated with John Phillips's Finsbury gang and were now friendly with Dodger Mullins's Bethnal Green Boys, which was enough to frighten the staunchest of hearts. Hickman's Folly was just a razor's stripe from where Tommy Benneworth was born and probably they all grew up together.

Jackson and Tobin were pronounced guilty, their sentence being deferred until other 'racing trials' had finished. Edwards and Arthur Phillips were found not guilty. George Fagioli, who was doing his bit for the Sabinis, was found guilty of possessing a firearm. Charges against Freddie Gilbert were dropped.

ON 1 AUGUST 1922, George Sage, Albert Medes and professional boxer Fred Rye were found armed with revolvers in the vicinity of Harry Sabini's home in Easton Street, Clerkenwell. Police officers had followed them from Rye's house in King's Cross. The police said they were one of four gangs who attacked each other with guns and razors, but would never prosecute each other. At the same time, a bunch of Sabini grifters, under the leadership of Vince Petti, a cousin of the influential Pasqualino Papa (Bert Marsh), set up a dice game on Brighton beach in order to fleece racegoers of their winnings – and by going through their pockets to get anything they had not already got. Several men were turned upside down and shaken.

Word reached Billy Kimber that sources of revenue, rightfully his, were being garnered by the Italian interlopers seeking to displace him. Kimber, who was at his London home and not keen to travel, telephoned Wal McDonald, who was closer to the scene and ready to go. Wal raided the beach and took everything he could find on the Italians. Those who resisted got a good hiding for a receipt. When the police arrived, all they found was Petti and some of his cronies tied together by their underwear. McDonald had taken no chances of missing any hidden plunder. Petti, on being untied, launched an attack on plain-clothes Constable Wood, something a magistrate was not convinced was in error, when he handed down prison sentences of three months and two months.

Throughout August, Freddie Gilbert searched racecourses for those who had attacked John Phillips. He, Sage and others forced Jewish bookmakers to pay compensation into a fund set up for Phillips. Harry Margolis was targeted on several occasions. Late in the evening of 19 August, three taxicabs pulled up outside the Southampton Arms in Mornington Crescent. Gilbert, Sage, Fred and Billy Rye, Albert Medes, Peter McNeill and about fourteen others, including several wives, stepped from the pub after a drink, having earlier been to Hurst Park races. Joe Sabini, Alf White, George West and two others jumped from the first taxi and fired shots at Gilbert and Sage. Even though Freddie must have been unsteady on his pins, they managed to miss him and everybody else. The shots were accompanied by exclamations of 'Take that', 'And that', and 'Here's another'. Seven more men jumped from the other cabs.

Unfazed, Sage went into action: he floored George West and a general melee erupted. Joe Sabini stabbed Gilbert with a stiletto attachment to his gun. The fight drew in passers-by and tramcar passengers, some of whom joined in. To escape, Sabini man Tommy Mack jumped onto a tram, pursued by Sage, Gilbert and Billy Rye, who had a wooden leg. As they fought, eighteen-year-old Amy Kent, on her way home to King's Cross, shielded Mack from some of Sage's blows then held on to him when she saw police boarding the tram. She fainted when she realised she was bleeding from a wound in her arm caused by Mack's knife, which he had thrust into his pocket as two constables approached to break up the fight. At the end of it, police made numerous arrests of King's Cross and Sabini gangsters.

False accusations of threats and assaults were swapped in court, in an attempt to cloud judgements about who was the guilty party. Joe Sabini had been arrested by two constables, who had retrieved his Browning automatic pistol-stiletto after seeing him throw it in the gutter as he fled. Alf White had jumped into a taxi and given an address which a constable, standing on the running board, amended to Albany Street Police Station. Sabini man Simon Nyberg, who was seen to drop a heavy hammer and run into the side of a bus, was knocked down by a passer-by. Nyberg claimed he was so drunk he did not know what he was being arrested for and West claimed he was not there at all. The fact that so many constables were on hand suggests that trouble had been expected.

To prevent further reprisals, George Sage was locked up in Brixton Prison on firearms charges related to his earlier arrest. From there, he wrote a note withdrawing identification of his attackers. In court, he claimed he protected Mack from a stranger who was hitting him with a stick: 'I seized the man with the stick by the throat and slung him off the car in order to prevent violence.' Mack, whose address was given as Rodney Road, right in the heart of Elephant and Castle, showed how thoroughly mixed were the abodes of rival gangsters. Sage and Gilbert were described by Detective Constable John Rutherford as frequenters of racecourses and being of uncertain character. Outside the courtroom, Detective Inspector Hancock noticed Joe Sabini swapping coats with his brother Harry, in an attempt to prove his pockets were not deep enough to conceal the pistol with its stiletto attachment.

Sage's wife, Ellen, made a statement identifying Alf White and West as the men who fired at her husband and Fred Gilbert. At a subsequent hearing, Ellen retracted her statement, saying it was too dark to see who the attackers were. Permission was given to treat her as a witness hostile to the prosecution and she was warned she could be charged with contempt of court. Even so, she denied she had been threatened or paid to change her evidence. Fred Rye also changed his evidence, saying he was so bitter about the attack he had lied about who the attackers were. Independent witness James Camp, who wobbled in the witness box, was urged by prosecuting counsel to 'show some backbone by doing your duty'. He withdrew his statement, insisting he had not been threatened but felt uncomfortable about giving evidence.

On 23 August 1922, four weeks after the Southampton Arms affray, Freddie Gilbert, John Phillips and others attacked Alf Solomon, George Langham, Harry Sabini and others as they were about to board a train for Bath races at Paddington Station. Only intervention by police, who were on standby for such eventualities, prevented a major shooting battle. Harry ended the argument by poking a gun into Freddie's stomach and waving goodbye as the train pulled from the station. He was arrested on his return.

The following week, Gilbert, Sage and Freddie Brett were arrested on a complaint made by Harry Margolis that they had terrorised him on several occasions. He claimed Gilbert pointed a revolver at him, while Brett and Sage threatened him with knives, demanded a tenner from him and ordered him to tell Alf White and the Sabinis that they were fifty-handed tonight and would fight to a finish. The twenty-seven-year-old Brett lived at Bonsor Street, Camberwell, and was a pal of Tommy Benneworth's. Sage was also charged with threatening Sabini man Sammy Samuels.

This was followed by the arrest of George Moore, Johnny Gilbert, Tommy 'Yorkie' Ackroyd and Joe Smith, for threatening Margolis and Samuels with corrective treatment if they did not withdraw their complaint. The whole lot was thrown out when it was suspected the complaints were a put-up job by the Sabinis, to counter charges against them for the Southampton Arms shooting at Gilbert and Sage. As Gilbert's defence had been that Margolis, a bookie's clerk with a bad criminal record, owed him £10 from a welshed bet, it is likely that the threats had been made and he was fortunate to get away with it.

That same August, Alf and Henry Solomon led an attack on the McDonalds at the Temple Bar in the Walworth Road, southeast London. That hammer blow must have still been ringing in Henry's head. They roughed up a few minor members but failed to find Wal McDonald, who had stepped out just before they arrived. He listened to events from behind a row of dustbins on the corner of East Street market, while his girlfriend Mary Stanford supplied the commentary. Wal retaliated by hunting for the Solomon brothers at the Bottle Club in Aldgate, where he shot up the place. People on both sides were arrested and charged with intent to cause physical injury and attempting to corrupt witnesses. Much of it was trumped up and was eventually thrown out by the courts.

When the courts had wrapped up their business, they got down to sentencing. Albert Medes received nine months imprisonment under the Prevention of Crimes Act; Fred Rye received six weeks and George Sage was discharged over the carrying of firearms. Joe Jackson received seven years, Tobin five years and Fagioli nine months for the Gray's Inn Road shooting fracas. Harry Sabini was lucky to be only bound over to keep the peace for his threats to Freddie Gilbert on Paddington Railway Station. He was ordered to find a surety of £200 or go to prison for six weeks. The money was put up by Eddie Emanuel. Joe Sabini received a two-year sentence for his part in the gun affray outside the Southampton Arms; George West was acquitted. Tommy Mack got eighteen months for riot, plus six more for wounding young Amy Kent. Simon Nyberg, who had many previous convictions, received twenty-one months.

Amid pandemonium in court, Alf White was sentenced to five years for attempted murder, plus two years concurrent for being in possession of a firearm. He was released when he won an appeal based on Ellen Sage's retraction of her identification, while being examined as a hostile witness. She had been branded by a magistrate as thoroughly untrustworthy and asked if she had accepted payment for her memory lapse. Appeal Judge Lord Justice Darling, who was given to referring to history during hearings, reminisced that in olden days she would have been given another turn on the rack or be asked to walk on hot bricks. Reluctantly he allowed White's appeal, but one by Nyberg was refused.

On 13 October, Camden Town gang members Peter and Jimmy McNeill were acquitted of assaulting James Camp, the witness who had withdrawn from giving evidence in the Mornington Crescent shooting. Camp was viewed as unreliable by the court and it is likely he had been put up to being a witness by Sage and Gilbert, in order to turn the screw on the Sabini gang. No doubt, he was knocked about for withdrawing from the arrangement. He had convictions under the name of Frederick Court.

In that same year of 1922, a series of letters, postmarked Leicester and signed by 'Tommy Atkins', the name used to refer to British soldiers during World War One, arrived on the Home Secretary's desk. 'Atkins' complained of attacks on Birmingham men by a gang of foreigners, led by Edward Emanuel and 'Girchen' Harris. He meant Gershon Harris, born in Whitechapel in 1880, to Russian-Jewish immigrants. In 1901, his father was a tailor living in Mile End. Young Gershon was the same age as Emanuel and, presumably, his partner in the race card business.

The letters still exist in Metropolitan Police files in the National Archives held at Kew. The letter writer has never been identified. He must be a Birmingham man: his list of victims includes Andrew Towey, attacked at Epsom; the shooting of Billy Kimber; the slashing of bookie Michael Sullivan, Ted and Jumbo Joice [sic]; George Phillips [sic] at Brighton; an assault on Evening News racing correspondent J.M. Dick; the attack on Bob Harvey at London Bridge (Harvey was a Brummagem who had moved to the Walworth Road). 'Atkins' writes that George Moore, of Tottenham, London, died as a result of an attack on him and his sons, something police could not confirm. In the general recording of racing gang warfare, it is said that a man died in a fight in Tottenham Court Road, but no one has named this victim: Barnett Blitz, killed in 1924 close to the northern end of Tottenham Court Road, has always seemed the most likely candidate. Atkins' letter points to an earlier incident in 1921 or 1922 and suggests the victim was Camden Town gang member George Moore. Possibly he was a victim of the Sabini-King's Cross alliance who died some time after a beating.

Atkins makes no mention of the Good Friday attack on Freddie Gilbert, a free fight outside the Brixton Empire Music Hall, in which Elephant and Castle men Alby Edwards and Billy Taylor were badly cut, and the Southampton Arms shooting affray. His naming of John Phillips as 'George' and his inclusion of the Joyce brothers, who were attacked by Freddie Gilbert, suggests he was not aware who were Brummagem allies, something that a Camden Town or Finsbury man would have known. My guess at the letter-writer, from the names known to us, would be Tommy Armstrong, who was acquitted of the manslaughter of Philip Jacobs in 1920; Billy Kimber and Wal McDonald must also be possibilities.

ON 20 NOVEMBER 1922, there was a serious falling out between the Sabini family and another of similar ilk. The Cortesis were an Italian immigrant family who arrived in Britain from France, the country where their gangster element were born. The first offence traceable to any one of them is the 1907 attack on a young man named John Tower, in Caledonian Road, Islington. George Cortesi held him while Dominic Marini, aged eighteen, slashed the top of his head and part of his face with a razor, inflicting a five-inch cut down to the bone. In 1910, George Cortesi was convicted of wounding Francisco Pacifico; he was stated to have many convictions, including being confined in a reformatory at the age of ten for warehouse breaking. On this occasion, a Vincent Sabini was acquitted. But the Sabini-Cortesi friendship broke down when the Cortesis remained allied to Freddie Gilbert, after the Sabinis had fallen out with him. Harry Sabini subsequently waved a revolver under the noses of the lesser known Cortesi brothers – Gus, Enrico, Paul and George – in the Fratellanza Social Club at Great Bath Street, Clerkenwell.

Such grievous insult required serious closure by the Cortesis. Darby and Harry entered the club, which was occupied by a few women at one table and six men at another. Unfortunately for the Sabini boys, the six were Cortesis, one of whom flung a cup of hot coffee over Harry; others pulled guns from their pockets. Gus Cortesi's hand was knocked away by the club secretary's daughter, Louisa Doralli, as he took a shot at Darby: the bullet passed through a window. Having saved Darby, Louisa next jumped in front of Harry Sabini, who gallantly pushed her out of the way, allowing Enrico Cortesi to shoot him in the stomach. Darby was floored by a blow from a full wine bottle, delivered by the hand of Alex Tomaso – the real name of Sandy Rice, who had been one of the attackers of Joe Sabini at Greenford Trotting Track. Even though the Cortesis favoured it as their watering hole, they wrecked the place.

When police tried to arrest Enrico, they were prevented from doing so by a crowd of sympathisers. Obviously, the Sabinis were not universally recognised as being the social benefactors of Little Italy that they claimed to be. The five assailants later surrendered to police. At the local magistrates' court, Mr Bingley commended Louisa Doralli for her bravery. Gus and Enrico received three years each for attempted murder, while Tomaso and Paul and George Cortesi got off. Harry recovered and Darby retired from leadership at this point. In May 1925, Harry Sabini put matters right by attacking Enrico Cortesi in Gray's Inn Road: he broke his nose and gave him a good few kicks, for all of which he was discharged by forbearing Clerkenwell magistrates.

Not happy with Alf White's successful appeal against his sentence for the Southampton Arms affray, the McDonald brothers staged a punitive attack on his gang, right in the heart of their territory near White's house in Farringdon Road. The attack took place in the Bull public house on the corner of Wynyatt Street and St John Street. Alf and some of his men were so badly injured – Alf being covered in paint and thrown onto the deck of a lorry – that he decided from then on to take a back seat. With Joe Sabini out of circulation and Darby tired of taking the leading role, command of the Sabini-White faction went to Harry, the youngest of the fighting Sabinis, who was generally called 'Harry Boy'. Alf Solomon continued to lead the Jewish branch.

The following year, White, George Drake and George Sabini sidled up to warders in the street outside Maidstone Prison. Drake, who knew one of the warders, introduced him to White, who asked what could be done for inmate Joe Sabini, offering a weekly £2 bribe to make jail life more bearable. The warder did his duty and the pair were jailed: White for eighteen months and Drake, who had a dreadful record of violent behaviour, for two years. George Sabini, who had hovered nearby, was released without charge.

On 4 June 1923, Darby and Harry Sabini and George 'Do Do' Dido attacked Maurice Fireman with knuckledusters, a chair leg and a knife at Epsom Downs in Derby Week, in a dispute over a pitch. In court, it was said that Fireman was an alias of Jack Levene: born in Russia, he was a notorious Whitechapel gangster and one of those jailed for the Salisbury disturbance. Dido said he was having a stand-up fistfight with Levene when Darby and Harry tried to separate them. No knives or knuckledusters were found at the scene. In a master stroke, the defence called Sergeant Major Michael O'Rourke, VC, a pensioner patient at Epsom Hospital. The Canadian

O'Rourke, who had won his Victoria Cross as an heroic stretcher-bearer near Lens, France, naturally said it was all Levene's fault. The trio got off. Dido and his brother, Tommy, were known associates of Eddie Emanuel.

In July 1923, Alf Solomon, Alf White and James Harper were found not guilty, at the Central Criminal Court, of conspiracy to cause grievous bodily harm to Islington bookie Bill Homer: he had denied them a 'score' (£20), the inflated fee to avoid a razor stripe. Matt McCausland, who had thrown punches, was found guilty of assaulting Homer under provocation and was bound over for twelve months. Detective Inspector John Gillan had told the court the event was not a continuation of a feud between racing men and that in fact the feud had been more or less wiped out, most of the men becoming fast friends. In view of commonplace attempts to bribe witnesses, it must be considered that this one was successful. In his defence, Harper denied having been in the fight, but admitted threatening to get Homer slashed. Solomon denied slashing Homer, but admitted being in the fight in order 'to rescue Steve Griffin from that bastard Kimberley, who was trying to cut his hands off'.

In a separate trial, William Kimberley, a thirty-one-year-old commission agent of Harrow Road, Paddington, was remanded on a charge of wounding Stephen Griffin with a broken glass, in a Camden Town pub. He was sentenced to twelve months imprisonment with hard labour. The same Detective Inspector Gillan gave evidence as to the violent character of Kimberley and his associates, who were known as racing pests and who made their living by blackmailing bookies. Kimberley was a Camden Town gang member who was actually born in Aston, Birmingham. It is tempting to think William Kimberley was Billy Kimber, but his age is wrong, as Kimber would have been forty-one. However, these rascals could be relied upon to dissemble, and frequently altered their personal nomenclature.

The violent behaviour of the Sabinis had not abated. At

about midnight on 1 December 1923, Jim Ford, George West and some others smashed up Freddie Ford's New Avenue Club and stole money from the till in an attempt to extort protection money. Police described Ford and West as part of a racing gang who would intimidate witnesses if allowed bail. They got off anyway. On 20 September 1924, there was an assault by Pasqualino Papa, an ex-professional boxer, Antonio Mancini, Harry Sabini and Tommy Mack. They attacked Lambeth bookmakers Harry Fellowes and Joe Taylor at Wye races, near Folkestone, Kent. According to police, over a dozen men were fighting and they found the two victims lying on the ground, having been badly kicked about. Harry was arrested, but the three others gave themselves up and said they had done it and Harry was not involved. Charges against him were therefore dismissed, with the three others receiving a month's imprisonment each. In 1924, a savage brawl outside a Birmingham pub, believed to have been an attack on the Brummagems by the Sabini gang, left a number of men badly injured.

Darby Sabini made an effort to disassociate himself from accusations that he led a gang of blackmailers, the common description for racecourse thugs who demanded money with menaces. Publishers D.C. Thomson ran an article in their April 1924 edition of *Topical Times* naming him and Harry. Darby sued, tried unsuccessfully to withdraw the action, and then failed to show up for the final showdown. Judgement was in favour of Thomson with costs against Darby. In June 1926, Darby did not attend a meeting of his creditors, including Thomson, who were owed £737 in costs. At a following meeting, it was put to him that he earned considerable money by selling race cards to unwilling punters and pitches to bookies, who were afraid to refuse. Darby denied this, claiming he received only £8 commission for organising the selling of cards and was not involved in the business of 'pricking' the cards (Kimber's dot-and-dash speciality). The following month he was declared bankrupt.

It is likely Darby had had enough and was feeling the effects of police interest and attacks from the other side of the Thames by Wal McDonald and Tommy Benneworth, who led the Elephant gang in Wag's absence. There was also a resurgence of Dodger Mullins, aided by the Phillips brothers. Increasingly, Harry was taking over leadership of the Sabini gang.

ON 23 SEPTEMBER 1924, Barnett (born Barnard) Blitz, one of the Finsbury crowd and said to be a bookmaker, though in reality a bookie's runner, was stabbed to death in the Eden Social Club at Eden Street, Camden. He was attacked just before midnight, although police were not called until two hours later. In that time, Blitz's body lay in Eden Street, after unsuccessful attempts to walk him to University College Hospital. The Eden Club was nothing more than a spieler occupying two floors above a garage, with a bar, card tables and a roulette wheel. It had been open only two weeks. Detective Inspector Steele found a scene of wrecked tables, splodges of blood on the floor and more smeared on a broken beer glass. On a small table, still standing in a corner, was a bloodstained carving knife.

After interviewing barman Edward Trinder, police went to a fruiterer's shop owned by Alf Solomon in Gerrard Street, Soho. Acting on further information, they drove to Covent Garden where they arrested Solomon, who was sitting in a taxi outside the market. At Albany Street Police Station, he was charged with the murder of Blitz and the attempted murder of Michail Abelson, a part-time doorman who had been stabbed in the thigh.

The story according to police was that Blitz was present in the bar when Solomon, Harry Mansfield and Eddie Emanuel arrived at about 11.30 p.m. The new arrivals engaged with others in a game of faro and Emanuel got up from the card table to go to the bar, where Blitz was sitting. A row broke out, in which Emanuel threw his drink in Blitz's face, sparking a fight. Blitz, a twenty-eight-year-old former boxer and an extremely tough man, knocked Emanuel to the floor, fell on top of him and smashed a glass in his face. Several men intervened and pulled the men apart. Emanuel, who was bleeding from a gash over his eyes, continued to curse Blitz, who went at him again. Manager Isidore Hyams, who shared a flat with Blitz in Gower Street, asked them to 'take it outside'. As they were heading to the doorway at the top of the stairs, Solomon, who seems to have been acting as a minder for Emanuel, darted across the floor and plunged a carving knife just below Blitz's left ear. As he raised his arm to strike again, Abelson grabbed him and they fought. Solomon slashed at him with the knife, driving him backwards until he fell into an armchair and received a deep wound in his thigh and a lesser one in his side.

Blitz was helped from the club by two men, but died in the street, where they left him. Hyams took Abelson to hospital. Solomon's story was that he was one of the men who got between the two to stop the fight. Blitz then offered to fight them all. When Blitz again attacked Emanuel, he tried to separate them. He saw Abelson, who had a knife in his hand, strike at Blitz. He then fought with Abelson: he did not see how Blitz came by his wound and said Abelson's wounds were self-inflicted in the struggle.

Police said the row was between two rival racing gangs. Blitz had accused Emanuel of grassing on him, causing his arrest for affray after a disturbance at the 1923 Spring Epsom meeting. At an inquest, witnesses, many of whom were racing men, said they saw Solomon stab Blitz and Abelson. The coroner's jury returned a verdict of wilful murder. Solomon appeared at the Central Criminal Court on 17 November 1924, where he pleaded not guilty. The prosecution made a quick attempt to cut away the defence's first plank that Blitz was a small-time criminal. They described him as mixing within the lower circles of the racing world and stated that, although his correct name was Blitz, he went by the name of Buck Emden, under which he had boxed professionally. English-sounding names were often adopted by Jews and people of other nationalities to avoid prejudice. What emerged at the trial was that the argument with Emanuel stemmed from the printing of bookmaker's lists at Epsom: Emanuel believed he held the monopoly for sales of race cards there, something Blitz failed to acknowledge. Emanuel bribed police to put up a charge of being a suspected person against Blitz, for which he was sentenced to three months' imprisonment. The sentence was quashed on appeal; even so, Blitz was certain that it was Emanuel who had put him in the frame.

When Blitz saw Emanuel come to the club bar, he chided, 'There's the copper.' Emanuel, who must have had more bottle than sense, responded with a blast of bad language, then threw the contents of his beer glass into Blitz's face. Blitz licked his lips and, believing beer would not be a sufficient response, smashed his glass into his antagonist's face, causing a deep cut across his forehead, which spurted blood. It was the crimson stream that stimulated Solomon: he saw his friend 'bleeding like a pig'. Spying a carving knife lying amid the cold cuts, he grabbed it and plunged it into Blitz's head. The wounded man rushed downstairs and died in the street. While this was happening, Solomon fought with doorman Abelson, amidst a sizeable scramble of the shady brigade to exit the club.

Sir Edward Marshall-Hall, who knew he could not get his client off altogether, conducted Solomon's leading defence. There was none better to turn a charge of murder into manslaughter. He set about this by branding Blitz as the cause of the trouble, saying he was a boxer who was not particular about using his fists: 'He was a dangerous man in a scrap.' In 1916, Blitz had been convicted of jabbing a glass into a victim's face and, in the same year, of stabbing a police constable with a bayonet. The jury shuddered when shown the jagged points of a broken glass. Solomon had a statement read out by the clerk of the court, in which he stated he thought Blitz was about to attack his friend again. He said he did not have a clear recollection of what happened that night.

The judge, Mr Justice Salter, helped Solomon's cause in his summing up, when he suggested to the jury that there was no premeditation and if the blow was not intentional this could be considered manslaughter. The jury deliberated and returned a verdict of not guilty of murder but guilty of manslaughter. Sir Edward told the court that Solomon had served in the Royal Fusiliers through most of World War One, until 1921 when he was demobilised. He was entitled to service medals. The prosecution pointed out that immediately on leaving the Army he was convicted of welshing at Windsor races, for which he had to pay £10 damages. He had also been accused of shooting Billy Kimber and was known to be a member of the Italian or Sabini gang. He was sentenced to three years penal servitude. Without Marshall-Hall, he would almost certainly have spared the world any more grief by going to the gallows.[1]

At the time of his fight with Blitz, Emanuel was living in a fine house at Elm Corner, Finchley. At forty-four, he would have been no match for Blitz in a fight. The incident probably caused Emanuel's temporary relocation to Brighton, where he lived in semi-retirement.

1 James Morton, in his book *Gangland Volume 2,* reveals that Alf Solomon was still causing trouble in February 1930, this time at Clapton Dog Track in east London in a quarrel with Dodger Mullins.

1925

SOHO BECAME, MORE and more, a magnet for London's crooks. It was the centre of their underworld, within which were gambling and drinking dens and clubs of all sorts, from desperately tawdry dives to swanky nightspots. Illegal dens would be open from 6 p.m. to 6 a.m., or from 2 p.m. to 6 a.m. on days when there were no race meetings and bookmakers would be among the clientele. Cheap eating houses provided temporary hangouts from late afternoon to early morning for crooks dressed in hand-made suits, usually comprising a three-buttoned jacket, waistcoat and slack trousers with turn-ups, all finished off with a patterned silk tie. They would lounge around a wireless set blaring out dance music or sit in a corner hatching dark deeds, from hotel theft for short-term working capital to blackmail plots. Visitors to Soho were often from outside London and were open to blackmail when they availed themselves of Soho's dubious delights. Goodtime girls went through their pockets to obtain letters, addresses and diaries to pass on to boyfriends, who would then threaten exposure to a victim's family, friends and work colleagues unless they purchased the items back. Billiards rooms, or a comfortable sprawl in an Italian barber's chair for a shave, were other relaxations. Gangsters dressed well and liked to be well manicured. It was a demeanour that could turn instantly nasty when they reached for a knife or razor.

In co-operation with the McDonald brothers, Billy Kimber moved into the West End club world, brushing aside Eddie Manning and Freddie Ford, who passed for Soho's bosses. Kimber became a silent partner of society nightclub queen

Kate Meyrick, whose clubs attracted the early flapper society embarking on the Roaring Twenties. Meyrick was born Kate Nason in County Clare, Ireland, in 1876. The daughter of a well-to-do family, she married Doctor Ferdinand Holmes Meyrick before immigrating to England some time before 1911. They had eight children before the marriage broke up on the grounds of his cruelty; three of their daughters married peers. Kate opened her most famous club, the '43', in Gerrard Street, Soho, in 1921 and went on to be constantly fined and jailed for allowing after-hours drinking. Her early business career had the backing of Kimber, who helped set up the 43 and Silver Slipper in Regent Street. When Meyrick was beaten up by a gangster outside her Dalton's Club, next to the Alhambra in Leicester Square, it was Kimber who tracked him down and beat him nearly to death.

Gangsters and decadent nobility plagued the clubs. In 1929, while Kimber was out of the country, Meyrick was jailed for bribing Police Sergeant George Goddard to tip off impending police raids. Goddard, who made a small fortune from her, possibly by adding blackmail to his sins, went down for eighteen months. Meyrick, weakened by her prison ordeal, died in January 1933 at the Marylebone home of her son-in-law, Earl Kinnoull. She succumbed to influenza, contracted during one of the great 'flu pandemics that wreaked havoc across Europe. Many Soho nightclubs dimmed their lights to mark her passing.

Edgar Manning was an enigma. He did not know himself if he was African or West Indian, or what his age was, which was given at various court appearances with ten-year discrepancies. He may have been born Freddie Simpson, or Alfred Mullin. Because he was a black nightclub owner, he received a good deal of attention from police, who branded him a vice king and described him as a 'man of colour'. There is no doubt he operated a ring of prostitutes and ran a number of opium dens, but he does seem to have attracted more warmth because of his colour. In August 1920, when forced to look after himself, he shot and wounded three men in a fight in Soho's Little Newport Street, for which he was jailed for sixteen months. His targets had been dope racketeers Charlie Tunick and Frank Miller, who failed to show up to give evidence; the third casualty was an unfortunate passer-by. On this occasion, police generously described Edgar as an upright citizen practising as a jazz drummer. He was released after a few months on orders of the Home Secretary.

Manning received further prison sentences for possessing drugs, running disorderly houses, harbouring undesirable women and illegal possession of a firearm. His final sentence came in 1929, when he received three years for stealing jewellery and a fur coat from the car of Lady Diana Cooper, a socialite and silent movie actress considered the most beautiful woman in the country. A hoard of stolen goods, including furs and jewellery, were found in the flat he shared with Dora Lepack, a Russian woman with much criminal form, who claimed to be his wife. Both were recommended for deportation. Edgar, who prosecuting counsel described as 'the worst man in London', had the last word; he died in Parkhurst Prison on 8 February 1931, aged forty-one.

Frederick Ford, the son of a Brixton plasterer, was born in Kennington, southeast London, in 1876. He was yet another villain associated with the Elephant and Castle gang. Although a big chap, he is not remembered for an ability to fight: more for his sociability and ownership of disreputable drinking places. In his memoirs, Police Superintendent Robert Fabian described him as having the bearing of a guard's officer. He had a reputation for being a good organiser who operated many clubs throughout east, central and west London. Before his entry into London's clubland, he served sentences for burglary, fraud and robbery. Later he owned hotels in King's Cross that were used by prostitutes servicing punters from the busy rail terminus.

On 3 February 1925, fifty-nine men and women were

arrested in an early morning raid on the Cursitor Club, in Holborn: they and were brought up before Bow Street Police Court. Frederick Ford, an engineer of Wardour Street, was stated to be the proprietor, and Jack Marshallsay, the secretary. They were charged with being concerned together with selling intoxicating liquor after hours. Clientele had been 'bussed' from Ford's New Avenue Club in Ham Yard, Soho, for an all-night drinking session. Many of the accused appeared in court wearing evening clothes. Thirty-four pleaded guilty, including Billy Kimber, and were fined. Matters were adjourned to 17 February and Ford and Marshallsay were granted bail.

When the case returned to court, Ford and Marshallsay faced further charges. Police claimed Ford pretended to be only the manager, on £4 a week, but was in fact the tenant and paid the weekly rent. Ford was said to run the New Avenue Club in Ham Yard. Customers had paid one shilling for a ticket, for a Bohemian evening of dinner and dance in pretence of the Cursitor being a club, but it was more like a pub: 242 people had been found on the premises, 156 men and eighty-six women and girls. In the confusion of the police raid, tables were upset, drinks thrown on the floor and glasses smashed in order to conceal evidence. The case was further adjourned.

In March, Police Sergeant Hastings stated that the place was packed with intoxicating spirits and that customers were drinking until 6 a.m. Ford's defence claimed that no spirits were served, only port-flavoured drinks, ale and stout. Sergeant Hastings denied he had poured away forty-eight bottles of beer during the raid. Proceedings were adjourned again. Freddie was putting up a fight but, on 26 March, he was sentenced to three months with hard labour and fined £30 on each of four charges of selling intoxicating liquor. He was ordered to pay £65 costs; Marshallsay was fined £60. Magistrates struck the club off the register and disallowed the premises for use as a club for twelve months. Ford was allowed bail to appeal.

Before his appeal could be heard, he was back in court on

another charge of selling intoxicating liquor after hours, this time at his New Avenue Club. He was jailed for one month, with hard labour, to run on expiry of his previous three-month sentence. Peculiarly, the magistrate said he had treated it as a first offence: in other words, he had treated the two raids as one incident and yet given consecutive sentences. Marshallsay was fined £5.

Being fined or locked up for short periods was considered part of the game of running drinking clubs. In 1926, Ford was back in court for selling intoxicating liquor without a licence, this time at his new club in Ham Yard, the Havinoo. It was Ford's prison sentences that left a weakness for Billy Kimber to exploit. Freddie was still active in the 1950s, when he backed Jack Spot and Billy Hill in a nightclub venture.

AFTER WAG McDONALD decamped for America in 1921, his brother Wal led the Elephant and Castle gang and, although a good fistfighter with many boxing bouts behind him, was not drawn to violence other than stand-up fistfights. One of his one-to-one straighteners, with early Titanic number one George Measures, became gangland folklore. Like Kimber, Wal was more interested in business, although continuing trouble with the Sabinis, Whites and East End Jews meant that fighting had to continue. In the mid-1920s, the vendetta was at its peak and constant attacks on Wal and Kimber's interests required the resurrection of a fighting arm. To lead it Wal chose Tommy Benneworth.

The Benneworth family trace back to James and Sarah Benneworth and their son, Cooper, who owned a small plot of land at Raydon, Suffolk, in the heart of 'Constable country' in the early 1800s. It was Cooper who moved their branch of the family to southeast London, somewhere around 1860. He appears to have joined the Royal Navy, afterwards settling in Southwark, where he married Sarah White in 1842.

Benneworth's grandfather had been a dock labourer on the Thames. His father, Charles, was born at 6 Victory Place, Bermondsey. Louisa Davis (McDonald), aunt of the fighting McDonalds, lived at number one and knew the Benneworths. Victory Place was adjacent to a cooperage yard where Thomas McDonald, senior, worked as a cooper at the time of his death in 1870. Eleven years later, gangster Eddie Emanuel would be born around the corner in Jamaica Road, making it one of those nice little clusters of criminality. It is likely that Tommy looked upon the likes of Wag and Wal McDonald as uncles.

Thomas Edward Benneworth was born at Gratwick Street, on 13 February 1894. The street was just off Bermondsey Square at the southern end of Abbey Street, Bermondsey, where it was overlooked by the ruins of an old abbey. His father was a machine printer while his mother, Julia, was the daughter of Irish immigrants from Cork and Limerick. He had an elder brother, Alfred, and a sister, Kitty. Tommy was a Bermondsey Boy along with the Jackson brothers, Joe and John, who all graduated to be Elephant Boys. In 1911, aged seventeen, Tommy married a pregnant sixteen-year-old Southwark girl, Esther Hawkins. She was the daughter of Henry Hawkins, a barman born at the Elephant and Castle, and his wife Mary Ann Gorman, a professional actress and the sister of Albert Gorman. Albert worked as a cooper with William McDonald, father of Wag and Wal, and was the leader of the Elephant and Castle gang for a spell in the 1900s.

Tommy was a bad man. He was heavily built and given to any amount of violence to achieve his ends. When given his first custodial sentence in 1917, for stealing canvas, he rebelled by knocking out a warder, for which he was lashed with the 'cat'. In 1919, Tommy and Ed Marchant slashed John Hazell with a razor in a local gang bust-up, but got off because it was 'an accident'. Benneworth is said to have mounted a raid on the Sabini heartland at Saffron Hill, Clerkenwell, which resulted in the rallying of the Italians and the delivery of a punch by

Max 'the Baron' Shinburn was a master criminal known as the 'Napoleon of Crime', before that moniker was taken by his bitter rival, Adam Worth.

The international thief 'One-eyed' Charlie King, who lost his eye in a gunfight in Whitechapel.

Adam Worth, the German-born criminal genius of the Nineteenth Century, pictured on horseback in France, before dissipation set in.

This historic photograph of the leading gangsters in London was taken at Hammersmith Broadway early in 1919, at a time when the Brummagems, McDonalds, Cortesis and Sabinis were still friends.
On the coach, from left to right: bookmaker Claud Fraser, George Hatfield, Joe Sabini, unknown, unknown, John Gilbert, Harry Sabini, Al Scasini, Brummagem leader Billy Kimber and Bert McDonald.

Front row: charabanc driver, unknown, George Sage (unconfirmed), Wal McDonald, Billy Endelson, Jim McDonald, Tom McDonald, Enrico 'Harry' Cortesi, unknown, unknown, Billy Banks, George Cortesi, Bert Banks, Wag McDonald, Italian leader Darby Sabini, charabanc assistant.
Within months, their various gangs had fallen out, leading to the long and bloody conflict that became known as the Racecourse Wars.

Hoxton-born thief Eddie Guerin, photographed in Pennsylvania in about 1887, when he was wanted for shooting an American cop.

Camden Town gangster William Kimberley was described by police as a most dangerous man. He made his living by intimidating and blackmailing bookmakers.

East End villain Arthur Harding and some of his boys on a trip to Brighton around 1923. Front row, from left to right: Benny Hall, George and Arthur Harding. Back row: unknown, 'Edgy', Jack Lincoln, Tom Allcorn and Harding's brother-in-law Dave Jones.

A rare photograph of Alf Solomon, the ultra-tough Jewish gangster who teamed up with the Italians and played a major role in the racing wars.

A young Jack 'Spot' Comer when he worked for bookie Wal McDonald, in about 1931. He went on to become the most important figure in the London underworld.

Left to right: Harry, Johnny and Eugene Carter, drinking in an Old Kent Road pub in 1956. They had just seen Dido Frett and Ray Rosa jailed for seven years for attacking Johnny. He claimed to be a humble barrow boy but was in fact a razor king who terrorised South London for years.

Ellen Brooks, circa 1920. She took up with Camden hardman George Sage and was embroiled in a sensational gunfight outside the Southampton Arms in Mornington Crescent, which led to numerous arrests.

Florrie Holmes, one of the Forty Thieves, who was once arrested for collecting bets for Bert McDonald while sitting in his Sunbeam beneath the railway arches at Waterloo, and was the girlfriend he left behind when he fled to the USA. Her sister married a notorious burglar.

Maggie Hughes, Billy Hill's sister, on her release from Holloway in 1922. She married Alfie Hughes, one of a gang of burglars and motor car thieves.

Alice Diamond, Queen of the Forty Thieves, from either a locket or a wallet photo found in the pages of Bert McDonald's World War One diary.

'Italian Albert' Dimes, pictured with his wife Rose after he was acquitted of attacking Jack Spot in 1955. Dimes was an heir to the Sabini gang and later allied with Billy Hill. Brash but popular, he was involved in some of the most notorious incidents in London gangland in the 1950s.

The ornate gravestone of legendary ganglord Charles 'Darby' Sabini, who lies in Hove cemetery.

The lurid life story of Jack Spot, Hill's arch-rival. Both collaborated in memoirs, but Spot broke the arm of Hill's ghostwriter.

The dapper Billy Hill, gang leader and self-styled boss of Britain's underworld.

Darby Sabini that broke his jaw. The event is probably folk-lore. Chronology puts the incident at around 1920, although these accounts are often found to be wanting. Benneworth, although twenty-seven years of age, is not noted as a leader of the Elephant Boys at that time; in the same account he is described as the 'Trimmer', a nickname of dubious veracity, however he did like to be known as 'the King of Walworth'.

In April 1921, he was given three months for loitering with the intent of picking pockets at Epsom racecourse. At that time, he was living at Myatt Road, Camberwell, well within the orbit of the Elephant and Castle. It is interesting to note that Wal McDonald once lived in the same road and, in later years, the Richardson family owned a confectionery shop just around the corner.

In January 1922, aged twenty-eight, Tommy appeared at the Central Criminal Court as Thomas Cooper Benneworth (for some reason he was using his father's middle name): he was up on charges of conspiring to receive cases of crème de menthe and other liqueurs. A warehouse had been robbed and police kept observation on a pub where they believed the goods were being stored. Benneworth arrived and, supposing one of the police officers to be 'the governor', offered £100 to be allowed to 'shift the stuff'. He helpfully added that he had a customer who would pay £200. The police officer then disclosed his identity. Benneworth offered no resistance; however, it came to light that two men, said to be acting on his behalf, had intimidated two policemen. The magistrate took the unusual course of directing a policeman to warn the men that, if any more threats were made, they would be called before the court and dealt with severely. Even though Benneworth had not been involved in the theft, he received a substantial sentence of eight months imprisonment with hard labour for receiving, perhaps because of the threats. In 1924, he was arrested on Epsom Derby Day for threatening behaviour and given three months, to reflect on the direction his life was taking.

There is not much good to say of Benneworth. In his memoirs, Detective Ted Greeno alluded to him as a burglar before he began mixing with racecourse toughs. He did not flinch from using a razor or a cosh spiked with nails, blades, coiled wire, or whatever took his fancy. He talked constantly of chivving people and had a threatening presence, locally and in the West End. In some incidents, he teamed up with the Hackney/Bethnal Green gang, led by that equally fearsome rogue Jack 'Dodger' Mullins, a ruffian about Tommy's age and his mirror image in the netherworld of east London: in the 1920s, he was continually at war with Alf Solomon's East End Jews, sometimes referred to as the Yiddishers.

Dodger was a shifty, violent villain who mirrored Benneworth well, although he most likely appreciated the large, violent nature of Tommy when big game was on the menu. Also with Benneworth were Eddie Connell and the Jackson brothers from Long Lane, Bermondsey; Freddie Brett and Len Winter from Elephant and Castle; Edgar Saunders and John Clarke from Camberwell; and a coterie of the meanest type of villains imaginable.

Winter, a barman from Burman Street, off London Road, was a particularly vicious associate. In 1921, he, Hector Matthews, Jim and Johnny Ransford, Dick Garner and Arnie Lee were described as 'the London Road mob', a sub-division of the Elephant Boys, when they went in search of a man called Josh Collins. Matthews thought he saw their quarry standing on the corner of Burman Street and stabbed him in the neck. It proved to be plain-clothes constable Benjamin Hooker, who nearly died. Attempts to pervert the course of justice, through threats and bribes, ensured that only Matthews came to trial: the judge decided he was just a naive young man under the influence of undesirables who frequented the Elephant. He let him off lightly with a fifteen-month sentence.

Nineteen twenty-five was a busy year for Tommy Benneworth. One Sunday night in February, Moses Levy was sham-

bling along after a merry evening of drinking in the company
of his friends in their East End manor. Moey, as he liked to
be called, was a bookmaker; not only that, he was a friend
of Alf Solomon who, like him, operated under the protection of the Sabinis. He was also a serious villain, who had
graduated from pickpocketing to running a series of East End
spielers, a dangerous occupation at any time. He hailed from
Whitechapel, then a largely Jewish quarter that housed buyers
of stolen goods, jabbering in Yiddish, among hovels jammed
into its dark and narrow streets, streets that would shortly be
stalked by Jack the Ripper. His confidence in this support of
the Sabinis caused him to turn down an offer of protection
from the Solomon crowd's persistent enemy, Dodger Mullins.
Dodger did not command a large gang at the time, however
he did know more than one way to skin a bookie. He offered
his services to Benneworth as a 'spotter' for a share of the take
from Jewish bookies, and Benneworth knew how to deal with
recalcitrant bookies: he chivved them.

As Moey moseyed along Aldgate High Street on his lone-
some, the terrifying sight of Benneworth, Mullins, John Jackson, Ernie Watts and Steve Martin confronted him. All except
Dodger were from the south side of the Thames. Whatever
was said is not recorded but, after an exchange of words, Moey
was slashed with an open razor, punched to the ground, and
kicked until he resembled raw chopped liver. Through broken
teeth, he told Detective Inspector Crocker who had done him.
Soon Crocker had rounded up the five suspects and brought
them before Alderman Jenks, at the Justice Rooms in the
Guildhall. They were charged with being concerned together
in unlawfully and maliciously wounding Levy, by cutting him
with a sharp instrument and further assaulting him.

Unfortunately for Crocker, he had no evidence to offer
other than the statement by Moey Levy, since forsaken by its
author. Defending, Mr Hardy said it was 'a most objectionable
practice that the police had lately adopted of putting men

in the dock on charges unsupported by any testimony, other than that of arrest and then to ask for remands'. At all events, he suggested the accused should be released on bail. Crocker responded that if bail were given, he would be compelled to arrest three of them on another charge. The canny Mr Jenks observed that, as the police had experienced no difficulty in getting in touch with the accused, and at present had not produced any direct evidence to connect the prisoners to the attack, he would accept bail for each in the substantial sum of £500. The sureties were immediately forthcoming. Tommy cheekily asked Mr Jenks if he wanted payment up front. After that, he was oft referred to as 'Monkey' Benneworth – that being the racing term for £500.

Later that month, the five returned to court where it was discovered Moey had developed latent amnesia. All were acquitted. It is not only in the Twenty-first Century that victims' needs are secondary to the criminal's ability to manipulate the law through fear or fancy lawyers.[1]

All this was to be too much for Home Secretary Sir William Joynson-Hicks. By the time the story reached his ears, over fifty men had been battling it out in Stepney with hatchets, knives and firearms. At the same time, a drunken ex-soldier shot up an East End pub and a bank robber, traced to his Waterloo Road hideout, attempted to do the same to two policemen who courageously wrestled him to the ground. He was also recoiling from gang wars in Sheffield, Birmingham, Glasgow and other places. It was the 1925 strife that brought 'Jix' into action, not earlier racing gang troubles as is sometimes stated. He leaned on courts to give little shrift to accused gangsters.

---

1 At the time of the attack on him, Levy was in decline as a gang leader and his operations were being taken over by the ubiquitous Eddie Emanuel. A year after his slashing by Benneworth, Mullins and retinue, he was cut again by Arthur Harding and Charlie Orrick. His downfall is reminiscent of that of Jack Spot. It was a bad career move to pass your prime.

The violent period between 1921 and 1925 had alarmed the Government. It came at a time when poverty was endemic in the land. Only a year ahead lay the General Strike of 1926, when workers and those desperate for work would vent their feelings in a countrywide show of anger at mismanagement of the economy following World War One. In addition to racecourse troubles, friction between Catholic and Protestant adherents had been resulting in street battles. While Joynson-Hicks was deliberating, a riot in Clydebank, Glasgow, at an Orange demonstration, brought scores of injuries, many of them to police, as Catholics surged to tear down Protestant banners. Arrests were made, followed by more violence as attempts were made to free the prisoners.

The danger Joynson-Hicks sensed was a breakdown in discipline. Desperate men and women would fetch for themselves in any way they could. Many people involved in crime did have work, but work that paid so little that it was only a means of basic existence. Wages often did not provide enough to ward off hunger and so crime increased across the country. Slum areas in big cities bred resentment, leading men and women towards crime or bad behaviour. Some women turned to prostitution to survive hardship. In an effort to become better off, men gambled and, when that did not work, they drank.

It was not only in London that gang warfare caught the headlines in 1925. In Sheffield, gambling followed the usual favourites of horse and dog racing, on both official and unofficial courses; bareknuckle boxing contests; street corner dice and pitch and toss; and their own variety of coin pitching which they called 'tossing'. A mark stood in a ring of scores of punters who predicted the fall of five pennies or half crowns, heads or tails. Bookmakers handled bets just as a croupier would in roulette. There was also considerable side betting between individuals. It was a consummate method of facilitating the exchange of large amounts of money. It attracted the usual hangers-on plying their crown and anchor boards, find the lady, spinning the wheel and all manner of cash-accumulating scams.

Sam Garvin and George Mooney led gangs that extracted money from bookmakers at the edge of a razor. The situation exploded when the gangs became so large their bosses could not bring in enough 'gravy' to keep members happy; there was one gang too many. In April 1925, a group of men attacked ex-serviceman William Plommer near his home in Sheffield. The attack was in response to Plommer being present at a club when one of his pals beat up Wilfred Fowler who, with his brother Lawrence, had once been affiliated to George Mooney's gang but had now joined Sam Garvin. It is probable that Plommer had only tried to stop the fight, but as Wilfred had been badly knocked about and required stitches and a bandaged head, it was felt by the Garvin mob that reprisals were in order. Plommer also ran his own small pitch and toss game under some railway arches, making it doubly important he should receive corrective treatment.

The group came on Plommer on the corner of the street where he lived. Bystanders heard Lawrence Fowler tell Plommer, 'You have done our kid, now we are going to do you.' Plommer offered to fight them one at a time. Lawrence Fowler thought about it and then hit him with a poker. Then they all got stuck in. Razors, rubber hoses bound with wire, and boots when he fell, made a bloody mess of Plommer. Witnesses saw a man jabbing him with what looked like a short bayonet. Plommer's mouth gaped open as one of the stabs drove into his abdomen. He got up again, staggered to his house, and collapsed in his front room. He died twenty minutes later in hospital.

The inquest concluded with a verdict of wilful murder against the Fowler brothers. The coroner spoke at great length in favour of the practice of inquests publicly questioning witnesses, who later would give evidence in court. He was not impressed with the new practice adopted in two recent murder cases, where the inquest had been adjourned until court proceedings had been completed. He felt it was contrary to the traditions and practice of the coroner's court that had existed for a great many years. In spite of his protests, the practice of coroners questioning witnesses to murder would soon be ended.

At 9 a.m. on 3 September 1925, Wilfred Fowler, aged twenty-three, was hanged at Armley Prison, Leeds. The following day his brother Lawrence, twenty-five, was executed at the same jail. The double execution concluded the business of the Sheffield gang wars. If either of them had any hope of a commutation it ebbed away in Aldgate High Street with Moey Levy's blood. An example had to be made.

TOMMY BENNEWORTH SEEMED to be enjoying more than his fair share of luck. In May, he was at it again. John Jackson left his flat in Mowbray Buildings, a cramped dwelling tenement tucked away between Borough High Street and Red Cross Way, in Southwark. He took the number thirty-five bus to Leytonstone, arriving at 6 p.m. There, using the name Dickenson, he hired a large car and a driver. They drove first to Bethnal Green, where they picked up Dodger Mullins, then to the West End, where they scoured pubs and clubs in search of rival villains who were on their list for chastisement. At 9 p.m., they arrived at the Queen's Head pub in Southwark, where they crammed another six men into the car. Benneworth levered his bulky frame into the seat beside Mullins, Jackson and the driver. That left Bert McDonald, George Watts, Lennie Winter, Eddie Marchant and Georgie Hughes to squeeze into the back.

Johnny Jackson must have spotted something tasty on his scout. The gang drove directly to the Oak Leaf Club in Ham Yard, Piccadilly, where, on finding their quarry had left, they comforted themselves with hard liquor until 11 p.m. They then went next door to Freddie Ford's New Avenue Club. Freddie did not need this sort of trouble. He had a good clientele who enjoyed after-hours drinking in his several nightclubs and the sight of such obvious gangsters was not good for business. To get rid of them, he let slip information that Alf White had been in and gone on to the Diamond Club and Card Room in Bouverie Place, Paddington, a little yard just around the back of Praed Street.

The gang arrived at about midnight and smashed their way in. Alf White was big and game: he did his best but, battered with bottles and chairs, he was left slumped in a doorway. The boys dished out the same treatment to White's pal Harry Parkinson. They had intended to ask White where the Solomon family was residing; as Alf Solomon was then locked up, they must have been seeking his brothers Henry and Simeon. But having rendered their prime source of information speechless, they picked up Parkinson and carried him to an open fire, where they held him against the flames until he remembered an address for Henry. It fitted. Henry Solomon's legitimate occupation was a fruiterer and greengrocer and he was known to frequent Covent Garden market.

As it was a chilly night, Jackson helped himself to a hat and overcoat. Somehow, Alf White managed to slither into the night and make it to St Mary's Hospital, just a short crawl away. From there, using the name Weiss, he alerted police with a stroy that shots had been fired from a big blue car carrying ten armed men, on the corner of Harrow Road and Edgware Road, and they set out to investigate.

The gang arrived after midnight at Maiden Lane, near Covent Garden, home to a number of betting clubs and drinking holes frequented by the racing brotherhood. These included: the Spooferies, a dive that saw regular 'choppings' and one murder before it was closed, and the Old Adelphi, which catered for theatricals who 'followed the turf'. They battered down a door expecting to find Henry Solomon. Instead, they found Lionel Bartlett, a tailor, and his wife hiding beneath the sheets. They did not know anyone named Solomon and helpfully suggested, 'Try number twenty-seven.' Faced with another door, they proceeded to break it open. Upstairs a light went on and a face from a window enquired if he could be of assistance. Realising it was not either of the Solomon brothers, and observing two constables approaching from Bow Street Police Station, just around the corner, one of them called out, 'It's all right, we're Nobby's pals.' Then they strolled back to the car, where the forbearing driver was waiting, by now fearful for his own safety. A wild chase followed as police cars latched on to the suspect vehicle. The driver dropped the gang at an Aldgate coffee stall and, under the pretence of turning the car around, sped off, leaving eight men on the pavement. When he inspected his rear seat, he found it had been slashed to ribbons.

Coffee stalls featured regularly in criminal social activity. In May 1923, Mr Fry, the magistrate at Tower Bridge Police Court, when sentencing Elephant Boy Freddie Brett to twenty-eight days for assault, commented that such stalls had figured in a number of cases and seemed to be an underworld meeting place. He said it would be well for the police to keep an eye on them. He did not state which coffee stall he had in mind. Ones at London Bridge and the junction of Long Lane and Borough High Street were within his catchment area. A bit further afield was the coffee stall adjacent to the Trocadero cinema on the corner of Tarn Street and New Kent Road, Elephant and Castle. It survived into the 1950s and was a late-night watering hole of many of south London's criminal fraternity. Mr Fry's comments brought a swift response from William Cole, Hon. Secretary of the Coffee Stall Keepers' Protection Society, who issued a statement condemning the remarks. He pointed out that police did keep an eye on them and stall-keepers always assisted the police in every possible way. He suggested that criminals not only congregated at coffee stalls but could also be found in West End hotels and restaurants. He said stall-keepers carried on their little businesses under very difficult conditions – as evidenced by the need for his protection association – and were always being blamed for things for which they were not responsible.

Alf White's drubbing and Harry Parkinson's part-roasted hide were sufficient for the hospital to inform the police. In early June, Benneworth, Watts and Winter were arrested; Jackson and Mullins gave themselves up and McDonald, Marchant and Hughes sat and hoped for the best. The five were brought up at Bow Street Police Court, charged with four other men with breaking into a house occupied by Mr Bartlett at Maiden Lane and with stealing a hat and coat from the Diamond Club. Alf White, when interviewed by police, could not identify his attackers. He mischievously stated that he was sure he had heard revolver shots, something police were unable to confirm, as there were no bullet marks anywhere in the club and no other witnesses had heard shooting. The police said that the trouble was the result of one racing gang hunting another.

Magistrate Sir Chartres Biron could not see how a burglary had been committed when nothing had been taken and the event was signalled by so much noise as to draw attention to it. He thought the evidence of the hat and coat being stolen was less than satisfactory: it relied on the driver saying he saw Jackson leaving with a different hat on. He did, however, think something curious was going on. Mr Hardy, again selected to defend, asked for dismissal of the charges. The magistrate decided to sleep on it and remanded the prisoners on bail until the following morning. On the morrow, Sir Chartres bound over all five defendants in their own recognisance of £100 each and ordered them to find another £100 surety, to keep the peace and be of good behaviour or go to prison for three months. They all promised to be good. Lennie Winter was promptly re-arrested on a charge of threatening a shopkeeper. The charge was withdrawn when the complainant failed to appear in court.

Another man the Elephant Boys had wished to interview was Alf White's brother-in-law, Charlie Wooder, who had good connections in the boxing world, where he promoted an occasional fight at Hoxton Baths in Pittfield Street. He and some of his boxers had roughed up friends of Dodger Mullins outside the Spread Eagle pub, after they had strayed onto the White's patch. In the East End and east central parts of London, rival gangs lived side by side, rendering it almost impossible not to transgress boundary lines, which were not clearly defined. Punishment was automatic and reciprocal. Wooder's home was in Farringdon Buildings, Clerkenwell; the people he attacked came from nearby Goswell Road. According to Mullins, this was a 'right liberty' and it may have been the reason Alf White had been hunted down.

Charlie Wooder was fortunate, or not, according to the way you see things. He had skedaddled to Dover to carry on his main occupation of pocket picking. He was a leading light of the recently defunct Titanic, due to his light touch, and was credited with the invention of 'steaming': the practice of a large mob rushing through trains on their way to the races and removing wallets by force; they also did this in racecourse enclosures. Although the Titanic had practically ceased to be, habits die hard; alas skills die too. Charlie was caught on the gangway of a Channel steamer with his hand inside an American tourist's jacket. Accused of attempting to rob Henry Schmidt, of Michigan, of a wallet containing £155 10s, it was found he already had the gent's watch in his pocket. He got six months.

In June 1925, George Marsh, a racing tipster from Lambeth known as 'The Major', was sentenced to three years penal servitude for slashing the throat of Brighton man John Didier with a razor during an altercation in the Strand.

The Brummagem Boys were also at it in 1925. On 29 July,

Whitechapel bookmaker Isaiah Elboz attacked Birmingham man Sid Payne in Brighton's Embassy Club. Payne took his cuts and bruises to the hotel where he was staying and showed them to Tommy Armstrong, the man who had been acquitted of the manslaughter of Philip Jacobs at the escalation of the troubles in 1921. Although aged fifty, Tommy was still a fighting man and he returned to the Embassy with Payne and Bill Glynn, where they sliced up Elboz and several stewards who tried to intervene. Elboz was seriously injured. At a following court appearance, the victims suffered the usual lapse of memory and Elboz was treated as a hostile witness, enabling a remand for further serious charges to be brought. The matter appears to have ended there.

By this time, Tommy Benneworth must have been feeling untouchable. On 7 August, he, Johnny Jackson, Len Winter and four others sought out Billy Smith, a racing man who owed Dodger Mullins a payment of some kind. They called at his home in Waterloo, where they received no reply. On their way back to Jackson's home at the Borough, they chanced upon Smith and his wife in Marshalsea Road and asked if he had Dodger's money. He said he hadn't. An onslaught followed, in which Smith was slashed and battered senseless and his wife was cut across her arm as she tried to protect her husband. Charges were dropped when Mrs Smith, who had named Benneworth, Jackson and Winter, withdrew identification.

A week later, sixteen men were questioned by police who arrived in response to a flood of emergency calls reporting a mass brawl. in Shaftesbury Avenue, Soho. Benneworth was among those who had lingered at a pub in order to refresh themselves after exercising their muscles. Police could find no victims and the matter was allowed to rest. A hunt for Henry Solomon at Goodwood races followed. Somehow, Solomon, Jim Ford, George Langham and others got wind of the ambuscade and found it prudent to give up a day's wages. Benneworth was furious and wanted to know who had snitched. This may have had some bearing on what followed.

On the evening of Saturday, 22 August, Ed and Charlie Marchant and Bert McDonald drove to the Old Kent Road and visited several pubs. Dan Kempley was sitting with his wife and a friend in the public bar of the Bricklayer's Arms, on the corner of Old Kent Road and Tower Bridge Road, when the three walked in. Bert returned to the car to get the engine running whilst Ed and Charlie walked up to Kempley and spoke to him. Talking later with a detective, Kempley said he did not remember what had been said to him; he did recall a loud bang and feeling a pain in his head. In hospital, he underwent an emergency operation. Up to this point, police did not believe a shot had been fired. The operation, however, showed that a bullet had been fired downwards, injuring Kempley's right eye and passing through his nostril. Had the shot had been fired from a level position, it would have killed him. He identified Charlie Marchant as the man who spoke to him, at the same time taking something shiny from his pocket. He had known Marchant for several months and they were not on friendly terms: Marchant had accused him of being a police informer, which he insisted he was not. Marchant was jailed for attempted murder. Could it be that Marchant had thought Kempley had overheard plans to attack Henry Solomon and had collected payment for a tip-off?

Three days later, Tommy Benneworth rode his luck again when he got into a fight in Waterloo Road, south London. At about 7 p.m. on a Monday evening, Benneworth, Ed Saunders and Bert McDonald arrived there by bus. They were met outside the Old Vic Theatre by a man named Keeves. A policeman, who recognised Benneworth, decided to keep observation. Keeves walked away and the three remaining men went into the Royal Victoria Tavern, next to the theatre. The bobby was about to depart when he saw Arthur Flatman, a Soho pickpocket and King's Cross gang member who was known to him, go into the pub carrying a parcel. In a few minutes, he heard a commotion and saw women fleeing from the pub, followed by Flatman, who was bareheaded, wild-eyed and running frantically in the busy road. On reaching the other side, Flatman stopped and stood watching the pub before returning.

The policeman summoned the assistance of another constable. As they approached the pub, Flatman again came running out, this time with Benneworth and the others in pursuit. Benneworth, who had a broken bar stool in his hand, chased Flatman across the road, where he ran into a hairdresser's shop directly opposite and locked the door behind him. Tommy was not easily put off. He slammed the stool through the door window and his pals kicked and barged the door in an attempt to get at Flatman.

The constables went into action, shouldering through a gathering crowd and grabbing Benneworth. Bert McDonald, ever alive to the dangers of being caught, took off. Saunders tried remonstrating with police, then seeing it was of no use, he also walked away. Benneworth did not put up a struggle; he knew he was too well known not to be picked up later for assaulting policemen. He walked with them to Kennington Road Police Station. On the way, he continuously swore and said no witnesses would come forward as they knew they would get chivved. He also threatened the constables with reprisals if they did not release him.

Charged with causing wilful damage to Mr Suhl's hairdresser's shop on Waterloo Road, Tommy gave his version of events. He never was in the Royal Vic; he was in the Olive Branch on the corner of Oakley Street, just a few doors away from Suhl's shop. He was having a drink with his friend Keeves and emerged to see what the fuss was about. He followed the action to the shop where he joined the crowd. Then someone punched him in the mouth, which is how he came to have blood on his hand and had taken on a fighting attitude. He was amazed when police arrested him. Keeves testified likewise.

Benneworth said he had not threatened anyone on his way to the police station and he was not there when the window was broken. The magistrate pointed out that Benneworth's evidence appeared to place him in two places at the same time, in the Olive Branch and in the crowd outside the shop.

Flatman was called as a witness. He said Benneworth was not the person who had attacked him and a man called Charles Hayes (in fact Timmy Hayes, the partner in crime of Dodger Mullins; either there had been a falling out or Hayes had lent himself to a colourful story). When he had first gone into the pub he joined Hayes at a table. Three men were sitting at the table next to them who, without any provocation, threw their glasses at him, rushed over and started fighting. Hayes fell down and he (Flatman) ran from the pub. When he realised he was not being pursued, he went back to see if Hayes was all right. Attacked again, he ran from the pub to Mr Suhl's shop to escape. He did not know who the three men were or why they had attacked him. Suhl testified that his door window had smashed when Flatman slammed it after him and was not broken by another person. No doubt, both men did not fancy one of Benneworth's chivvings.

The magistrate, Mr Waddy, dismissed suggestions that this was a fight between rival racing gangs, although he said he had received several letters saying that it was. It seemed some people had it in for Benneworth. He would treat it as a simple case of wilful damage to the shop window, as he was not satisfied Suhl's version of events was truthful. He found Benneworth guilty because he could not see how a policeman so close to the action could get it so wrong. Interestingly, Flatman's parcel had been found to contain a jemmy. Previous convictions were proved against Benneworth, including his being bound over to keep the peace in June. Even so, Waddy passed the lenient sentence of a £5 fine, plus a small sum to replace the window, but he did order Benneworth to forfeit his surety, with time to pay of course. Tommy smiled.

TYPICAL OF THE gangs ranging throughout south London in this period were the Battersea Boys, who caused trouble during their frequent binges and dance hall punch-ups. There are stories of hundreds of Battersea Boys patrolling the streets and frightening the local populace. In the 1920s, they were led by Wandsworth-born Billy Rowlett, who even in his late twenties was having difficulty finding direction after adolescence. Perhaps inevitably, they too were caught up in the general mayhem of 1925.

On Sunday, 30 August, at 10.30 p.m., on the suburban platform of London's Victoria Railway Station, over forty Battersea Boys and Girls caused havoc while waiting for a train to take them home. They were returning from Gatwick horse races: Gatwick Racecourse was a popular venue for Londoners until it was closed in 1933 for the building of the airport. By the time they had located the platform to return to Battersea, they were well bevied. Inevitably, they began to quarrel, first among themselves, then with other travellers, then with railway staff.

Rowlett, then aged twenty-nine, was drunk and vomiting profusely over the railway's fixtures and fittings, making the platform surface slippery. He slumped down on a bench and refused to be reconciled with his friends, with whom he had been quarrelling. When Charlie Newman tried to pull him up, he slipped in a squish of Billy's outpourings, thereby ruining his suit. He got up and clouted his drunken friend. Harry Taylor tried to calm things by pulling his mates about and succeeded only in making them more unsettled. A general fracas followed, girls included, with language as colourful as Rowlett's bodily fluids.

Into this stepped fifty-four-year-old Southern Railway Constable William Gatford, whose remonstrations were not welcomed. Asked if he was a first-aider, he replied in the negative, at which he was told he was not wanted and should 'take a train'. Gatford was not cowed and took hold of the sozzled Rowlett, who was unaware of who had hit him and was looking for someone to 'stick it on'. In his hand was a broken glass tumbler which he jabbed twice in Gatford's forehead, badly cutting his scalp. Gatford, who was a determined character, grappled with Rowlett, who quickly needed the help of his pals. Some of them grabbed the constable, pummelled his already bleeding napper, dragged him to the platform's edge and threw him onto the line, where he lost consciousness.

Other police officers arrived in time to hear the cheers as Gatford's limp form arched its way through the air, in his sudden and violent expulsion from the platform. Railway Constable Harry Rollins was floored by punches and kicks when he went to Gatford's aid. Metropolitan Constable Leonard Collins arrived next. He was made of tough stuff and waded into the crowd with his truncheon in an attempt to rescue Rollins. When Billy Rowlett grappled with him, Collins smashed his truncheon down on his head with considerable force, laying him out. As the gang tried to carry their leader away, Collins and the injured Rollins, with the assistance of several travellers, arrested five men, including an unconscious Billy.

Rowlett was brought from hospital to the London Sessions to face charges of maliciously causing grievous bodily harm and assault. Appearing with him were Charles, James and Joseph Newman and Harry Taylor, all charged with assaulting Gatford, Rollins and Collins. Rowlett, who had previous convictions for assault, was sentenced to fifteen months with hard labour. James Newman received twelve months, his brother Charles was acquitted and his other brother, Joseph, was remanded in custody for further investigation. Chauffeur Reginald Edwards, who went to the aid of the police, was awarded £1 for his courage. William Gatford recovered after a spell of convalescence.

This is one of many incidents that have been put down to racing gangs instead of being recognised for what they were: a brawl between racegoers that got out of hand. The incident on Victoria Station still pops up in racing gang folklore, while an attack on three police constables in Tooting, soon after the Gatford affair, is generally forgotten, as it was not attributed to racing gangs.

Charlie Newman took advantage of his acquittal to become leader of the Battersea Boys. When the deposed Rowlett, now over thirty, was released from jail, he tried to regain leadership. The Newman brothers decided he was not of the right mettle to lead such a bunch of young lions and gave him a beating, after which he accepted his relegated place in the Battersea pride. Not much different to animal behaviour in the jungle.

YOU CANNOT REALLY blame someone of Tommy Benneworth's standing for believing he was on a roll. On Sunday, 27 September 1925, he visited the basement Union Club in Frith Street, Soho, with Ed Saunders, John Jackson and Sam Ashley. He got into a fight after Jackson had annoyed customers by singing at the top of his voice. The proprietors, brothers Nicola and Luigi Cavalli, attempted to push Jackson up the stairs towards the exit but suffered terrible wounds for their efforts.

Four days later, Benneworth, Saunders and Jackson appeared at Marlborough Police Court accused of maliciously cutting and wounding the two men. It was stated that Benneworth and Jackson were doing most of the fighting and that Saunders had been seen driving them away in a large, silver-coloured Daimler, which police had traced. References were made to protection racketeering and racecourse gang feuds, the inference being that Jackson was making a point that money should be paid to silence his raucous tonsils. All three strenuously denied the charges; Benneworth stating that he had gone to the club to meet George Sage to arrange some ground at Epsom. They were remanded on £100 bail.

It would have come as no surprise to Benneworth and his pals that, when they reappeared on 14 October, the police had no evidence to put before the court. The victims were no longer certain who had attacked them and other witnesses were too terrified to come forward. Ed Saunders, who lived on his scrapyard premises at New Church Road, Camberwell (later the site of Charlie Richardson's Peckford Scrap Metal Company, the elder Charles Richardson, father of Charlie and Eddie, being an associate of Tommy Benneworth), was charged with intimidating witnesses, but no one came forward to support the charges. No prizes for guessing why. But Benneworth's confidence in his untouchability took a knock when he was locked up in Pentonville Prison for not having paid his forfeited surety. It took several frantic phone calls before friends put up the money.

Within days of the Elephant gang's attack on the Cavalli brothers, there was evidence that the Sabinis were still in business. Police arrested Giovanni Periglione, a thirty-seven-year-old acrobat; George Modebodze, a thirty-three-year-old general merchant; and twenty-eight-year-old Wilfred Cooper, all living in the heart of Soho. The three were charged with being concerned in feloniously demanding £110 by menaces from Gaston Reynaud, who owned a small cafe where he cooked meals to order for small groups of clients. Cooper, who seems to have been in command, said he represented the Sabini gang, who had signed a truce with the Cortesis and were back in business: he invited Reynaud to pay up or be glassed. There had previously been a fight between Periglione and Reynaud, who both lodged in the same house run by a Madame Roux in Old Compton Street. Reynaud had been bound over to keep the peace. This may have been a case of opportunists using the Sabini name to blackmail small Soho businesses. In any event, Reynaud, after offering Cooper money to square the police over a previous incident, was again threatened with having his throat cut with a razor or his face glassed. He went to the police. Detective Sergeant Lander hid under a bed in Reynaud's room and overheard Cooper's threats and his claim that 'I am the chief of the Sabini gang'.

In December, a plain-clothes policeman overheard Len Winter threatening to cut the ears off a coffee stall keeper with a razor. No doubt, the poor chap was a reluctant trader on Benneworth's list of donors. Winter got three months with hard labour and the stall owner kept his ears. Len's £100 surety, given after the Maiden Lane trial for his good behaviour, was forfeit on pain of an additional three months. John Clark, who had also put up a £100 surety for Len's good behaviour, was ordered to forfeit £50 of it. He was told he deserved no sympathy because he had stood surety for a dangerous and violent criminal, who had ten convictions for housebreaking, wounding, and other bad behaviour.

The Guv'nor of Camden Town

TOMMY BENNEWORTH'S reference to George Sage proved the continuing link between the Elephant and Castle and Camden Town gangs. It indicated that Sage, not the Sabinis, was in a position to decide who should have favourable positions at Epsom, where he likely represented Billy Kimber. Sage's career with the Birmingham and Camden Town gangs has already been noted. For many years, he was a prime player in racing feuds and was known as a fighting man. He was at it again in 1925, when at the age of forty-nine, he was arrested following an affray in the West End. In December, he appeared at Westminster Police Court with Robert Penfold, a twenty-seven-year-old costermonger from Catford, charged with disorderly conduct by fighting at Knightsbridge. The matter was said to be a betting dispute. A police constable said that he saw a crowd of between 300 and 400 outside Tattersalls. The prisoners were engaged in a fight in the centre of the crowd and he attempted to take them into custody. A general rumpus prevented the arrest of the prisoners and several people needed first aid. Sage and Penfold, who were said to be the originators of the disturbance, subsequently surrendered themselves to police. Penfold claimed to have been set upon. Both were remanded on bail by the magistrate, who said the matter deserved further investigation.

The likelihood is that Penfold had been gypped in some way by Sage and had demanded his money back, Sage declined and they squared up in a ring made by onlookers. At forty-nine, George must have still fancied himself good enough to take on a twenty-seven-year-old. No further police action seems to have been taken. At this time, George was still living beside the majestic sweep of palatial Mornington Crescent, Camden Town. He must have made a few bob.

Among the early Sage family were brothers Francis and John and their cousin Charles, who all resided at Her Majesty's pleasure in 1881. Frank, who was born in Birmingham in 1842, occupied his time in Cheetham Prison, Lancashire; John, born in 1847, whiled away his ten-year sentence for being an habitual criminal in Portland Prison in Dorset; while Charlie, born in 1843, was serving ten years as an habitual criminal in north London's Pentonville Prison. John and Charlie were born in Whitechapel and, although the family had connections with Birmingham, they seem to have originated in London.

George Sage's cousin, Frederick, known as Frank, was also born in Whitechapel. He had his own dubious pedigree. He served five years, plus twenty lashes of the 'cat', for robbery with violence. The 1881 census shows that he was then a seventeen-year-old serving this sentence in Holloway, in its final days as a mens' prison. In December 1891, he received another seven years for shop breaking. Soon after his release, he was at it again. In May 1899, aged thirty-five, he and nineteen-year-old Charlie Stuart intervened to prevent the arrest of burglar Bill Brown, who was being taken from his home in Bethnal Green to the police station. Sage came up and wrestled Brown free from Detective Handley, who was struck with a club by Stuart, before Brown took his truncheon. Handley chased the men and closed on Sage, who pointed a revolver at him and fired a shot that whizzed past his face, saying, 'Take that you bastard.' Handley ducked into a boot-mender's shop, snatched up an iron last and pursued Brown, bringing him down by throwing the last at him. Brown dropped the truncheon but managed to take off again. Meanwhile, public-spirited citizens were trying to capture Sage and Stuart: Sage waved his gun at them. Two constables responded to Handley's police whistle and one knocked Sage down with a truncheon blow to the head while the other grabbed Stuart.

At the Central Criminal Court, Sage claimed he only fired one warning shot in the air, and could have shot all the policemen if he had so wished. Expert examination of the revolver showed that it had jammed after the first shot. He was lucky to receive only three years; Stuart was jailed for six months.

In July 1909, Frank, as Frederick, appeared again at the Central Criminal Court. He was charged with the violent robbery of Patrick Kelly, who had been invited by Sage, John Humphreys and Mike Crawley to Spitalfields market to see a bareknuckle prizefight. For some reason the fight did not take place; instead Kelly was held by Humphreys and Crawley while Sage went through his pockets. Kelly was warned not to spout to police, but courageously summoned two constables, who caught up with the robbers and were assaulted by them. Frank Sage got two years with hard labour, Humphreys two years less one week and Crawley two years less two weeks. The reason for this strange sentencing was that Judge Lumley Smith did not want them all released on the same day. When released, Humphreys engaged in a rash of burglaries with Dick Vincent and Wally Bowen. Police described them as one of the most dangerous gangs in the East End. All had many previous convictions and were jailed for five years.

The 1919 electoral register lists George Sage and his wife, Ellen at Mornington Place, Camden. They were still there in May 1930, but had left by the time of the 1938-39 register. The property, which could accommodate six adults, is on three-storeys and George and Ellen (erroneously named Helen in some newspaper reports) were able to afford it for just themselves. The Sages, in fact, were not married but had at least three children between 1918 and 1926: Gladys, Edward and Ronald. When Edward was born, George was described as a racing commission agent. A commission agent took bets for other people. George was also one of the pests that infested racecourses before the war and after his demob. He would have been thirty-seven at the start of World War One.

GEORGE NEAVES SAGE was born at Red Lion Lane, Stoke Newington, on 16 March 1877, to Charles Sage, a waiter at the Red Lion Inn, and Bessie, a child of the 'Old Nichol', that notorious slum nestled between Shoreditch and Bethnal Green. Young George, however, did not have a poor beginning. Stoke Newington was a prosperous, middle-class borough, populated by wealthy trades people living in pleasant streets, one of which, Church Street, had a large number of desirable residences. On its corner with Red Lion Lane stood the Red Lion Inn, dating back to the Sixteenth Century. The district was undergoing change: house building on green fields and the arrival of railway and tram services brought an influx of working-class wage earners, particularly in the expansive brickfields that occupied large tracts of former parkland. Stoke Newington was located on 'brick earth', which decided its destiny as a brick making industrial site.

His father may have taken up a better paying job as a labourer in the brickfields. At any rate, the Sage family moved to Brick Fields, Willesden, where George's father worked in the gigantic brick factory established by the Furness family. Labourers lived in rows of cottages with basic amenities, coated with red brick dust that also polluted the local water supply, stored in the West Middlesex Water Works reservoir. Also living in cottages in Brick Fields were Charles's parents – George's grandparents – and their six children, not counting William who, aged twenty-four, was an inmate of Clerkenwell Prison. The grandfather was a foreman at the brick works. Charles's brother, Robert and his wife and four children lived next door to him.

It may be that George took a lead from his uncle, William, by becoming a crook. In 1894, he was convicted at Clerkenwell

Police Court of theft. In 1896, aged twenty, along with two others, he broke into his Uncle Robert's house at Edmonton and stole goods and cash, for which he received nine months with hard labour. Things seem to have settled by 22 April 1900 when, aged twenty-two, he married twenty-year-old Lilian Bussey in a St Pancras church, at which time he is listed as being a coal porter living at Hampstead Road. In 1906, police charged George (as 'William Johnson'), Lily Sage, Frederick White, William Baker and George Dunsdon with the theft of clothing from Brailey's in Pentonville Road, Islington. Police said windowpanes had been removed and the tailor's shop effectively cleared of suits, materials and cash. Lily got off but George received five years. He had other convictions for theft under the name William Johnson.

By now, he was set on a criminal course, reinforced by a 'prison education' and indoctrination. He separated from Lily and took up with Ellen Brooks, who was two years younger than Lily. Ellen was born at Berwick Street, in the heart of Soho, and her father was yet another criminal: he was an inmate of Borstal Convict Prison, Chatham, in 1881 and was recorded as a prisoner in Pentonville twenty years later. Lily refused to divorce Sage and it was not until June 1942 that he and Ellen were married, following Lilian's death.

Sage's entrance into the wider world of villainy did not get off to a good start. Having served his sentence, he came up against Lambeth's Dick Burge, once a highly-ranked boxer who was now promotiong contests at The Ring in Blackfriars. On June 1910, Burge staged the first big contest at his recently-opened venue, featuring the great American Packey McFarland. He was talking to some newspaper men in the gallery when he spotted 'Brummy of Holloway' and some of his mob. Burge had not only been a formidable boxer but had also served a ten-year prison sentence for bank fraud and was harder than nails. Figuring the hoodlums were there to pick pockets, and possibly snatch his takings too, he nimbly climbed down the balcony and flattened Brummy with a right-hander, before wading into the rest with fists, feet and even his head: he left three unconscious and the fourth running away. Burge later apologised to his horrified wife Bella, who had witnessed the whole scene: 'Sorry about that, Bella, but if you have much to do with this lot you'll learn that you've got to be able to give them more than they can hand out – and you've got to hit first. It's the only sort of rule they understand.'[1]

Sage joined the Army and served in World War One. He also put aside his burgling tools and became an associate of the McDonald–Kimber combine during its war with the King's Cross/West End Boys in the 1910s. Much of the brawling was in Soho, outside Ellen's street door. Florence Brooks, the girl Billy Kimber lived with at the time of his shooting in 1921, is likely to have been related to Ellen.

Sage also had at least six professional fights out of Hackney. His street fighting skills were probably learned with the fabled Hackney and Finsbury gangs in association with Freddie Gilbert, which continued when George took over leadership of the Camden Town gang (so described by Scotland Yard at the time of the Portpool Lane shooting affray) and also known as the Birmingham gang, because of its association with Kimber. He was regarded by Wal McDonald as a stand-up, toe-to-toe fist fighter; both men revelled in their reputations as 'top men'. George must have been party to the expulsion of Alf White and Dodger Mullins from racecourses in 1920. However, his association with Tommy Benneworth in 1925 shows he was back on good terms with Mullins. At that time, he appears to have been the dominant rogue in racing gang activity, even more so than the Sabinis.

His nickname, 'Brummy', appears in Metropolitan Police files in 1922. He may have taken it because of his association with Kimber's Brummagems. Ex-detective Tom Divall related

---

1 Quoted in Leslie Bell, *Bella of Blackfriars*, Odhams Press, 1961.

a tale of Sage and Joe Gandley helping him to quieten some riotous behaviour at a racecourse, and Gandley lived in Birmingham, close to where Kimber was born. No doubt, George Sage's London origin is the reason he knew the Elephant and Castle gang and he is likely one of the men who brought the gangs together. Police files on the Southampton Arms shooting describe him as an oft-convicted thief; his association with Gilbert suggests he may have been one of the Titanic.

Alice Diamond and the Forty Thieves

IN DECEMBER 1925, just four days before Christmas day, Tommy Benneworth's pal Sam Ashley got into more trouble. It concerned the other half of the Elephant and Castle gang, the 'Forty Elephants' or 'Forty Thieves', as they were variously known. This was the girl's branch of the business. Their specialities were taking bets on behalf of the boys and indulging in the largest operation ever seen in this country of systematic shoplifting. They benefited from prudish attitudes of the times by taking shelter behind the privacy afforded to women in large stores. Dressed in specially tailored garments, with hidden deep pockets and voluminous knickers, they mounted raids on the West End, where they plundered shops and stores of goods worth thousands of pounds.

They became so well-known in London that panic erupted when they were seen near high-class shops and stores, causing them to expand their enterprise to countryside and seaside towns, which were strategically blitzed. To escape, they used high-powered cars to outrun police pursuit. If they were stopped, they were found to be clean, having 'posted' stolen goods to a number of receiving depots around Elephant and Castle, all under the protection of hard men from the Elephant. Bert McDonald is most associated with the organisation of events; however, Tommy Benneworth would have been in there somewhere. Many a husband lounged at home while his missus was out at work, and many an old lag was propped up by a tireless shoplifting spouse.

The shoplifting enterprise of the Elephant and Castle gang began in the Nineteenth Century. Charlie Pitts, born 1865, is generally credited with creating the original large-scale network. The Pitts family, who came out of Lambeth and Southwark Bridge Road, passed their skills on to their progeny, who became leading practitioners. Mostly, the girls lived within a mile circle of Elephant and Castle.

The head of the Forty Elephants/Thieves came to be called the 'Queen'. In 1896, twenty-five-year-old Mary Carr, of Southwark, known as 'The Queen of the Forty Thieves' and the leader of a gang that infested south London and the Strand, was convicted of stealing the male child of a gypsy woman at Epsom races, either to sell or use for prostitution. Her cohort, who got off, was Philip Jacobs, alias Phil Oker, the man who was killed by Tommy Armstrong at Sandown races in 1921. There would be a succession of 'queens': Alice Diamond in the 1920s and '30s, Maggie Hill in the '30s and '40s, and Shirley Pitts from the 1960s to her death in 1992. In the 1920s, Tommy Benneworth liked to be called 'King'. Alice Diamond, the most infamous Queen, was born in 1896, when her parents lived in Southwark. Both of her parents had criminal records: her father for shoving the head of the Lord Mayor's son through a plate glass window during a riot over housing conditions. In 1920 (as Diana Black), she was said to be a married woman who had been deserted by her husband six months after their marriage, when he discovered her true character.

The girls led by Alice Diamond included veteran hoisters Maggie Springett and Ada Barrett, both with many convictions dating back to the 1910s. Newer members were Ada Wellman, Florrie Holmes, Christina Noon, Maud Seymour and Bertha Tappenden. There was also Maggie Hill, whose thirteen-year-old brother, Billy, would one day claim to be Boss of Britain's Underworld; Gert Scully, a tailoress who made their specialist couture; and Dollie Mays, all of whom were constantly before the courts for practising their craft. The girls were rarely caught with significant amounts of booty, because hoisters quickly passed their goods to boosters. They then spirited them away to cars manned by the flat-nosed brigade, who discouraged enquiries from pursuers. When working other towns the girls would sometimes use the rail network, depositing empty suitcases at railway stations, which they filled with booty for the return trip.

Police were amazed at just how much loot could be stuffed into specially tailored coats, cummerbunds, muffs, skirts, bloomers and even hats. Stolen shoes, hats and garments would be worn on to the street. In one variety of operation, two or three women would go towards different exits; one might be stopped by a sales assistant or security guard, in which case she would say she was taking the items to the doorway to see them in the light. The others, once they had made it to the street, quickly passed their goods to confederates, who were accompanied by tough men who would make apprehension hazardous. If caught, they could look forward to three, six, nine or twelve months with hard labour, escalating to three years penal servitude, depending on previous form.

In July 1923, three fashionably dressed Elephant and Castle veterans, Marie Butler, Emma Hinds and Laura McLean, entered the Debenham and Freebody's store in Oxford Street: there one was observed to grow significantly in size. They were arrested in the street after a fierce struggle. Marie had three frocks under her dress and the others had garments stuffed inside their clothing. Six months with hard labour was the result.

The girls targeted preferred stock, particularly items of jewellery, designer clothes, furs, hosiery and leather goods. Store sales were a bonus for them. In the rush, they would grab all they could, leave and come back for more. Many of the girls were well built and grew even more in size as they stuffed plunder into their garments. Some speculate that they were called the Forty Elephants because of their build; however, Bert McDonald always claimed to have changed their name from 'Thieves' to 'Elephants'. They were referred to as 'thieves' in 1921 when Ada Wellman, who lived in Southwark and was a sometime girlfriend of Wal McDonald, was described in court as a member of a south London gang known as the Forty Thieves. She was convicted of relieving the Army and Navy Stores at Victoria of a body-load of goodies at their July sale. The name seems to have changed around 1924. In 1939, Ada was still at it and was this time described as a member of the notorious Elephant Gang of shoplifters, when jailed for four months.

One veteran of the Forty Elephants, Alice Turner, was arrested in 1925 after leaving the upmarket Bon Marché store in Brixton's shopping centre, with a fur she had been seen stuffing inside her coat. In court, she burst into tears, crying, 'I don't know what made me do it.' The magistrate lost all sympathy when he was told twenty-five other stolen articles had been found in her shopping bag. 'Three months,' said he.

The girls hit the headlines in 1925, after a fight in the bar of the Canterbury Arms Club in The Cut, Waterloo. Maria Jackson attacked Bertha Tappenden with a broken wine glass after an exchange of insults. Maria was the married daughter of Bill Britten, a leading light on the male side of the Elephant and Castle gang, who joined in and punched Bertha. He then got into a scrap with Alice Diamond's brother Tommy. This led to a falling out between gang members. On the night of 21 December 1925, Alice Diamond, Sam Ashley, George Hughes, Phil Thomas, Bert Conway and Maggie Hughes, with other angry females and minders, drank themselves into a frenzy in the bar of the Canterbury. They then departed for Britten's home in Lambeth, just around the corner from the earlier Benneworth brawl in Waterloo Road.

Alice knocked on Britten's door. He opened it and threw a jug of water over the Queen of the Forty Elephants. To his horror, from the shadows came the harridans of hell. Although Britten managed to get his door shut, they broke it down and chased him from room to room, cutting him with knives and clubbing him with iron bars. Those who could not fit inside showered his home with bottles and bricks. By the time police had reached the scene of a reported riot, Britten had suffered wounds that would require more than twenty-five stitches, with only his stout resistance saving him from even more of the surgeon's catgut. Also wounded was his fifteen-year-old son. Sam Ashley later got three years and six months for his part in the attack; George Hughes, who had waved a revolver under the nose of Bill's wife, received five years; and Maggie Hughes got twenty-one months, as did Gert Scully. Alice Diamond and Bertha Tappenden each received eighteen months. Dollie Mays and her husband, who stood trial as Bert Conway, were acquitted, only to be jailed the following year with her husband for a burglary in Hampstead. The girls would have rued missing the January sales.

Maggie Hughes was a serial shoplifter with convictions from the age of fourteen, after running away from home. In 1915, she was acquitted of stealing letters from a business premises, abetted by her husband Alfred and Harry Teague. They had covered her movements as she slipped her tiny hand into a letter box in search of envelopes containing cheques, which they could doctor with an assortment of acids and inks. In 1920, she and Alice Diamond raided five West End stores and stole valuable furs and expensive gowns worth over £1,000. They were traced to Alice's southeast London home, where no trace of the stolen goods was found and no assistance given to recover them. Police described the pair as the cleverest of thieves, who lived with notorious shop breakers. Maggie was jailed for twelve months and Alice (as Diana Black) for eighteen. In 1921, Maggie was described as an expert thief, addicted to drink, and of loose morals, when she was convicted with Madeline Partridge. In 1923, she was put away for three years after running out of a jeweller's shop with a tray of thirty-four diamond rings, straight into the arms of a policeman. Her cheeky attempt to avoid identification, by swapping clothes in her cell with confederate Ellen Mead, did not help her defence. After release from prison in 1928 for her part in the attack on Bill Britten, Maggie was jailed for five months, as Margaret Gray, for stealing from a West End store. Agnes Ross, who was arrested with her, was most likely Alice Diamond.

Diamond began thieving at a young age and already had a police record for petty theft when, as a seventeen-year-old, she was arrested with Christina Noon in 1914 for stealing from a hat shop in Oxford Street: for this both were bound over. By the age of twenty, she was the accepted 'Queen' and Maggie Hughes was 'Baby Face'. Diamond demanded loyalty from men and women and was a genius at organising the gang into cells of four or five to raid one store, or in groups of cells simultaneously to loot major stores across the country. At times, several cells would descend on one store and ransack it, while confused store watchers were pulled in all directions. She was a big woman, five feet eight and one-quarter inches, according to her criminal record. She had a punch to match that of her minders and fists studded with diamond rings, that could put out an eye. To the police she was 'Diamond Annie'.

The girls bullied outsiders who they suspected of thieving. They would demand a percentage of their take and be very unpleasant if they were denied, arranging beatings and even kidnappings until money was shelled out. Other sidelines included using false references to obtain work as maids, quickly clearing the jewel box and clothes closet. In 1916, Alice Diamond was arrested for obtaining a position in a munitions factory by using another girl's identification card; her exact purpose is unknown and she seems to have got off with a warning. Blackmail was not beyond the girls' morals, especially the prettier ones, who would lure men into disreputable dalliances, which they then had to pay the girls to get out of. On the plus side, they threw the liveliest of parties and spent lavishly at pubs, clubs and restaurants.

Their lifestyles were in pursuit of those of glamorous movie stars, combined with the decadent living of 1920s aristocratic flapper society. They read of the outrageous behaviour of rich, bright young things and wanted to emulate them, the problem being that they did not have the wherewithal to pay for it. Their answer was to steal and dispose of huge quantities of top-quality merchandise and reward themselves from the profits. They rarely wore what they stole, preferring to buy legitimate high fashion.

The various branches of the Elephant and Castle gang liked to keep things in the family. Maggie Hughes was Maggie Hill, of the north London family, who married Alfred Hughes, the brother of George Hughes. This was how she and Dollie Mays came to be members of the Forty Thieves. The Hughes family, all born in north London, were 'big' around Elephant and Castle. Another brother, Teddy, was given five years in 1930 as one of Billy Hill's smash-and-grab gang and was one of the London Airport bullion raiders in 1948. Maggie, a vivacious, short, round, fiery vixen, was jailed many times for wholesale shoplifting and assaults on police. Her sister Dollie, real name Dorothy Hill, married Albert Mays: they were described by Billy Hill in his memoirs as burglars who targeted vulnerable homes spotted by him on his delivery round for a local greengrocer. They were sometimes referred to as the Hampstead burglars and included Albert's brother George.

Yet another of Billy's sisters, Alice Amelia, married George and Alfie Hughes' brother, Billy. Gert Scully married Phil Thomas; Bert McDonald had a dalliance with Alice Diamond before moving in with Florrie Holmes, whose sister Bertha married burglar Billy Tappenden. Dan Johnston, another minder, married Ada McDonald; Tommy Benneworth married Esther Hawkins; Tommy Diamond married the sister of Maud Seymour; burglar Billy Benstead later associated with Billy Hill, had a son who married the daughter of Alice Diamond. Benstead's partner, Harry Pitts, became the father of future 'queen' Shirley Pitts; Emma Hinds belonged to a family of notorious thieves in Walworth, where she and husband George became parents of Albert Hinds, a robber who amassed many convictions. Albert lived with Gert Cottrell, another of the Forty Thieves, and their son became the infamous prison escapee Alfie Hinds.

Stolen goods were disposed of through a chain of fences in south and north London. Small-value items went to street market traders, jewellery to pawnbrokers, and clothes to an assortment of dealers, some of whom operated as 'wardrobe sellers' of low-cost items: others ran better class establishments in lingerie and dresses. Furs usually went to dodgy furriers in the East and West ends of London, who skilfully replaced labels and remodelled coats. Much was shifted through Ada McDonald, who lived in Stead Street, Walworth, where she dealt in goods bought from the giant Houndsditch warehouse in the City. Her house was turned over in 1910, when she was suspected of being a receiver for five notorious gangs; she produced ledgers to prove rooms full of stock had been legitimately purchased.

Jim Bullock, who had a long career as a receiver of stolen goods, operated out of Islington with Jane Durrell, who lived with him as his wife. The Bullocks relied on others to do their thieving, including members of the Forty Thieves. Numerous attempts to convict them of theft and receiving ended in failure. In 1911, he and Jane were charged with receiving the proceeds of shoplifting sprees from West London shops. These included Selfridges, Bourne & Hollingsworth, Derry & Toms and Whiteleys. The goods were stolen by a group of women who police observed going into stores, coming out looking stouter, going into pubs to parcel their goods and becoming thin again, before delivering them to Queen's Head Street, Islington. They then set off for more raids. Inspector Tom Divall raided the house and premises close by and found the Bullocks examining a quantity of chemises, table linen and other items. Three shoplifters, Elizabeth Cooper, Amelia Evans and Florence Roberts, pleaded guilty and received prison sentences. A jury could not decide whether the devious duo knew the goods, valued at hundreds of pounds, had been stolen, and said the magic words 'not guilty'.

Thus ended the remarkable gang violence of 1925, much of it under Tommy Benneworth's stewardship. At some time, Wal McDonald took him to one side and suggested an easing off. Tommy took the hint and, although he remained active, he no longer grabbed the headlines. He may have joined Johnny Jackson in becoming one of Ruby Sparks' smash-and-grab specialists.

Dodger Mullins

IN SEPTEMBER 1927, a former welterweight boxer called David Lewis was attacked by five men in the centre of Cardiff, the Welsh capital. The next day he died, aged thirty-one, from loss of blood caused by knife wounds to his face. Two men were subsequently sentenced to death for his murder. On the morning of 27 January 1928, a church bell tolled as more than 5,000 people massed outside Cardiff Prison. Inside, thirty-four-year-old Danny Driscoll, a traveller and racing man, and Edward Rowlands, a bookmaker, took their last walk.

The Welsh tragedy made national headlines and showed that gang violence was not confined to the English capital city. It also took the spotlight from a colossal free-for-all that had taken place three days earlier, just off Gray's Inn Road, between Alf White's King's Cross Boys and Dodger Mullins's Bethnal Green gang. The east Londoners had provoked the fight by doing the rounds of Clerkenwell pubs. Mullins's crowd came unstuck when White countered with a bigger gang and cornered them in Acton Street. Shots were fired and several men were taken to the Royal Free Hospital with head wounds. No arrests were made.

By 1928, Billy Kimber and Bert McDonald had departed for the United States to meet up with Wag McDonald after firing shots through the doorway of the Griffin Club in Theobald's Road, Clerkenwell, a drinking place of the Sabinis. The Sabini gang had now become known as the Italian gang, but still had its old guard in place, among them many non-Italians. In March, they sought out and attacked Elephant and Castle men John Carpenter and Mad George Moss, in the Optimist

Club in Edgware Road. However, they got the worst of it when Carpenter pulled a knife from his sleeve and cut George Langham. In November, ex-boxer Jim Ford was jailed for assaults on bookmakers Lester Montague and Charlie Ricketts. Montague was attacked by Ford, his younger brother Harry and Jim Paul in the Horse Shoe Hotel, near the corner of Tottenham Court Road and New Oxford Street (in the 1960s, a watering hole for Eddie Richardson and Frankie Fraser). The assault took place in front of police officers, including the redoubtable D.C. John Rutherford, but they were unable to prevent Montague from being seriously injured. The trio remained at large to attack Ricketts at Paddington Railway Station. A letter to the Home Secretary concerning the attack on Ricketts, signed 'A Londoner', complained that in certain parts of London it was not safe to sing 'God Save the King', but it was safe to sing 'God Save the Emperor, Darby Sabini'.

On 22 September 1929, George Sewell and Johnny McCarthy, the man who had once shot Eddie Emanuel, attacked John Phillips in Dean Street, Soho. Sewell was a Shoreditch bookmaker, who also boxed twenty or so bouts as a middleweight. Arthur Harding had once rescued him after he had foolishly biffed Harry Sabini when Sabini tried to pull him off a stand at Brighton races. The Sabinis threatened to do him at the Ring boxing venue in Blackfriars, but were discouraged by a group of Harding's Bethnal Green Boys and their allies from Elephant and Castle. It was an example of the ever-shifting alliances in the muddled world of London's gangs.

Shortly after the attack on Phillips, Jim McDonald, the youngest of the McDonald brothers, was approached at Hurst Park races and threatened with a razor cut if he did not hand over a tenner. McDonald, who had been a good amateur boxer, used his left hook to good effect, to leave Sabini man Sid Baxter lying among the furnishings of a beer tent. McDonald worked for Billy Kimber, who had now returned from America, but was not in the mainstream of gang warfare.

To prevent a comeback against him, Kimber turned to another Elephant man, Charlie Furlong, to sort it out. Furlong decided to recruit from north of the river. Kimber, meanwhile was building up a 'respectable' partnership with gambler Andrew Towey, in which he no longer sought the spotlight of notoriety. Many years later, it emerged that the unobtrusive Towey, who had criminal convictions under the name of Cochrane, had been the ringleader of a group of unscrupulous bookmakers and an organiser of illegal gambling, principally at Epsom during Derby meetings.

It was not all one way. Dodger Mullins's hatred for the Sabinis and their allies spilled over into a loathing of all things Italian. On 25 January 1930, Jack Mullins, Henry Barton, Jack Sangers and brothers Charlie and George Steadman, all East Enders, together with many others, forced their way into the Argus Club in Greek Street, Soho, after licensing hours had ended and demanded drinks. The club secretary, who knew Mullins and Barton, obliged and waived payment, hoping his unwelcome guests would depart. Mullins swilled his beer, drew his sleeve across his mouth, rubbed his hands, and inquired if there were any 'Raddies' (Italian radicals) in attendance. Not receiving a satisfactory reply, he pushed his way into a clubroom, picked out the first olive-complexioned gent to meet his blood-red eye and set about him. After Mullins put him on the floor, they all joined in and gave him a merciless kicking. Still not satisfied, Mullins pulled him up by his waistcoat and began beating him with a cosh, assisted by Barton, who whacked him with a chair leg. The man, Angelo Costognetti, soon resembled a rag doll. Courageous Edith Milburn stepped in to stop the beating and immediately joined the Italian on the floor. Undaunted, she grabbed Mullins' legs and screamed, 'Stop them Jack, stop them,' at which some of the gang kicked her off Mullins so he could continue his work.

The five were soon arrested and charged with malicious wounding with intent to do grievous bodily harm. In court, club secretary John Lewis said there was blood everywhere: men were cowering in corners, and other men had revolvers, life preservers, legs of chairs and bottles, which they were throwing about. One man was running about waving a gun in the faces of terrified club members. Asked what he had done, Lewis replied he had gone behind the bar and fainted. When he came round, the gang had gone and he telephoned for an ambulance. Mullins reappeared as he completed the call and demanded to know what he had done. Told he had only phoned for an ambulance, Mullins told him, 'I hope you have not spouted against me. God help you if you have. You know I am a thick 'un, and you know what it means for me. I shall do you if you have.' Could Dickens have written better of Bill Sikes?

Lewis, as it turned out, was using an alias that Mullins' defence lawyer used to discredit him as a witness. He also had a history of mental illness. Even so, bail was refused the prisoners and Lewis was given police protection. Soon, friends of the Dodger invited Mr Costognetti to a pub in King's Cross, where they offered him a sum to square the matter. This was related at the resumption of proceedings by Divisional Inspector Horwell, who must have thought, 'I've got them now.' The accused were sent for trial at the Central Criminal Court, where Costognetti, Edith Milburn and John Lewis all developed a case of the jitters and impaired memory cells. All five were found not guilty.

In the same court on the same day, Minnie Dore, Dodger's 'wife', appeared on a charge of having stolen a woman's handbag. She got off as well. Minnie, a terrifying amazon, married Joe Cooper in 1911 and had 'I love Joe Cooper' engraved on her forearm. Her volatile affair with Dodger began after her release from prison in 1918 and produced at least one child. Her convictions were mainly for shoplifting from jewellery stores and pawnbrokers, sometimes with her sisters Daisy and Lily.

IN FEBRUARY 1930, Charlie Furlong, John and Arthur Phillips, John Daly and Walter Rance caught up with their quarry, Sid Baxter. They found him in the Admiral Duncan public house in Old Compton Street, Soho, drinking in the public bar with George Sewell. Unfortunately for Sewell, the Phillips brothers had it in for him too for deserting Dodger Mullins to take up with the Italians and for the recent attack on John. The six attacked with furniture and broken bottles, leaving the pair seriously disfigured and needing an abundance of stitches. At the Central Criminal Court, it was stated that Sewell and Baxter were members of the Sabini gang, now called the Italian gang.

John Phillips has an interesting pedigree as a gangster. He had connections with the Elephant and Castle gang and was a prominent member of the Finsbury and Hoxton gangs. He was born in Hackney Wick in 1900 to the much-convicted, Birmingham-born Arthur Phillips and Londoner Annie Ryan, both unwed, and members of the Titanic. The Phillips family lived in Lambeth before moving back north of the river to Finsbury. In the 1910s and '30s, they were at Macclesfield Street, Finsbury. John's younger brother, Arthur, was born in 1904, followed by another son, James, in 1908. Their father, when he was given a hefty five-year sentence for pickpocketing, in February 1921, had twenty-three previous convictions dating back to 1893 and a current twelve-month sentence for a similar offence. He was an extremely violent man, something that would have future significance.

John had the usual early brushes with the law, collecting bets for Freddie Gilbert and keeping watch for policemen, no doubt sometimes rewarding them for not reporting the illegal practice of street bookmaking. He worked variously as a greengrocer and fishmonger. The streets around Finsbury, Hoxton, Clerkenwell and King's Cross all had their gangs and

John was proud to be one of the Finsbury Boys, with whom he practised the skills inherited in his genes by becoming a proficient pickpocket. In July 1922, he and Arthur were drawn into the racecourse gang wars when Harry Sabini slashed John with a razor. They mounted a comeback with allies from Elephant and Castle, which developed into the shootout in Portpool Lane. In June 1923, John was acquitted of picking the pocket of a woman on a Tube train. In 1924, he and Tommy Scott were acquitted at Westminster Police Court of being suspected persons.

In 1925, John and Arthur added to the general mayhem by attacking Sabini man Billy Presswell in a café in Upper Street, Islington. The victim said he was hit with iron bars and slashed with a knife handed to John Phillips by Harry Sabini. John quickly pointed out that he had himself been cut with a razor by Sabini at Brighton in 1922, which requited twenty-six stitches to repair the damage. The muddying of waters worked and everyone got off. A year later, charges of assaulting a clergyman in an office in Chancery Lane were withdrawn, when both men said they had settled their differences. John paid one guinea for repairs to the Reverend Pawson's teeth.

John was a follower of Fred Gilbert, one of the nasties who infested racecourses and the trains travelling to and from them. He fitted in well with Freddie's enterprises. Last known of his career is in 1939, when he was jailed for two months as part of a combination of Finsbury Boys and Elephant Boys, targeting the pockets of passengers at Charing Cross Underground Station.

Charges of occasioning actual bodily harm to Baxter and Sewell, and causing £200 of damage, brought John Phillips five years, brother Arthur three years, and Daly fifteen months, all with hard labour. Rance was luckier; he was referred to the Probation Service to 'see what could be done for him'. Eventually he received a conditional discharge for causing damage. What Recorder Sir Ernest Wild did not know was that Wally Rance was a close friend of Tommy Benneworth and worked for his father, Charlie Benneworth, in his Camberwell print shop. Charges against Furlong and a sixth man, Dave Chinsky, were dismissed.

THE BETHNAL GREEN gang dates back to the mid-Nineteenth Century, when it was a bunch of footpads and pickpockets. The first recognised leader, Moey Levy, was shoved aside by newer arrivals Arthur Harding, Dodger Mullins and his pal, the unwholesome squirt Timmy Hayes. Hayes hid behind a razor's edge while demanding protection money from shopkeepers and stallholders and extorting money from bookmakers and punters.

Timothy Hayes was born in Bethnal Green in 1891, the illegitimate child of fifteen-year-old Frances Hayes. He spent much of his time in prison and seems to have been the leader of the gang by 1910, when he was arrested, with Billy Driscoll and Tommy Nicholls, for assaulting police officers and two managers of a dosshouse in Seven Dials, Holborn. A savage fight had erupted after they were refused entry, in which police and civilians were bitten, kicked and head-butted. The fight continued at the police station, where Hayes kicked one of the managers in the groin. He was in Pentonville in 1911.

Hayes had been a thief from an early age and, by 1914, had already racked up ten convictions when he was sentenced to three months for attempting to pick pockets. His accomplice Billy Driscoll had eight previous, one of which was for assaulting a seaman and stealing a parcel from him, at a coffee stall in Commercial Road. His victim caught up with Driscoll but was given a good kicking from six or seven others, who also went through his pockets – most likely Hayes was in the gang, which police said infested the neighbourhood.

Another of the gang, Issy Conn, was a street trader who could whip up a crowd with his 'spiel' and sell them almost anything. In 1924, he was jailed, along with his brother Harry,

Rube Phillips and Harry Goldman, for kicking the stuffing out of Police Inspector Kirchner and Major Griffith Turnbull, the superintendent of Wembley Exhibition, who had asked them not to flog 'iffy' merchandise outside the Canadian Pavilion. Their arrest came about because Kirchner recognised them as members of the Bethnal Green gang. The impetuous Major never fully recovered from his kicking.

Jack Mullins was a throwback to Jack Sheppard in looks and manner. Jim McDonald described him as scruffy, often with food hanging from his mouth, and always scrounging something from someone, whether he had a need for it or not. He was not a favourite of Billy Kimber, who drove him and other bad elements from racecourses. No doubt that is why Dodger kept to the East End, where he operated a vicious protection racket among bookmakers, shops, pubs and clubs. Opposed to him were tough characters such as Alf Solomon and his brother Henry, who took it upon themselves to protect Jewish bookmakers.

Convictions racked up by Dodger commenced in 1908 when, as a sixteen-year-old, he was jailed for wounding. In January 1921, with Timmy Hayes, Tommy Salmon and George Askew, he broke into a warehouse to steal tailor's cloth, for which Mullins and Hayes received three-years sentences, the others received lesser terms. In 1924, Mullins, with Albert Deighton, was acquitted of passing dud pound notes.

In early 1926, he worked for Arthur Harding as a bodyguard for strike breakers during the General Strike. Strike breakers were paid to keep goods moving from the docks, particularly food that would have spoiled. The employment of bodyguards for them first came about during a twelve-month strike in 1912, that paralysed the east London docks. Thousands of dockers attended meetings, formed processions and marched on dock gates that had been locked against them. When police tried to prevent them pulling down gates by throwing hooked ropes over them, they were attacked with fists, banners, missiles and fire bombs. Vans and lorries were overturned and their loads set on fire. Employers recruited strike breakers from men, desperate for work, many of them from southeast London. East London gangsters were paid to escort blacklegs into work, to keep goods moving.

By this time, Mullins had a considerable reputation for violence. It is interesting that he fought the Sabinis and their Jewish allies and yet was driven off the racecourses by their enemy Billy Kimber. He just was not popular.

Dodger's career had its next setback in July 1926, when he and his equally vicious and ruthless pal, Timmy Hayes, were convicted of demanding £10 with menaces from a Bethnal Green billiard marker. Hayes, who had since called on the unfortunate victim and kicked the chalk dust out of him in an attempt to get him to withdraw his complaint, was also found guilty of causing actual bodily harm and of being a habitual criminal. Two of Mullins' gang, Charlie Harvey and Benny Hall, were charged with a similar attack on another billiards hall but were acquitted. This was typical of the bloody terror inflicted by Mullins on small businesses in the East End.

Dodger informed the Central Criminal Court that he could prove the case had been 'got up' by the Sabinis and the Yiddisher mob, who wanted him and Hayes off the streets. Detective Sergeant Donaldson pointed out that the defendants, who had previously been convicted, had a history of violence and intimidation in the East End and other parts of the country. They were pioneers of gang warfare in east London and on racecourses, where they levied blackmail. Both defendants were sentenced to four years penal servitude. Hayes received a further five years preventive detention. East Enders breathed a sigh of relief. Dodger would be back, but for a while a cloud had been lifted from over small traders' and bookmakers' heads, including those of Alf Solomon's Yiddisher gang.

At the time of this conviction, Mullins was living in Eastman Street, Bethnal Green. It was just a splash away from where 'brides in the bath' murderer George Joseph Smith, who killed three women for their life insurance, was born and close to Vallance Road, where Mr and Mrs Kray's little boys would one day pull the wings off flies, as they practised to succeed Dodger. As described at various trials, Dodger was a fish porter, then a labourer, and later, a bookmaker's clerk.

Jack Mullins was born on 8 March 1892, at Alma Road, Bethnal Green, to John Mullins, a Jewish confectioner, and Louisa Giles. Louisa, who could not write her name, was of Irish descent but was born in Bethnal Green. Alma Road lay behind Old Ford Road, at one end of which was the Grand Union Canal and, around the corner, Hackney's Victoria Park. The Cranbrook Estate has since obliterated the road. At the peak of his career, Dodger, as he was known from an early age, was lucratively employed as a fish porter at Billingsgate market. His father is popularly believed to have been a fairground worker; however, he was working at Batger's Sweet Factory in Poplar when Jack was born. Two years later, in 1894, he was listed as a beer retailer.

Now here is a poser: John Mullins, who was born in 1862 to Uriah and Jane Mullins, grew up in the St. Luke's rookery and was by all accounts a knife-happy villain feared around Bethnal Green. In June 1890, he knocked down an old gent to steal his watch and chain, then gave him a hefty kick in the head. Sentencing him to ten months with hard labour, the magistrate said he was lucky police had not charged him with highway robbery. In the early hours of 13 February 1891, shortly after his release, occurred the last of the nine possible Jack the Ripper murders, when Frances Coles had her throat cut in a dingy railway arch in Whitechapel. It is known that Frances visited Bethnal Green about seven hours before her death, before returning to a number of places in Whitechapel. The killer was almost caught by a police constable, who saw him run off after the attack. Unfortunately, the young constable stayed with the body instead of giving pursuit.

Mrs Mullins must have become pregnant around 8 July 1891, about four months after the final 'Ripper' murder. John seems to have settled down from that point. In March 1892, a baby son was born: John named his son … Jack! And this at a time when fear still stalked the streets around the East End. Did he have a macabre sense of humour or could it be that John had extracted a living from the tortuous lives of street women in that area, and made an example when they did not cough up a few pennies for his pub expenses? For those who have difficulty with the usual Ripper suspects, why not enjoy another one?

Police Constable Thompson was known for a while as 'the man who lost the Ripper'. The joke stopped in 1900 when he himself was stabbed to death by Barnet 'Narky' Abrahams at an all-night coffee stall in Commercial Road. Abrahams was roughed up by two arresting constables, to such an extent that his defence lawyer was able to claim his wounds were inflicted before he stabbed Thompson, bringing a conviction for manslaughter instead of murder. He still got twenty years.

The world Jack Mullins was born into was one of abject despair endured by miserably poor people, many of whom turned to drink or crime, often both. Jack's situation was made worse by his father's desertion, followed by his mother's death in 1903, when he was eleven. Some sought their fortune in the boxing ring, including Jack, who gave up after three bouts. The Whitechapel district was infested with criminals, many of them immigrants who brought their criminal skills with them. When Jack was ten, the talking point had temporarily moved from the 'Ripper' to the turf war between the Bessarabians and Odessians.

IN 1930, AFTER his acquittal for the Argus Club assault, Mullins turned on his old pal Arthur Harding, who was now married with four children and displaying the dissipation of an old lag. Mullins and Jackie Berman demanded £2 from him, something they had done before. This time Harding, who was more terrified of his wife than he was of Dodger, slammed the door in his face. When they broke open his door, he pointed an old pistol at them. It was not in working order, but they did not know that and fell over themselves scrambling over garden fences to get away.

Harding went to the police and Mullins and Berman were arrested. Mullins asked Charlie 'the Office' Barwick to square the situation. Barwick, who specialised in office walk-ins to pick wallets from coats hanging in cloakrooms and to lift handbags, had been an earlier pal of Harding. But, bolstered by his wife's fortitude, Harding rejected offers of cash to twist his evidence and stood firm in the face of threats to his bodily well-being. Mullins, in spite of an expensive defence paid for by contributions from local gangsters and compliant shop-keepers, received a six-year sentence for demanding money with menaces from Harding, with whom he had once worked a protection racket. Berman received a lesser sentence.

Mullins found himself in Dartmoor prison, a veritable who's who on London gangland at that time. Almost inevitably, there was trouble there. In January 1932, thirty-two convicts, most of them London gangsters, were separately charged that: 'they being riotously and tumultuously assembled together to the disturbance of the peace, feloniously, unlawfully, and with force did demolish, pull down or destroy or begin to demol-ish, pull down, or destroy a building devoted to public use, or erected or maintained by public contribution, contrary to section 11 of the Malicious Damage Act, 1861'.

The accused were William Henry Beadles, Thomas Bullows, Harry Burgess, Anthony Castor, Joseph Conning, Patrick Cosgrove, James Del Mar, Thomas Elliott Dewhurst, William Gardner, George Garton, Alfred Greenhow, Herbert Hardy, Alfred Hart, Albert Henry Hill, James Horn, James Ibbesson, John Jackson otherwise (Alex) Robb, Edward James, Patrick

Kavanagh, Victor Kendall, William Mason, Walter Francis Moore, Alexander Muir, John (Jack) Mullins, Frederick John Richardson, Frederick Roberts, Charles Alfred Saxton, Frederick Smith, Charles John (Ruby) Sparks, Harry Stoddart, Sidney Tappenden and Joseph Taylor.

Mullins was the well-known East End terror; John Jackson, Ruby Sparks, Ed James, Sid Tappenden and Joe Taylor had past connections with the Elephant and Castle gang (Jackson was Tommy Benneworth's crony); Taylor was the Camden Town bookmaker friend of George Sage who had been cut up by the Sabinis at Wye races, he had also been a runner for Wag McDonald and was a 'jump up' specialist, raiding lorries and vans; Tappenden was a minder for the Forty Elephants and his sister-in-law, Bertha, was one of them; Ruby Sparks was the foremost smash-and-grab merchant of his time and would later tutor rising boss Billy Hill in the art of gang leadership; Victor Kendall was a member of Sparks' gang.

Charles Watson had renamed himself Charles 'Ruby' Sparks. He was born 25 June 1895 at Benhill Road, Camberwell, close by Tiger Yard, right on Camberwell Green and just around the corner from the Camberwell Palace of Varieties. This was a popular music hall, featuring comedy and dance acts and singalongs before it became a cheap sort of Follies Bergère and closed through sparse attendance, even from the grey mac brigade. Ruby must have visited the Golden Domes picture palace, a phenomenon in its time. His first gang experiences were with the delinquent Tiger Yard Boys. His parents were born in the East End. His father, Charles 'Alf' Watson, a water inspector, earned money on the side by boxing at fairs and in bareknuckle street bouts around south and east London; he had five professional fights out of Fred Duffett's gym in the Walworth Road, the same place where Wal McDonald trained. Ruby's mother, Emmie, was a receiver of high-class stolen goods, brought to her by the Forty Thieves.

Ruby's family moved to the Bermondsey end of Long Lane,

where he teamed up with Bermondsey Boys Freddy Smith, Joe Jackson and Tommy Benneworth. Like them, he forged links with the Elephant and Castle gang and became part of that conglomerate. During his long criminal career, which began with Borstal at the age of fourteen, he practically invented motor smash-and-grab and spent summary years in prison, later escaping from Dartmoor and remaining at large for five months.

The technique used by Ruby, or another of his gang, was to quickly tie the handle of the door to a jeweller's shop to hinder interference, then take a position on the pavement outside the front window. A car would be driven on to the pavement, scattering and confusing passers-by, the man then smashed the window with a club hammer and the jewels were gathered up, often at the cost of badly cut hands. Escape was along a pre-planned route with little chance of pursuit – that is until the introduction of the Flying Squad, formed specially to combat motor crime. Some say Sparks got his nickname by giving away a swag of rubies stolen from a maharajah, believing them to be worthless. He was not as foolish as that, and probably put that story around about himself. Jim McDonald said he was called Ruby because of his florid complexion.

All thirty-two prisoners were remanded to appear at Princetown Town Hall the following week. To accommodate the prisoners and their escort a special wooden dock and benches were built by Dartmoor convicts, all of which were bolted to the floor as a precaution against any outbreak of violence.

The mutiny had resulted from dreadful food and harsh conditions imposed by Prison Governor A.N. Roberts, who was a firm believer that prisoners should experience hardship for the good of their soul. They may have put up with his soul-cleansing activities; his mistake was to serve up food that even hardened lags could not eat. Empty bellies made bad tempers and trouble flared in the exercise yard and spread quickly to the central administrative core of the prison. Prisoners tried to get access to their prison records to destroy them; when that failed they set light to the offices.

The mutiny was quickly put down by a large contingent of police, who handed control back to prison warders. The result was some brutal clubbing for what had been in some ways a jolly jaunt. At a magistrates' hearing, it was clear that there had been a regime of beatings and other brutal behaviour at Dartmoor, some of which had occurred in the weeks leading up to the hearing.

Sparks and Jackson were cited for leading factions of rioters and for protecting officers. Mullins had played it pretty quiet. He and some others broke into a workshop and stole ropes, which they used to scale a wall. By this time, prison officers were on guard outside and some of them were armed. When Mullins stuck his head over the parapet, he heard a shrill whistle, then shots, and dropped back into the yard. Another prisoner, Billy Mitchell, was not so lucky; he caught a bullet in his throat and crashed to the ground. He was carried by prisoners to the prison hospital. Another prisoner was shot and wounded 'by accident' in a laundry room, 'where steam obscured the guard's view'.

Much of the evidence concerned various groups of prisoners roaming about, smashing windows, starting fires and causing damage estimated at £3,000. It was claimed twenty-four prison officers were injured, though there were counter claims of severe clubbing by officers. There was a humorous moment when the assistant governor and chief officer were described exiting through a window, just before the mob arrived, after seeing the windows of their office disintegrate. Outside, Assistant Governor Turner attempted to reason with a group of men who promptly pinned him to a wall and were about to pour a plate of cold porridge down his throat, when he was rescued by officers. The Devon magistrates saw it as their duty to believe everything the prison authorities said and nothing proffered by the prisoners. This caused some serious muttering in the dock. Thirty prisoners were sent for trial, among them those highlighted.

Mullins and eight others were acquitted. Sentences handed down to others were less than jolly. Some had up to ten years added to their sentences. Ruby Sparks collected four years, which was later overturned on a technicality over his original sentence. His record was read out: 1920 and 1921, sentenced for housebreaking, sent to Borstal for three years. Joined Army and deserted. Back to Borstal. Sentenced in 1927 to three years for housebreaking and stealing property valued at over £1,000. On his release, he teamed up with Johnny Jackson, Len Fry, Billy Andrews and Larry Martin to mount a rash of smash-and-grab raids across London. Fry, Andrews and Martin were captured after a hot pursuit by Flying Squad officers, who saw them casing a furriers in north London. In 1930, Sparks and new recruits Ernie Harris, Jim Turner and Bernie Rayner were charged with conspiracy to rob, stealing cars, breaking and entering and receiving £2,000 worth of stolen rings, Sparks received his present sentence of five years penal servitude and five years preventative detention for being a habitual criminal.

It was stated he lived with the sister of an associate (Johnny Jackson); previously he had lived with a petty criminal girlfriend called Lilian Goldstein, branded by the Press as the 'Bobbed-hair Bandit';[1] he was concerned with smash-and-grab raids; he escaped from Manchester's Strangeways Prison and was recaptured the following day; he was known to police as one of the motor bandit type, without the slightest regard

---

1 Goldstein was born in Hackney. She became a focus for romantic newspaper reporting that obscured a tougher reality, including convictions for prostitution. She married Harry Goldstein, who had convictions for living off her immoral earnings. In 1940, she was bound over for harbouring Ruby Sparks after he escaped from Dartmoor Prison. Later, she shunned the criminal limelight, dumped Harry and married a respectable gent. Her brother, Victor Kendall, was a member of Dodger Mullins's smash-and-grab gang.

for other people's life and property; he and Jackson had been associated for many years, and he was a leader of criminals, as was Jackson, and came from the same district. When he was in Wandsworth Prison, the Bobbed-hair Bandit arrived outside in a motor car with other criminals and threw ropes over the wall. One man got away but was arrested afterwards. Sparks was caught just as he was about to climb out of the prison.

Mr Justice Finlay accepted evidence that showed Sparks had protected two prison officers: 'Whatever violence you might be prepared to use, or however destructive you might be, you did stop short of inflicting injury upon the two officers. You are entitled to some credit for that, but apart from that yours is a case of great gravity.'

Johnny Jackson was born in Bermondsey in 1892. He conducted his own defence and had six years added to the ten he was serving. In one piece of cross-examination, he accused an officer of bringing him round from unconsciousness by banging him with his stick. When the officer denied this, Jackson put on a look of horror: 'How can you deny it? I saw you do it!' The judge immediately wondered how, if he was unconscious, he could have seen the officer hitting him. Other than that, he made an able job of his defence. His record showed he was sent to Borstal in 1913. In 1918, he was jailed for six months with hard labour for possessing a forged Army discharge. In August 1921, he was sentenced to three years and six years penal servitude, to run concurrently (reduced to three years on appeal), and fifteen strokes of the 'cat', for highway robbery with violence. Eight other cases were taken into consideration.

In 1930, whilst living at College Street, Lambeth, he robbed a post office in Brixton. He was arrested while driving a stolen car through Bloomsbury and was sentenced to five years, three years and ten years concurrently, for offences including being in possession of explosives and an automatic pistol and ammunition with a view to endangering life. While being arrested, he had punched a policeman who had jumped on the running board of the stolen car, and attempted to pull a pistol from his pocket. It had taken several officers to arrest him during a violent struggle, in which the car crashed. It was said he belonged to a powerful and dangerous band of motor bandits, who had been a menace to society for some years. Jackson claimed, with some justification, that his last sentence was longer than he deserved, due to perjured testimony from the police. His adventures with Tommy Benneworth were not admissible as evidence.

Mr Justice Finlay told him, 'Your record shows, and your conduct throughout the trial shows, that you are a man who, if you had chosen a better path, might have done well. But you have chosen a worse. I have no doubt whatever that when you got from the cells you were a leader in this business, and indeed you were well fitted to be.'

Sid Tappenden received six months imprisonment after a recommendation for leniency by the jury. He was serving seven years for attempted murder, having hit a woman over the head with an iron bar during a robbery. Ed James belonged to the same crowd as Sparks and Jackson. He received eighteen months to add to his present sentence of five years for country house breaking. Joe Taylor received three years' penal servitude added to his present sentence of three years for theft. The toughest sentence was twelve years for Thomas Davis, for wounding a prison officer. Billy Mitchell, the prisoner who was shot, would suffer speech problems for the rest of his life. No officer saw who did it or heard any shots.

Some of the accused benefited by citing their World War One decorations: Harry Stoddart had won the Military Medal for escaping from the Germans and bringing with him information that enabled the capture of a village. Instead of ten years he received three, to add to his existing sentence of three years for burglary.

Interestingly, at his trial Mullins claimed to have been

awarded the Distinguished Conduct Medal. I can find no record of this. Was he just being artful? In April 1918, a John Mullins, born in the same year as Jack, was arrested as a deserter from the Royal Fusiliers. He was taken to Shoreditch Railway Station in handcuffs, but still managed to escape. Recaptured at Bethnal Green, he escaped from his police cell by pulling bricks from a wall. He crawled through to a room from where he climbed down a drainpipe. He was re-taken in Shoreditch and sentenced to two months with hard labour. Nineteen previous convictions were cited. Sounds like our Jack, who is often misnamed John.

The Demise of the Racing Gangs

WAG McDONALD RETURNED from America in 1931. Three years later, Isek Najmark, the head of a Polish forgery ring who posed as a horse trader, was introduced to Wag and his brother Wal at the Elephant and Castle horse auction, a gathering place for villains who used the market as a crude mechanism for money laundering. Najmark had survived the collapse of a banknote forgery scheme and was now involved in a new enterprise: the forging of National Health and Unemployment Stamps, which were to be printed in Poland and brought to Britain by couriers.

What Najmark did not appreciate was that the brothers, for all their dastardly deeds, considered themselves patriots. Wag thought about the deal, which involved his selling the stamps on to interested parties as a buffer between the forgers and the receivers, and decided it was not in his interests, nor those of his country. He met Detective Edward Greeno at Kempton Park races and dropped information about what was afoot. Greeno was a keen racing man, who knew all of the principals in the racing gangs and used them for information to gain favour with his superiors; at the same time, he gave them some measure of protection.

Wag was asked to go along with the plan and to tip off Greeno when the stamps were due to arrive in England. The result was that Najmark's couriers were arrested after stepping off the boat train at Liverpool Street Station, carrying suitcases filled with well printed, but worthless, stamps. Najmark arrived alone, carrying only samples of his wares, which was enough to convict him. He received four years and was then deported. Greeno's memoirs state that Wag went to Warsaw as part of the sting, but Wag insisted he had not gone that far, for fear the fiercely ambitious Greeno would double-cross him. Greeno got his promotion and Wag's identity was protected, although he was identified as 'Mac'.

DARBY SABINI SEEMS to have led a comfortable life even after being declared bankrupt. He left London and settled in Hove, just along the coast from Brighton, in Sussex; today he may have chosen Marbella. In 1929, he suffered a loss when police raided an Italian club, managed by immigrant Amy Gabba, which had his financial backing. Gabba, who was suspected of paying bribes to police officers, fled the country, taking the club's cash with her. In the same year, Darby seems still to have been in association with Eddie Emanuel: he was described as a printer's agent when being fined for assaulting Hove bookmaker David Isaacs in a greyhound-racing dispute. Isaacs refused to give evidence because 'he and everyone else were in fear of Sabini'.

The last serious attempt at extracting protection money by Harry Sabini occurred in May 1935: the Majestic Social Club in Wardour Street, Soho, was wrecked because its owner, Jack Isow, refused to shell out. Tommy Mack, James Sabatini, Sid Buonocore and Michael Tiano foolishly informed Isow that he had better call the police, as his club was about to be trashed for ignoring warnings he was 'ruining Harry Boy's finances'. Isow locked the four in the club, giving enough time for police to arrive and nab them in the act. They were ordered to pay for damages to the club's fixtures and fittings and bound over to keep the peace, when it was suspected Isow had exaggerated his evidence.

Remnants of the Sabini gang remained active, however. In March 1936, three north London villains walked into an inadequately protected strong room at Croydon Aerodrome and removed three boxes of gold bullion, worth £80,000 (about £12 million at today's values). Cecil Swanlund, a forty-eight-year-old, incorrigible thief, born in Barnet, was later sentenced to seven years for theft. John O'Brien and Silvio Luigi Mazzardi were acquitted. The gold was not recovered. All three at that time were denizens of Clerkenwell. Mazzardi was an affiliate of Darby Sabini. In 1921, he and Solomon Cohen were arrested for fighting with Fred Gilbert and Billy Moore over the outcome of a dice game on a Paddington street corner. O'Brien was the one-time member of One-eyed Charlie Woolgar's gang of Hoxton ruffians.

Soon after the onset of World War Two, Darby and Harry Sabini were ordered to be interned under Defence Regulation 18B, as persons of hostile origin. This had more to do with their reputations as suspicious characters than being security risks; after all, they had little real connection with Italy. Joe was not interned, the reason for which would have been his good record in World War One; he was wounded in 1916 while fighting in France with the Cheshire Regiment. Harry had been named as being both Sabini and Handley and described as a violent and dangerous criminal of the gangster type, liable to become involved in internal insurrection in this country. He applied for a writ of habeas corpus, on the grounds that his Italian father had died eighteen months after his birth and he regarded himself as entirely British. He denied ever being known or arrested as Harry Handley. The writ was denied and, a short time after, he was charged with making a false statement when it was discovered that Handley was his mother's maiden name and that he had been convicted under it. His internment continued.

A sad aspect of this is that the RAF Volunteer Reserve had trained Darby's son, Flight Sergeant Ottavio Henry 'Harry' Sabini, as a pilot at the age of eighteen. In August 1943, aged twenty-one, he was shot down near the Suez Canal during the final expulsion of Rommel from Africa. He lies in the Fayid

War Cemetery, near Ismalia, Egypt.

When Dodger Mullins was released from prison in 1936, he took up his racecourse activities without the involvement of most of his old gang. He soon ran into trouble with Alf Solomon's Yiddishers, who chased him and three of his pals from Yarmouth races: he had demanded payment from a Jewish bookie for a bet he had called out, but had not put up his cash or received a ticket. This was a common trick of 'the boys', who would claim if the horse won, but would not pay their bet if it lost. The row continued on the train back to London and on to Liverpool Street Station, where Mullins offered to fight any one of his tormentors. They declined, but followed him to a pub where blows were exchanged and Mullins' group, who were outnumbered eight to three, were forced to run for their lives.

Later that evening, Mullins visited the Bedford Hotel, near Tottenham Court Road. He walked into a bunch of Alf Solomon's men, who attacked him and slashed his face and back with razors. The damage was bad enough for an ambulance to be called to take him to the Royal Free Hospital, Hampstead, for a length of the surgeon's catgut.

This incident led to the infamous 'Battle of Lewes'. Mullins appealed to Jimmy Spinks and the Elephant Boys to make peace and unite against the common enemy. Spinks, born in Shoreditch in 1910, was the great-uncle of bareknuckle street-fighter Lenny McLean, who appeared in the film *Lock, Stock and Two Smoking Barrels* and whose autobiography, *The Guv'nor*, was a bestseller. As a seventeen-year-old tearaway, Spinks had led a score of Hoxton Boys in a raid on the Dalston Boys at a Hackney fairground, where a young man, who did not belong to a gang, was slashed with a razor. Spinks was discharged for lack of evidence. In the 1930s, Spinks, who weighed around twenty stone, was the leader of the Hoxton-Shoreditch gang that had affiliated itself to the Bethnal Green Boys, who were without a definite leader since the jailing of Dodger Mullins.

Among Spinks' gang was Albert Blitz, a brother of Barnett who had been killed by Alf Solomon. In 1933, Spinks was set about by a crowd from Elephant and Castle and badly beaten with iron bars.

On 8 June 1936, a combined gang of between thirty and forty hard men armed with hammers, iron bars, hatchets and knuckledusters, descended on Lewes races in Sussex in search of Solomon. Spinks led the Hoxton Boys and Wag McDonald led the Elephant Boys. Before racing started, the gangs split into their respective branches and went searching for Solomon and any of the Italian or Jewish gangsters they could find. The plan was for the Hoxton crowd to rush the Jewish bookies and drive them into the Elephant Gang's arms.

Police, alerted to the presence of so many known ruffians, sent for reinforcements. Solomon saw the Hoxton mob arriving from the three-shilling car park and hid behind a charabanc. His clerk, Mark Frater, was not so lucky; by the time he saw the danger it was upon him. He was beaten to the ground and held there by Albert Blitz while Spinks hit him with a hatchet. Solomon's luck did not last. After deserting Frater to his fate, he ran across the car park and found Wag McDonald and others on his heels. He was dragged over a fence and pummelled with a fence post. Police swooped on the Hoxton contingent and arrested sixteen of them. Mullins and most of the Elephant Gang slipped away, leaving Solomon with a busted head. There have been hints that Wal McDonald passed around a number of £5 notes to dull police memories.

At Sussex Assizes, Mark Frater apologised for not having previously appeared in court as a witness. He explained that, after leaving hospital, he had gone to live with relatives without leaving a forwarding address. Of the incident, he said he had seen a large crowd rush up the hill towards him; he was knocked down but could not say who had hit him. He added that he worked for bookmaker Alfred Solomon, had no quarrel with anyone and did not know why he had been attacked. Questioned in court, he agreed he had met Spinks in a Harringay pub when Spinks was out on police bail. He had gone to Spinks and asked him if he was the man who was charged with attacking him. They had a conversation in which he acknowledged that Spinks was not his attacker. He denied he had been threatened. The prosecution did not pick up on the fact that Frater lived in Maida Vale, some way from Harringay. Alf Solomon had disappeared and did not appear as a witness.

Charges of malicious wounding and riotous assembly were proved against all sixteen accused. All but three had previous convictions. Their sentences included: Spinks and Charlie Spring, five years each; Albert Blitz, four years; George Gilder, John Tyler, Tommy Mack, Arthur Boniface and Steve Bennis, three years; George Gardiner, Mickey Illingworth and Eddie Hain, eighteen months; George Churchill, Harry Bond, Johnny Kilby, Tim Bennis and Harry Wilkins, two years.

Arthur Boniface was the son of Titanic veteran William Boniface. Thomas William Mack was born in Clerkenwell, just around the corner from his one-time friends the Sabinis; his criminal convictions date back to 1915. He was the same man who was convicted for the Southampton Arms affray and for assault at Wye races. At one time, he was a professional boxer. He appears to have assigned himself to the Hoxton gang on this occasion. His brother, Dominic Mack, was another Titanic veteran. Interestingly, an uncle, Ernest Mack, was convicted in 1921 as one of Billy Kimber's racecourse pests and his address was given as Garrison Lane, Birmingham. A relative of Albert Dimes, the Sabini heir, married Tommy's sister, Emily. Harry Wilkins was the cousin of Bert Wilkins who would, later that year, be convicted of the manslaughter of bookmaker Massimino Monti-Columbo.

The Battle of Lewes spurred Graham Greene to write *Brighton Rock*, later made into a film starring Richard Attenborough in his most chilling role as the razor thug Pinkie.

An Italian gangster bears a resemblance to Darby Sabini. A fight at Brighton races, in which Pinkie is cut with a razor, is based on the Lewes fight. Intriguingly, in the background of the genuine Brighton races set is a bookie's stand bearing the name Jim Ford. The movie is highly regarded, but British films generally poorly serve London gangs. *The Frightened City*, made in 1961, starring Herbert Lom and Sean Connery, comes closest to the reality. There are shades of the six gangs that ran London, backed by an Eddie Emanuel-type character. The gangs merge in order to maximise profits, then fall out when the south London gang pulls out. Their leader, who is akin to Billy Kimber even to the point of Birmingham support, is shot and then avenged by his enforcer. Sean Connery plays a role not unlike Wag McDonald. Just over a year later, Connery made his first appearance as James Bond in *Dr. No*.

On 1 September 1936, at Wandsworth Greyhound Stadium, Massimino Monti-Columbo and his brother Camillo were attacked by what was now described as the Italian gang. Massimino was stabbed to death. The killing was executed by Pasqualino Papa and Herbert Wilkins, after Papa, the progeny of a huge family of Italian immigrants who worked around north London as ice cream vendors, was knocked about by Massimino and Camillo. Wilkins stabbed the victim in the neck and several other places, inflicting seven wounds from which he died the next day in St. James's Hospital, Balham. Most probably, the row was over rights to plum pitches. Papa, who already had a number of convictions for demanding money with menaces, had been a professional bantamweight boxer under the name of Bert Marsh, with at least fifty bouts behind him, and was a long-standing member of the Sabini gang. He was sentenced to twelve months and Wilkins to nine.

In their later years, Dodger and Jack Berman were greyhound racing ruffians. Dodger acted as cockily as ever and hung around with Jack Spot's and Billy Hill's West End gang. He was a sort of court jester, but not everyone found his antics

funny and he was beaten up a few times by young tearaways.
Jim McDonald, who did not like Mullins, believed he always
went 'mob handed' and on occasion, when he was 'called out'
on his own, he backed off: 'I never had much time for those
who could dish it out, but couldn't take it. He made a big mistake in having a go at drunken Jock Russo and Jim Emmett,
who were sober enough to cut him and Billy Hill's older
brother Archie pretty badly.' It took Billy Hill several years
to repay the cuttings in like fashion. This attack happened in
April 1947, when Dodger should have been celebrating his
fifty-fifth birthday with a cake and not a razor. He was cut a
few more times after that for being 'flash'.

The days of the racing gangs were now numbered.

> Eventually the Jockey Club, in conjunction with the
> police, embarked upon an organized and thorough
> campaign to exterminate the rats. Numerous detectives,
> policemen, and others were employed in this. Entrances
> to the race-courses were carefully guarded; many of the
> leading railway stations were barricaded and watched;
> and even booking-clerks at some of the the stations
> had by them men who knew members of the gang so
> as to avoid letting them have tickets in the event of
> their managing to sneak in. It was a long struggle, but
> gradually the scissors tightened. Denied their means
> of livelihood, members of the gang became desperate
> and lost their cunning; some of the leaders got arrested;
> many of the others quarrelled amongst themselves. The
> feet of the police tread slowly, but they tread wondrous
> small, and what now remains of the Sabini gang must
> defy all recognition.[1]

1 Norman Clark, *All In The Game*, Methuen & Co., 1935

A number of detectives wrote their memoirs, describing how they personally curbed the racecourse bullies, although in fact it was mostly local police who did the job. Edward 'Ted' Greeno, of Scotland Yard, wrote *War on the Underworld*. In it he occasionally struggles with the sequence of events and the identities of certain villains he came across. Greeno was a racing man himself but was not seriously involved in quelling racecourse mischief.

In his recollections in *Britain's Godfather*, by Edward T. Hart, which is the only full-length biography of Darby Sabini, Jack Capstick has events in 1938 happening in the 1920s and has the shooting of Billy Kimber occurring after the Epsom affray instead of before it. The chronology is all over the place. Tommy Benneworth is said to have been beaten up by Darby Sabini at about the time of the Battle of the Nile, although this is unlikely; his story intimates Benneworth's age as forty-two, which would place the event in 1936, way outside the time window. Alf Solomon and George Sewell are said to have had a pub fight after Darby Sabini died; however as Darby expired before Alf, Sewell must have been sparring with a ghost. Misspellings of Benneyworth for Benneworth and Mazzarda for Mazzardi suggest Capstick gained much of his information from newspapers of the time.

Tom Divall worked as a railway carman before joining the Metropolitan Police in August 1882. He knew his business as a policeman in south London and later east London, and knew all the racecourse villains. Even so, he has George Sage seriously injured and at death's door in the Southampton Arms attack. By 1901, he was a Metropolitan Police Inspector at Mile End, where he helped break up a villainous German gang of thieves, led by Bertha Weiner, her brother Ludvig, and his sons, Johann and Wilhelm, who operated out of Shadwell, east London. Divall's fistfight with Wag McDonald outside the Wellington Public House, opposite Waterloo Railway Station, was a classic informal boxing bout held in a circle of spectators, most of them racing men. Divall was bigger but older than McDonald, making the contest equal in the nous of betting men. The fight ended when McDonald connected with Divall's bullet-like head and broke his hand. After leaving the police force in March 1913, due to ill health, Divall became a member of the Jockey Club and a racecourse security adviser where, sensibly, he was on friendly terms with racing's villains. His book *Scoundrels and Scallywags,* published in 1929, is good reading, although he uses aliases for most of the racecourse rogues. With today's knowledge gained from court proceedings and family recollections, it is possible to identify the principal villains. He planned to write a second book; alas, he died in 1943 at his home in Hove.

Fred Porter Wensley was born in Taunton, Somerset, in 1865. He wrote *Detective Days*, published in 1931, in which he relates many East End stories. His career began in 1888 as a constable in Lambeth, where he received a sharp lesson when he was thrown through a plate glass window in New Cut. Shortly after, he was again hospitalised after confronting rowdies outside the Ring boxing venue. Not having learned the wisdom of summoning assistance, he was next sliced up by a sword-wielding madman. His transfer to east London must have come as a relief. He describes Bertha Weiner as the head of a ring of burglars and receivers. Her gang of twelve operated out of a house in Shadwell. She was arrested at her home in Ship Alley, a dingy row of villain's dens close to Cable Street, Whitechapel, where she lived with Max Rebork, who hid under the sheets of their bed. The Shadwell house was raided in 1901 and a van loaded with stolen articles was recovered. Thirty-six burglaries were laid at the gang's door. Bertha received seven years penal servitude, others five years, including her brother Ludvig and Max Rebork. A fight broke out in the tightly packed dock between prisoners and officers.

It was Wensley who interrogated burglars Smithson and Ingram; unfortunately he named them 'Grey and Green', depriving us of their identities. He became a chief constable in 1924 and is renowned as one of Scotland Yard's first 'Big Four'. He retired in 1929 to become a private investigator, before his death in 1949.

Sharpe of the Flying Squad, written in 1938 by Frederick 'Nutty' Sharpe, is a good read. He does not identify those still alive at the time, which is a shame as he could have provided much information and corroboration. He was a leading player in the suppression of pickpocketing gangs in the East End. His chapter on racing gangs gives the usual account, with the usual omissions and repetition of errors; at least he does not claim to have single-handedly wiped out the racecourse terrors. One person he does identify is 1920s Australian smash-and-grab specialist Denny Harris, who rivalled Ruby Sparks. Harris died in 1934 and is believed to have secreted his spoils in safety deposit boxes under various names. Could they still be there?

Charles E. Leach started out as a constable in Kennington before moving north of the Thames. His book, *On Top of the Underworld*, published in 1933, is one of the best accounts of good, honest coppering, much of it centred on Hoxton. There are tales of pickpockets, van draggers, screwsmen, con men, forgers and much more. The book is now rare, but worth hunting for. His father, retired Police Superintendent Alfred Leach, worked for Lloyds in 1913 as a private enquiry agent, in pursuit of the stolen oriental pearl necklace.

Many detectives miss important players such as the McDonald brothers. In some memoirs, they can be recognised by references to unnamed persons and those with dashes instead of names. To be fair, there was always the possibility of a libel suit from people still alive. It seems that to become famous, a villain must first be caught. Yet others with strings of convictions are overlooked, such as Sabini neophyte Simon Nyberg and Finsbury Boy John Phillips. The problem with memoirs is that they often rely on previously published material, therefore little if anything new is introduced and much guesswork fills in the gaps. Worse still, errors are passed on as fact. I have tried to keep guesswork to a bare minimum but, even so, where consecutive events need to be strung together, it has been necessary to supply links that seem most logical.

JUST AS AMERICAN crooks came to Britain, some of ours, like Wag McDonald, exported their enterprise to the United States. Jimmy Spenser was born in 1905, at Well Lane, Allison Street, in the Digbeth area of Birmingham. As a youngster, he would have known of the tough reputation of the Aston area close by, although he does not seem to have been involved with local gangs. In his teens, he relocated to London with Billy Kimber and befriended the McDonald brothers, particularly Bert. As well as fighting the King's Cross gang, he and Bert ran a receiving ring centred on East Street market in Walworth. The two young men also sidelined in warehouse burglary, until Spenser was caught and sent to Borstal. In his early twenties, he was sentenced to serve three years in Dartmoor for a burglary in which some violence had been used.

After his release, he was hired as a deckhand at Southampton and voyaged to the United States, where he jumped ship. He burgled two properties in Pennsylvania before moving to New York, where he learned that things were too dangerous for a lone operator: many New York cops were in the pay of racketeers, thereby rendering small-time crooks vulnerable to policemen who needed to show arrests. Sentencing in New York was severe and prisons were diabolical places of disease. He decided to take the ferry to the less vigorously law-enforced New Jersey to resume his career in burglary.

After a dramatic scare while burgling a house in New Jersey, Spenser returned to New York to take up employment as a booze hijacker with small-time hoodlum Jack Brusseau. He then moved over to the Sheffield-born Owney Madden, whose risky racket was stealing other gangs' booze in large quantities, which was cheaper than paying to import the stuff. Such economies made Madden the largest supplier of affordable booze in New York.

In about 1927, after helping Madden to hijack a Dutch Schultz booze truck, which led to his pal Joe Batty being shot dead, Spenser stole Madden's car and drove to San Francisco, California. There he joined Joe Parente's mob of booze hijackers. Next he met up with Englishman Red MacDaniels, who took him on to Los Angeles to link up with Niley Payne, a small-time gambler and robber. Payne's ran an outfit that was under attack from early Los Angeles Mafia don Albert Marco.

Spenser was with Payne when he entered his home in Long Beach. Payne heard a noise upstairs and darted up the stairway, leaving Spenser behind, just as two plain-clothes cops, who had been searching the house, stepped out of a bedroom on to the landing. Payne pulled an automatic and shot them, wounding both. Payne and Spenser went into hiding. A short while after, Payne was wounded during a shootout with deputy sheriffs, after a two-mile running gun battle along Sunset Boulevard. Police later rounded up six more suspects, including Spenser, using the name Frank Swallow, who surrendered when he learned that the cops had orders to shoot him on sight. He was charged with being an accessory before and after the fact in the police shooting and with being part of the shootout. Payne was arrested as he lay in hospital and charged with attempted murder.

Payne's lawyers wrangled until his only conviction was for kidnapping and robbing a clothes salesman. Even so, his sentence was an indeterminate one to ten years. When the attempted murder charge against Payne was dismissed for lack of evidence, Spenser was released and went to work as a bodyguard to Nick Licata. He joined forces with Wag and Bert McDonald, at that time working for up-and-coming Mafia boss Jack Dragna, to rob a casino. In 1929, Spenser was sent to San Quentin prison for burglary and beating up a crooked cop (he is listed in the 1930 census for San Quentin under his real name, aged twenty-six). He had the pleasure of seeing Los Angeles District Attorney Asa Keyes, who had convicted him, arrive as a convict. Keyes had been accepting bribes from Marco. Marco was later arrested and sentenced to twenty years for an old murder.

In 1932, after serving three years, Spenser was deported to Britain. While in San Quentin he had been writing the story of his escapades. In an August 1932 edition of *The Passing Show*, he contributed 'The Jailbirds' Jamboree', describing entertainment in San Quentin. In 1933, assisted by H. Kingsley Long, he produced *Limey – An Englishman Joins the Gangs*, a curious mix of real and fictitious names to protect those still living. He wrote five more books, all concerned with crime: *Limey Breaks In*, 1934; *The Wheels, a Story of London's Underworld*, 1934; *The Five Mutineers*, 1935; *The Awkward Marine*, 1948; and *Crime Against Society*, 1938, reprinted 1973.

Jimmy Spenser was born Francis Harold Guest. He died in Birmingham in 1983, aged seventy-eight. Ralph 'Niley' Payne was born in Georgia in 1898. According to Spenser, he was paroled in 1932 and continued in the rackets until his death. Albert Marco was born Marco Albori in Italy in 1887; he was released for deportation aboard the 'stir train' to Italy in 1933. Federal courts blocked his efforts to regain entry to the United States. He died in Italy. Jack Dragna gradually assumed control of the Los Angeles underworld. He is remembered as being a weak leader who was supplanted by Mickey Cohen with the assistance of New York Mafia led by Benjamin 'Bugsy' Siegel, however deeper research shows that Dragna remained an influential Syndicate leader until his death in 1956.

ARTHUR, THE FATHER of the Phillips boys, was born in Birmingham in 1872 and was an associate of George Sage and

Billy Kimber. He grew up, however, among the grim streets of Finsbury, where he became a thief and burglar given to violence, and was an early member of the Titanic gang. Some time around 1897, he paired up with local girl Annie Ryan. His first conviction, in 1893, was as Arthur Flynt, followed by many more under various aliases – Arthur Flynn, Arthur Caine, Arthur Gunstone, William Phillips, Alfred Martin, William Johnson, Arthur Hill, Arthur Phillips/Philips, George Davies and George Harris – all around the country, including Manchester, Liverpool, Halifax, Bolton, Castleford, Whitby, Chester, Kingston, Penge and Lambeth, as well as on his Finsbury doorstep.

An example of his local enterprise took place in City Road in 1896, when he and three others knocked down Herman Conrad and stole his watch and chain. Phillips was pursued by his victim, who wrestled him to the ground and handed him over to a policeman. Phillips said it was all a mistake and suggested Conrad felt in his pocket; on doing so, he found his watch had been returned to him during the struggle. It fooled no one, including the judge at the Central Criminal Court who gave him three years for robbery with violence.

In 1903, again in City Road, a policeman saw four men attack Robert Austin and steal his watch. He blew his whistle and another constable mistook Phillips for a detective and called on him to assist, instead receiving a hefty bash over the head and a severe kicking from all four; the other constable was given similar treatment. Phillips was picked out at an identification parade and, again, received three years.

In February 1921, he and John Webber were arrested at Praed Street Railway Station, Paddington, after being observed by plain-clothes police officers who were on watch for the Titanic. Police described the pocket-picking operation in court. The two prisoners and seven other men hustled and shoved passengers boarding trains. The gang then broke up into small groups but came together again on a signal of

Phillips raising his hat. The gang surrounded an elderly man, forced his arms above his head, and went through his pockets. Both thieves were sentenced to twelve months. On a separate charge of stealing a wallet containing £82, Phillips was sentenced to a further five years.

By the age of sixty-five, Arthur Phillips had amassed thirty-six convictions. His last for theft was at Whitby in 1936 and his last for violence in May 1937: he was bound over for hitting his wife with a hammer and doing the same to her friend Emily Baggott, then biting the hand of his daughter Rosie, who intervened.

When his son, also called Arthur, was released from prison after serving his sentence for the attack on Sid Baxter and George Sewell, he went to live with his wife and two children in Essex Road, Islington. On 1 June 1937, three weeks after the hammer attack on his mother, he visited his parent's home in Macclesfield Street, Finsbury, where he became embroiled in yet another family row, one that again escalated into violence. Father and son had a fight when the younger Arthur stepped in to stop his father hitting his mother with a hammer. During the struggle, Arthur Senior grabbed a pair of scissors and stabbed his son in the face, neck and back, before he was knocked down and fell heavily to the floor: from there he stared up with a look that only the dead can give. Attempts were made to revive him by pouring water into his mouth.

A constable was brought to the house and young Arthur, covered in blood, was taken to Old Street Police Station, where he was charged with the murder of his father. In the Police Court, witnesses testified to the violent nature of the father, at which the prosecution withdrew the murder charge but sought a conviction for manslaughter. Death was certified as being due to a heavy fall. Magistrate Herbert Metcalfe took the view that the son had done everything he could to pacify his father, who was the aggressor from the very beginning. He had properly intervened to prevent his father striking his

mother with a hammer and had been stabbed. He was convinced a jury would not convict and dismissed the charges.

A Last Hurrah

IN A BRIEF chapter on English gangs in his book *Making Crime Pay* (concerned with his making money as a crime journalist and playwright, not with criminal enterprise), the popular author Peter Cheyney intriguingly drew attention to London gang activity. His book, published in 1944, does not specify in which year the following incidents occurred:

> June 8: A battle between rival gangs with rubber truncheons after an open-air dance.
>
> July 5: Twenty coloured men fighting with razors and clubs in Stepney, east London.
>
> July 15: A police constable attacked while investigating a disturbance. Another police constable almost thrown over a railway bridge.
>
> July 20: Michael McCausland died in hospital following a Soho gang fight.
>
> August 9: A police constable maliciously wounded in east London. Witnesses too afraid to give evidence.

He goes on to name the major London gangs: the Hackney gang, the Hoxton Boys, the Elephant and Castle Boys, and North London. He says the West End was ruled by the Hoxton, Elephant and Hackney gangs. According to Cheyney, the Hackney gang was supreme until 1927, when they suffered a serious setback in the 'Battle of Ham Yard'. He also notes that the Elephant Boys were led by a tough villain, who never paid for anything in south London and the West End.

In fact, there were many battles in Ham Yard, Soho. The 1927 one occurred when the Elephant gang, led by Wal McDonald, ambushed the Italian gang, led by Harry Sabini, in the yard by the side of the Lyric Theatre, just off Windmill Street. The yard contained Freddie Ford's New Avenue Club, a preserve of the Elephant Boys, where the Italians had been demanding money for protection. Ford complained, and the scene was set for battle. The ground outside Ford's club was a demolition site strewn with bricks, timber and metal. The gangs came together as the Italians were arriving to receive an answer to their demand. About thirty men fought on the rubble with clubs, knives, razors and anything else that came to hand. Wal McDonald cut Harry with a knife, forcing the Italians to retreat, carrying their leader. The fighting had spilled into the entrance to Ford's club where the stairs were stained with congealed blood.

Another battle occurred in June 1931, after the Italian gang had given their protection to Italian and Greek establishments in several Soho streets: an act that deprived the Elephant gang of a chunk of its livelihood. As a retort, they smashed seven restaurants in and adjoining Ham Yard. This expeditionary force, led by Tommy Benneworth, contained both south and east Londoners. Police arrested sixteen men and transported them by police tender to Tottenham Court Road Police Station; as ever, no witnesses came forward and no charges were preferred.

The 8 June battle Cheyney refers to concerned the Finsbury Boys fighting the Angel gang outside a Finsbury dance hall in a local territorial dispute, something not uncommon between the wars. Cheyney missed an attack on Jack Spot by Jimmy Wooder and other White gang members, who were attempting to stop him taking over their racecourse rackets. This indicates that Spot, later the don of the London underworld, was not well known at the time.

The name McCausland (see above) caught my attention, as did mention of the Elephant and Castle gang, of which I had been an adherent in my youth and my family had been leading lights between the wars. The McDonald brothers paid little for their personal upkeep, preferring to rely on the generosity of those they were protecting; however in the 1920s Tommy Benneworth also qualified for Cheyney's accolade for the tough Elephant and Castle gang leader who paid for nothing.

Investigation reveals Cheyney's year to be 1938. The Michael McCausland incident concerned gangs located north of the Thames. On 13 March 1938, McCausland, son of Mike and Julia, and nephew of Matt (both of whom had suffered at the hands of gang lord Billy Kimber, and had been solid members of Alf White's and Darby Sabini's racecourse gang alliance), was attacked by about twenty men in Moreland Street, Finsbury. It was in revenge for his involvement in a brawl in Dean Street, Soho, over protection rights. He was then a twenty-four-year-old street trader who had fallen under the influence of Freddie Gilbert, an old enemy of the Sabini alliance. Freddie lived in Moreland Street and it is possible the attackers were waiting in the shadows for him to appear and settled for young Michael instead.

As could be expected, a victim of a twenty-man attack was in serious trouble; Michael was knocked down and kicked by those who managed to get at him in the scrum. Before they were able to do him good and proper, John Phillips arrived. Phillips had a history of accomplished violence and was ready for action; he carried a scimitar, as you do on a night out. Once John got amongst them, striped a few bottoms and sliced at least one thigh open to the bone, there was a rapid decline in interest in kicking the stuffing out of young McCausland. The gang ran off, leaving the two men cut and bruised. Phillips' fight must have been heroic, for he suffered several deep gashes to his body and face and yet held the field. He then supported McCausland to Gilbert's house where they were 'fixed up'.

After a while and feeling better, McCausland left for his home just around the corner at Macclesfield Road. As he arrived at his street door, a car drew up and five men jumped out and attacked him with iron bars and razors. His wife, Kate, found him when she opened the door to see what the fuss was about. This time he had been seriously injured. He was taken to St. Leonard's Hospital in Kingsland Road, Finsbury. He died three months later.

At an inquest held in July 1938, it was stated that McCausland had been injured in a fight and had suffered a broken nose, a black eye and cuts to his face and hands. A doctor added that his wounds had been superficial and had healed satisfactorily. Pathologist Dr Temple Grey said the deceased suffered from kidney disease and, in his opinion, the death was a natural one. Kate McCausland, who had been married only seven weeks prior to the attack, said her husband had never been seriously ill and that he had not been the same since the assault. She believed he had died because of his injuries.

Evidence was given that two men had been arrested and charged with assault. The coroner was not convinced that injuries from the fight would have had a fatal effect so long after they occurred. The jury agreed and returned a verdict of death from natural causes. As soon as the verdict was announced, John Phillips leapt from his seat screaming, 'It was murder, it was no natural death! Let the jury see his clothes. Look at the cuts on my face.' Others joined in and there was uproar in court, causing it to be cleared.

The two men who had been arrested soon after the incident had already appeared at Old Street Police Court. They were Edward Raimo, a tailor of Gainford Street, Islington, and John Arthur Wyatt, a porter of Malta Street, Finsbury, both aged thirty-one. They were charged with being concerned with others, not in custody, in wounding McCausland with intent to do him grievous bodily harm. Both had been picked out from an identification parade by Kate McCausland, who was the sister of Finsbury villains John and Arthur Phillips, and had been in the house when her father was killed by his son. Raimo and Wyatt appeared again in April when a full account of the attack was given. Divisional Inspector Salisbury spoke of gang warfare. In May, they were found not guilty when police declared they had no evidence to offer.

In 1939, 'Italian Albert' Dimes – probably one of the five who made the final attack on Michael McCausland – and Eddie Raimo became suspects in what police described as a racing gang attack on an East End villain associated with Dodger Mullins and his allies, the Finsbury Boys. In the early hours of Sunday, 12 November, Charlie 'Chuck' Lawrence, who had strayed from his usual Hackney patch, got into an argument in Spitalfields which resulted in a car pulling up beside him, from which a number of men jumped and beat him to death in an alley whence he had fled. No one was charged with his murder.

Dimes' next adventure resulted in the death of Harry Distelman in a fight at the Bridge and Billiards Club in Wardour Street, Soho, on 1 May 1941. The murder followed previous trouble at neighbouring clubs between rival gangs, until this final incident, in which highly charged Antonio 'Babe' Mancini came running from the Palm Beach Club below to plunge a dagger into Distelman's armpit. Harry calmly remarked, 'Babe has killed me': he was right. Dimes and others were found guilty of wounding. Distelman. Dimes served a brief spell in detention before being returned to the RAF, which he had deserted. He began to flex his muscles on de-mob when he became heir to the Sabini throne. Mancini, who was a member of the Sabinis, would have fared better if he had been interned; instead, he went to the gallows.

These incidents are typical of the strife that took place in what, in gang terms, is broadly the Finsbury area, all the way from 1921 to the 1940s. One reason the gangs came together in so many violent clashes is that they all lived right alongside each other. When analysing these incidents, it is never easy to decide who belonged to what gang. For example, John Wyatt lived just three streets away from Freddie Gilbert. One rough guide would be to describe the gangs as the King's Cross gang, led by the White brothers, and the Finsbury gang of Freddie Gilbert and John Phillips and their new recruit, the senior Matt McCausland. He had turned away from the King's Cross lot after being jailed on their behalf in 1923: the others got off and he felt a bit miffed.

Alf White's King's Cross mob, later taken over by his sons Alf, Harry and Billy (born 1909, 1911 and 1914 respectively), and for a brief spell by Eddie Raimo, fought constantly with Freddie Gilbert's Finsbury mob, later to be taken over by John Phillips. Both gangs had alliances with other gangs: the Whites with the Sabinis, later called the Italian gang; Gilbert with the Camden Town gang led by George Sage, on behalf of Billy Kimber. To complicate matters further, White's King's Cross mob had been subjugated by the Elephant and Castle gang, who had also teamed up with Billy Kimber's Brummagem Boys and were therefore friendly with Freddie Gilbert!

Edward Raimo was born in Clerkenwell, London, on 17 January 1906, to Italian parents. His nicknames were variously 'Rainbow', a play on his name, and the 'King's Cross hit man'. The latter came about through his support for the White brothers, who had taken command in the West End in the 1940s. Raimo had been a young tearaway with the doyen of King's Cross villainy, Alf White, confirming that the attack on young Michael McCausland was a clash between King's Cross and Finsbury gangs. When Alf White stepped down, his sons, Alf, Harry and Billy, took over, using Eddie's brawn to keep them in power. Alf Junior was a fighting man. In June 1931, with Dick Maxwell and Antonio Nappi, he was acquitted of cutting up George Buckland and Arthur Bardsley, two up-and-coming King's Cross tearaways, in the jockeying for positions that occur when there is a void in gang boss supremacy.

Harry White put in a rare appearance in a violent incident that same year. He was one of four men, led by Michael Tiano, one of the Sabini gang's most dangerous new recruits, who terrorised the Phoenix Club in Little Denmark Street, Soho. Tiano demanded drinks and, when refused, went behind the bar and helped himself, then brazenly tried to pick the pockets of patrons. Staff forced the gang out of the club, where White and Eddie Fletcher waited and attacked two of them when they left after work. Mostly, Harry left the fighting to others.

John Wyatt, 'English Jock', was born in Clerkenwell in 1907, less than one year after his pal Eddie Raimo. His father was Scottish. Many immigrants settled in the area having got off the train at King's Cross Railway Station. Jock was not so much associated with racecourse gangs and protection rackets; he was more into armed robbery, having been educated into the ways of serious crime in Borstal, when he met Billy Hill. On his release, he joined Hill's early gang to perform smash-and-grab raids, burglaries and mail van and Post Office robberies.

In 1938, he had a narrow escape when some of Hill's men smashed their way into a furriers in Islington. The Flying Squad pursued their car, crashing into the back of it when it slowed. The impact tore off the back and hurled Charlie Davis into the road, where he lay dead. Police threw the book at Charlie Lemon, of Barking, and Arthur Morris, of Elephant and Castle, the illegitimate son of Nellie Morris, one of the Forty Thieves: garage-breaking to steal the car, shop-breaking to steal fur coats, larceny, receiving, and manslaughter of their dead colleague, to which they pleaded guilty. Jock, who had been involved in an earlier car accident, was having time off.

Jock served a number of prison sentences for robbery. In 1942, with Billy Hill and Teddy Hughes, he attempted to rob an Islington postmaster of a bag of cash being carried from a van. While he kept watch, the two others pulled up their car and leapt out to cosh the postie. Before they could land a blow, a lorry driver sussed what was happening and rammed their car. Hill and Hughes took off on foot and were apprehended by citizens. Jock, who should have just shuffled away, went to help his pals and the crowd nabbed him as well. He got four years for not being very bright.

In 1951, a series of Post Office raids occurred across southern England. Police traced a Post Office employee who had been copying safe and office keys and this led to the robbers, one of whom was 'Big Jock'. For that he got a big eight. Jock's part in the attack on Michael McCausland shows he was a part of the King's Cross gang in 1938. As a young man, he also received the cat o' nine tails, something that placed him in a select club of villains: Billy Hill, Frankie Fraser, Eddie Raimo and Tommy Benneworth all qualified for membership. It took a lot of bottle to suffer the murderous pounding of that knotted rope, though some actually asked for it to avoid a prison term.

By this time, the gang was known simply as 'the White brothers', although their father, Alf, was still a man to be avoided. The brutality of the gang is demonstrated through an incident on 17 April 1935, at a charity ball at the Wharncliffe Rooms of the Great Central Hotel in Marylebone Road. John Defferary, manager of the Yorkshire Stingo pub in Marylebone, made the mistake of opening his wallet containing twelve crisp pound notes, to hand one to the bar tender. This was seen by sour-faced, mousy-haired, five-foot six-inch Billy White. The twenty-one-year-old runt of the White brothers, Billy wanted the contents of that wallet. It may be that he tried to pick the pocket of Defferary, causing his hand to be brushed away.

Billy was miffed enough to report to his father that Defferary had touched his girlfriend, an insult demanding correction by the paterfamilias. They hunted for their quarry through the crowded ballroom, finding him as he exited from the gents' toilet. Billy punched him in the face and six or seven others rained blows and kicks. Defferary staggered to his feet, only to have a glass-topped table smashed on his head by Billy's dad. The glass shattered, causing severe cuts and the loss of an eye. Somewhere in the chaos, Billy helped himself to the wallet. Robert Sutters, who tried to help Defferary, was also set upon.

Sutters and hotel staff identified the attackers and picked them out at an identification parade, but withdrew from attending the trial when they were threatened. What they had seen happen to Defferary would have been fresh in their minds. Before Alf and his two sons, Billy and Alf, came up at the Central Criminal Court, police received several anonymous letters branding the family as vicious hooligans who blackmailed bookies, publicans and market traders, cut victims with razors and were greatly feared in north London. Carrie White, Alf's wife, was said to be as bad as the men. They were cited as claiming they could never be prosecuted because police were in their pay and witnesses would never come forward. It was suggested police should visit the New Arcade Club in Holloway, where they would learn about the violent nature of the gang. One letter reminded police that Alf, senior, had been sentenced to three months for kicking a policeman, who nearly lost the sight in one eye. Another referred to Darby Sabini and Alf Solomon and the killing of Barnett Blitz. The trial went ahead with only Defferary and his wife Queenie giving evidence for the prosecution, while twelve others said what thoroughly decent chaps the Whites were. They said they had seen a fight, but it did not involve the accused: all they saw was Defferary attacking some unnamed man.

During the trial, about forty Sabini gangsters sat in the court or patrolled outside. Prosecuting counsel Horace Fenton received a letter threatening the 'hiding of his life' if any of the three were found guilty. The jury saw through all of the ruses and found all three guilty, the judge sentencing each of them to twelve months with hard labour. Police files name other White gang suspects as Eddie Raimo, Tommy Mack, James Sabatini, Michael Tiano and Sid Buonocore. They also note that there were three brothers present, which could only mean Harry was there but did not assault Defferary.

Young Alf died of cancer in 1942, aged thirty-three, leaving his softer brother Harry in charge. There was a loose understanding between Harry White and the up-and-coming Jack Spot. This hardened when Spot cut Harry's cousin, Jimmy Wooder, thereby seriously weakening Harry's grip on Soho and, at the same time, causing him to relinquish his racecourse enterprises to the much tougher Spot.

In October 1946, Billy Hill, who was working for Spot, pushed matters so hard in the Yorkshire Grey, in Clerkenwell, that Eddie Raimo smashed his glass on the counter and shoved it in his face: it stuck, inflicting a wound above Hill's right eye that just missed putting the eye out. A saloon fight erupted between Hill's pals and the King's Cross gang. Hill carried a triangular scar thereafter to remind him that, when he picked on Harry White, the reply came from Harry's dad's pals. Raimo was something of a curiosity. He had grown up with American gangster films and mimicked his celluloid hero Alan Ladd, with Stetson, herringbone drape, cigarette drooping from the corner of the mouth, and a terrible phoney accent. On another occasion, he attacked George Sewell, his opposite number with the Sabini-Solomon combination, and went to prison for it. Sewell, who some called an enforcer, was more enforced upon than not.

In 1947, Jack Spot did what Billy Hill could not. He swept Harry White aside in a week of cutting and pummelling, doing Raimo along with Harry and others. Spot was coming into his prime at thirty-five, while Raimo was leaving his at forty-one. Showing stark signs of wear and tear, he never returned to prominence. In 1951, White transferred his interests to dog

---

stadiums, but even then he came under pressure, this time from Frank 'Ginger' Rumble's mob, who already had a foot in the door at White City Stadium. Rumble's gang are typical of small-time tearaways who blagged pocket money, free drinks and grub by leaning on local shopkeepers and bookies, mostly in Kensington and Shepherd's Bush. Harry turned to Spot and Hill to warn Rumble off.

BEFORE LEAVING THIS period, it is worth reflecting on the sleazy world of white slavers. Prostitution has always spawned violence. In the 1850s, Henry Mayhew wrote that there were about 9,000 prostitutes working in London. They ranged from desperate harlots of the seediest districts, prone to venereal disease and looking older than their years, who sold their bodies for the price of a swig of gin, to the more genteel variety of Haymarket and West End girls kept by wealthy men, who fared better than those run by bullies, or ponces, in less salubrious places.

In 1926, warfare erupted between Soho's two main gangs of white slavers: men who imported women, often by trickery, to be lured into prostitution. Forty-one-year-old Charlie Baladda was shot to death in the Union Club in Frith Street, Soho, by Emile Berthier on the orders of Juan Antonio Castanar. When Casimir Micheletti sent his 'boys' to kill Castanar in a revenge attack, police intercepted the attempt. The courts deported both Castanar and Micheletti to Europe. In 1930, Castanar shot Micheletti dead in Paris, for which he was sent to Devil's Island. In 1936, Emile Allard (Red Max Kassel), a Latvian immigrant, was shot dead at an apartment in Soho and his body dumped in a field near St. Albans, Hertfordshire. Chief suspect was Frenchman Marcel Vernon, a fugitive from Devil's Island. He was deported to France and returned to Devil's Island for a ten-year spell.

It is fair to say that organised prostitution was the forte of foreigners – Maltese, French, Greek, Italian and African – who were pretty much left to get on with it. London's regular gangs regarded them as 'low lifes' not worthy of rivalry, although that wily rogue Jack Spot charged a royalty for many of them to trade in peace. It was the Messina brothers who brought the trade into public view. Five brothers, Carmelo, Salvatore, Attilio, Alfredo and Eugenio, born in Malta and Egypt, had been operating a ring of prostitutes in Mayfair since the 1930s. Only Eugenio (Gino) had come to police notice, when they convicted him for slicing the tips off two of the fingers of Carmelo Vassalo, a rival Maltese pimp, who had convictions for running women. It took a 1951 exposé by *People* reporter Duncan Webb to reveal the scope of the huge callgirl ring. Four of the brothers fled abroad, leaving Alfredo, who had not been named, to tidy up the considerable financial labyrinth of hidden bank accounts, security boxes and spurious property ownership, worth many thousands of pounds.

The police, who had virtually ignored the operations of the gang, were embarrassed by further fervent newspaper reporting into taking action. They raided the home of Alfredo and found him living with a prostitute, well-known to them over a period of years, but who, apparently, they did not realise was keeping Alfredo in sumptuous circumstances. Alfredo shrugged, smiled and offered Detective Superintendent Guy Mahon £200 to let the matter drop, which was declined. Alfredo was jailed for two years and fined £500. He died in England in 1963, the police being unable to deport him, as no country would acknowledge his birthright. The other brothers were jailed abroad at various times.

4

BENEATH 'THE SMOKE'

London During and After
World War Two

The King of Soho

WORLD WAR TWO brought a respite in gang warfare. It did not entirely go away, but it did quieten down. Some gangsters enlisted in the forces; some were interned, including the Sabinis. There was less opportunity to find targets, as businesses became more security conscious and goods became scarce. There was contempt for criminals from the public, who saw them as having no excuse for such behaviour during wartime. The respect that gangsters enjoyed between the wars, for often being the ones who rebelled against the unfairness of British society, no longer existed. All that the public would tolerate was the spiv. He supplied goods not available from other sources and circumvented rationing. The fact that the goods he sold out of a suitcase in Oxford Street or outside railway stations were stolen was conveniently overlooked, in the quest for clothing and food bargains to bring some light into the grey war years.

The spiv was a common sight in busy public places during and just after the war. Often he is characterised by a raincoat and a trilby hat, reminiscent of a racing tout, which many of them had been. They would select pitches on the approaches to railway stations and bus termini as well as high streets. Not everything they sold was 'kosher'. Many an unfortunate examined their purchases out of public gaze only to find they were fake and useless. In these cases, the spiv would locate somewhere else the next day. Fights occurred infrequently over pitches because they could not afford a commotion and there was generally enough space to go around. Two or three pitches were about the most anyone saw in one location.

They would employ at least one lookout to watch for beat policemen and sometimes to drop a passing copper a half-crown for observing the skyline. Their sources of contraband were docks, warehouses, military depots and the arrival of over-supplied American servicemen. The word spiv is short for cockney 'spiffing', as in having a spiffing time or dressing spiffily, as they did in their flashy garb.

The post-War years, however, were to see a new man take over the London underworld. Jack Spot was born Jacob Colmore at Fieldgate Mansions, Whitechapel, to Polish-Jewish immigrants: Alick Colmore, a tailor's machinist, and Rachel (Lifschinsky), on 12 April 1912. Alick could not sign his name. Fieldgate Mansions was a razor's stripe from Vallance Road, Bethnal Green, where one day Mr and Mrs Kray's little boys would terrorise the local populace. Also in the vicinity was the birthplace of Dodger Mullins, and Sidney Street, scene of a famous police siege. In Fieldgate Street, Stinie Morrison was arrested for the murder of Leon Beron.

The Colmore family name appears in records as Comacho, Comer and Comor, but it was as Jack Spot he would become best known. As a youngster, he fought his way to leadership of a gang of Whitechapel ruffians. In his teens he was recruited into a gang controlling market stalls, where his job was to collect subscriptions on behalf of the 'stall trader's fund' of five shillings a week. Those who declined to sign up were not allowed to pitch their barrow; those who fell into arrears were charged interest and slashed on the buttocks with a razor by Spot or one of his boys. His reputation as a tough guy brought him to the attention of Morrie (Moisha) Cohen, who operated a similar business on small racetracks, where he bought bookies' pitches from gypsies and rented them out. Established bookies, who resented the intrusion, were thrown off the park. When some made a comeback, Jack was employed to sort them out. A series of fights with the sun glinting off flashing razors soon settled matters in Morrie's favour. Cohen also ran a number of gambling clubs in Birmingham and Leeds that benefited from Spot's muscle. When the British Fascist movement, under Sir Oswald Mosley, began a series of marches in the East End in the 1930s, there were counter-riots by Jewish residents. Spot claims to have led the attacks on fascists, but there is no evidence of this.

Spot arrived on the main racecourse scene in the mid-1930s, when he went to work for Wal McDonald. His first sortie was to attack Hendon bookmaker Eddie Emanuel and take over his pitch organisation. Emanuel was not young enough or hungry enough to stand up to a robust East End tough coming into his prime. Emanuel's hard men, Alf Solomon and Alf White, had been warned off horse racecourses and were plying their depredations at London's greyhound tracks.

Taking over from Alf White was his son Harry, a tall, tough-talking, well-educated bookie, whose talk was tougher than his spirit. He was frightened of Spot. To survive, he assisted Spot in the organisation of pitches at racecourses and point-to-point meetings. This continued until the onset of World War Two. By 1940, Spot had a flourishing bookie business that included allocation of pitches and supply of ancillary services. At the same time, he had built an East End empire of protection and club business, in which he specialised in operating low dives for drinkers and gamblers. When war broke out, his business suffered through increased police observation in the dark streets of his east London manor.

Spot's underworld rise suffered a setback in February 1937, when Jimmy Wooder, Benny Freeman, Charlie Wright and Moss Black attacked his chauffeur and bodyguard, the ex-boxer Nat Simmons, in Fox's Club. This was a nasty little dive in Dean Street, Soho, managed by former world welterweight champion Ted 'Kid' Lewis. A gang of between fifteen and twenty men forced their way into the club, which was protected by Spot, and beat up Simmons and Lewis. Only four came to trial, which they could have avoided if they had paid

Simmons the £50 he asked for to bring on a bout of memory loss. Kid Lewis, an East End Jew and one of Britain's greatest-ever boxers, kept links to the underworld all his life, standing bail for gangsters and appearing as a character witness, once for Alf White. He owned a succession of pubs and clubs in dangerous places. In the 1930s, he sullied his reputation by becoming a bruiser for Oswald Mosley's fascist movement, though he later claimed ignorance of Mosley's anti-semitism.

Simmons, who had supported Spot in his fight to control protection in the East End, built up his own following and went into business for himself. In 1938, he encroached on Spot's enterprises and for a while did very well with a gang numbering about thirty. Spot hit back on 22 March 1939, when he ambushed Simmons and others in the Somerset Social Club in Whitechapel. Nat was slashed with a razor and Hymie Jacobs was hit with a bottle in a fight that wrecked the club. Police responded to cries of 'murder' and fought to get the two injured men through the wreckage to hospital.

Spot, Bernie Schechter and Moisha Goldstein appeared in front of the Lord Mayor at Mansion House Court, where they presented the Mayor with an arrogance he could hardly believe. Naive police and officials allowed the court to be attended by two crowds of opposing gangsters, and the inevitable happened. When Goldstein was discharged for lack of evidence, Simmons' mob tried to get at him and a fight broke out, with Spot and Schechter struggling to get over the rails of the dock to join in. It took twenty minutes to get Spot and Schechter to the cells after they were given six months with hard labour. Schechter, who stuck with Spot right up to the 1950s, was later referred to as 'Sonny the Yank' in a 1955 conspiracy trial, although he was born in Germany.

WHEN SPOT WAS released from his six-months prison sentence, for the battle with Nat Simmons' gang, he did the decent thing and joined the Army, serving until his discharge in 1943 due to ill health. Because of his health, he manned an anti-aircraft battery and did not serve abroad. He thought it ironic he should now be encouraged to fight fascists. In 1943, he attacked George Drake, a sixty-year-old thug from Paddington, in a tiny spieler known as The Smoke Room at the rear of a pub on the corner of Chapel Street and Edgware Road. This was said to be because Drake had abused a Jewish bartender. As Drake was part Jewish, this does not seem likely. He nearly died, which would have been no great loss, as he once slashed a prostitute's face because she was late paying her dues in his trade association. Drake had once been jailed with Alf White for bribing prison warders to treat Joe Sabini with courtesy beyond normal expectations and this association probably was the cause of the disagreement.

Although Alf White's star had dimmed, Jack Spot returned to Leeds to avoid possible reprisals from his pals. He minded clubs for Polish émigrés, with whom he empathised, and interfered in the smooth working of pitch allocation at northern racecourses, becoming involved in a brawl at Pontefract that saw a local pitch distributor take a beating. This was most probably Billy Kimber's one-time partner Andrew Towey who, in his fifties, was no match for the burly Spot. When Spot returned to London, he reopened his racecourse pitch allocation business and stepped into the West End void left by the Sabinis and Kimber. He not only charged clubs, pubs and restaurants for protection but also took money from thieves and ponces. He headquartered in lavish style at the Galahad Club in Charlotte Street, was attended by a coterie of the London underworld. My father, Jim McDonald, recited the following tales to me of Spot and Soho after World War Two:

JACK SPOT WAS a friend to me. I had seen him around the racecourses when he was a young man, at which time we used to call him Jake. He had a reputation in the East End as being afraid of nothing and he ousted gangs that were blackmailing Jewish shopkeepers. Naturally, they returned favours. After starting out as a bit of a lout, he became well dressed and began to take care of his appearance. Compared to Dodger Mullins, who always looked a right scruff, Jack looked more like gentry. He was so well turned out that, at first, I didn't recognise him. My brother Wal sometimes employed him as a clerk and used his muscle to intimidate bookies into paying for Wal's and Billy Kimber's services.

The year after World War Two ended, Soho began to open up again. Not every club had closed: many had catered for service people billeted in London, with dances and show entertainment, but always the war had cast its shadow over those wanting to let go and have a good time. Somehow, it didn't seem right while others were suffering. My fighting had been done in World War One, yet I felt some awkwardness in not being in the front line.

The war had meant a dull time for everyone, except those frivolous people who put enjoyment above everything else. Sad to say a number of women did not do their best for soldier husbands and spent time with American servicemen, for the glinting reward of a cheap rolled-gold ankle bracelet that pretended to be something else. There were some tawdry times and it did breed resentment towards the Americans, who were seen as having an unfair advantage. Then again, it wasn't their entire fault.

Soho is roughly the area bounded by Regent Street, Oxford Street, Charing Cross Road and Coventry Street. North of Oxford Street, stretching to Warren Street and bounded by Tottenham Court Road and Great Portland Street, is an extension to Soho, less frequented by nightly tourists but popular with resident crooks of all sorts, who know where to get a fairer game of cards and where they can mix with other professionals. The area surrounding this we would generally call the West End.

Soho retained a village atmosphere just as Camden, Clerkenwell, Hampstead and Mayfair did. Its narrow streets were crammed with clubs and restaurants and some streets were taken over by various races, most of whom had come to this country as refugees from both wars. Frith Street was mainly Italian; Dean Street was more Jewish; Wardour Street I suppose you could say was English, inasmuch as it was not colonised by settlers. Greek Street, in spite of its name, was a real mix. Anywhere you could pass a Spanish restaurant, and then come on an Italian one, sandwiched between them would be a bottle club or a spieler, perhaps a barber's shop. The flats above them often provided accommodation for ladies of the night. There would be all kinds of eating houses catering for every taste and every price. Hot salt beef was a favourite treat when my wallet had more than just air in it.

Most evenings would find the streets teeming with people and on Saturdays, you could say it was jam-packed. In the daytime, the place was less busy. BBC and film producers would be everywhere, well that's what they claimed to be, and they would talk about their great success or prospects, and then search their pockets for enough change to pay for a coffee.

All over Soho, there were spielers: small seedy clubs with a bar and a card room and other rooms for hourly rent for those with other pastimes. A membership fee was charged and touts got money for bringing people in. Strangers would have no difficulty being signed in but would find it impossible to get out without being fleeced of all they had. Some were hit over the head and put out the back door, lighter by the weight of their wallet. Gambling went on through the night. Police regularly closed them, but there were so many joints opening and closing they just couldn't keep up.

Card rooms provided opportunities for faro, poker, rummy, solo whist, nap and a fun family game of Slippery Sam, in which almost any number of players gambled on the likelihood of one of their three cards being higher than the top card remaining in the deck. Played in clubs, it was a rapid way of depriving amateur players of their hard-earns. Roulette and chemin-de-fer were played in slightly more salubrious surroundings. There were also women-only cards clubs that were mostly respectable.

Official licensed drinking hours were from 3 p.m. to 11 p.m. Then the doors of many establishments closed, blinds came down and people not already inside would enter with a secret knock or by some other arrangement. The seedier places would have a fair share of villains leaning against fruit machines, scraping their finger nails with a clasp knife or the stylish stiletto that had been so useful to commandos during the war: it now had a place out of sight, tucked in the back of a belt or down the trousers, or contained in a sheath slung beneath the armpit. Knives were intended to wound not to kill; the death penalty did have some deterrent effect, although Tony Mancini was proof that not everyone took notice. Some gangsters carried guns that could be bought from ex-soldiers for as little as a fiver. Mostly they were kept at home ready for collection if the need arose.

Soho was a collection point for confidence men, hotel thieves and pickpockets. Because bona fide nightclubs were not allowed to harbour convicted criminals, racecourse thugs spent their off-duty hours splashing their day's pickings around seedy haunts crammed into back streets, where rents were cheap and premises less well illuminated. Tricksters fleeced mugs in crooked card games and Australian conmen worked every kind of swindle, and they were the best at it. Petty crooks always had some sort of deal to sell and were best left alone. It was usual to stick with your own crowd: Italians and Jews had their favourite places, I favoured the Intrepid Fox or the Dog and Duck pubs. They not only sounded English, they attracted cockneys and other down-to-earth people who enjoyed a pint of wallop and were lively meeting places.

Bottle clubs were all over the place. These operated through the night to provide sustenance to drinkers who couldn't wait around until 3 p.m. next day. Prices were exorbitant and the usual dangers were present. They cost £1 or more to enter, for which members were able to dance without moving far around the tiny floor. You could meet girls who encouraged you to drink for their commission. Extra personal services cost anything from £2 to £10. Most of the women looked tired and hard beneath their plastered faces and it was wiser to spend that sort of money on pleasures more wholesome. When the clubs closed at six in the morning, heads were sore and wallets empty.

Some people were addicted to dissipation and nowhere was it better provided than at those private parties whose title was a device to make them legal by payment of the membership fee. One cheeky proprietor set up opposite the police court in Great Marlborough Street.

Open all hours were the near beer joints, selling beer that was less than two per cent alcohol. The drinks might have been soft but drinkers hardened them from hip flasks that were replenished by errand boys, who were tipped for the service.

Contraband was stored in Soho cellars and outlying warehouses. The relaxation felt after the war brought a desire for luxuries denied during the conflict. People no longer worried about, or understood, the continuing need for rationing and were not at all concerned about subverting it by buying stolen goods on the cheap. After all, we had won the war. Jewellery, watches, cigarette cases, liquor, perfume, clothes and food, were eagerly demanded and supplied. The spiv became a necessity. Soho restaurants also depended on the black market. Cash opened warehouse doors and dimly-lit cellars for goods surreptitiously stocked during the war, creating a market niche for those able to replenish supplies. Bonded warehouses were raided; smash-and-grab gangs rammed quality shop windows with cars or cracked the glass with hammers; country houses, West End residences and factories were burgled; and dockyards were systematically pilfered. Pickpockets, who practised with the ease from years of experience, found willing purchasers for the personal effects they relieved from the careless. One benefit that American servicemen brought to peacetime Britain was access to military stores: Aladdin's caves of fuel, food and tobacco, which streamed goods onto the black market.

Some, like Billy Hill and Ruby Sparks, stole the merchandise for others to peddle. The wide boy, so-called because of his wide knowledge of worldly things, generally did the less risky selling. The Billy Hills of this world spent sundry years in prison, while shrewd operators like Jack Spot made their fortunes by imposing royalties on spivs, thieves and proprietors, and by protecting practically all of the illegal gambling joints. I was pleased to share Jack's bounty; he ate the bird while Billy Hill did it.

American soldiers were plentiful and were the means of subsistence for many small bars. Girls who tarried there were mock Americans, dressed in jive clothes, with bleached hair, bright lipstick, talking in broad accents, and always champing on a piece of flavoured rubber. Some girls would do anything for a stick of gum. Fights would break out when American servicemen realised they had been taken. They were easily outnumbered by touts who had reinforcements on hand in the event of trouble, even the girls steamed into the Yanks to protect their ponces; some called it the Third Front. There were frequent rows between white American servicemen and blacks because some Americans had difficulty understanding that Soho was a cosmopolitan mix.

Drugs were available and white girls would go with blacks to get a dip of cocaine or opium, usually the former as the old-fashioned opium den had mostly given way to parlour use of fashionable drugs. Substances were not plentiful because the war had made supplies difficult; even so, 'snow' was not expensive to buy for those who wanted it, because demand was not that high.

Jack Spot was good to me. He knew I had been an enemy of the Sabinis and he was respectful of my brother, Wal, who had guided him through the racecourse routines and scams and pinpointed weaknesses in the White's set up. Jack knew I had been a doorman at Kate Meyrick's Forty-three Club. It was there, in Christmas 1928, that I knocked out Harry Distelman, who was with a crew of pickpockets targeting patrons entering the cellar club. I cleared them out of the way and left Harry, who was a Jewish street bookie, lying in the middle of Gerrard Street. He was a big, ugly lug, who I was surprised went down from one left hook. What made it worse was that Harry was picked up by two coppers who went through his overcoat pockets and found stolen articles. He got three months. Wal made it known that there must be no comeback from the Yiddisher crowd. I was in demand as a minder after that.

I became doorman at Gennaro's when it was in New Compton Street, before Hitler bombed it. It is now on the Rendezvous site in Dean Street. Jack got me a job as a doorman at the Gargoyle Club, *which occupied the upper floors of 69 Dean Street, with another entrance in Meard's Street. The owner was Dave Tennant,[1] who was some sort of nobility, but was quiet about it. I was now fifty-eight and could only expect a low-paid job on the door, but Jack persuaded his lordship I was ideal to greet patrons and discourage bad faces who knew my family and friends' connections, so I did much better. On top of that I had generous tips. I was used to taking care of drunks and troublemakers. I don't think Jack was getting protection money from the Gargoyle, but he may have charged something for placing doormen and other sorts of minders.*

Doormen would train as fighters. We had a punchbag in a basement store, where potential doormen were tested on their ability to swing the bag past a mark with a punch from no more than twelve inches. The idea was to be able to give a discreet jab to discourage troublemakers and walk them away from the premises, or pretend they were ill and needed to be carried to the outside air. I had learned from my brothers how to battle with fists, bottles and chairs, which was not much use when dealing discreetly with a tipsy troublemaker. We all knew how to fight, but we liked to learn some commando tricks. I learned that the body is not comfortable leaning backwards or sideways: tumbling forward, you can go into a somersault and scramble up without losing much orientation, but backwards and sideways upsets equilibrium and makes you more susceptible to attack. One thing I found useful was to face a troublemaker, take hold of his sleeve, put my foot against the side of his lower leg and pull him sideways off balance, turning him at the same time. Many a drunk found himself twirling down Dean Street without quite realising what had happened.

The Gargoyle was a good class of club and I was expected to turn away anyone who looked like trouble. If I wasn't sure, I could look at a manager or the owner and he would nod or shake, a bit like Rick

---

1 David Tennant was the son of Lord Glenconner. The Gargoyle Club was established in 1925 as an avant-garde meeting place for theatrical people and their society hangers-on. It lost its charm after World War Two, when it became the haunt of disreputable characters.

in Casablanca. *If they were not to come in, then they didn't come in. On one occasion, Eddie Raimo tried to get past me and I had to block his entrance. He was a little bloke who dressed like the film star Alan Ladd and had a reputation as a razor man. I was nervous he may have some pals standing nearby who would rush me and turn the club over as a message that protection was a good idea. I explained he couldn't come in without the guv'nor's say so and instead of getting all cocky, he said 'Fair enough' and we had a friendly chat. Later, when I was in the Fox, he sent a drink over.*

A bigger threat was Vic Russo, a cousin of Albert Dimes, who had once cut someone's ear off with a chopper. He had been cut by Billy Hill's crowd and his face was a right mess. He was not afraid of anything or anyone, probably because they could only tame him by killing him; another cut would have meant nothing to him. He was often drunk and would try to blag free drinks in clubs and pubs. My technique was to stare him straight in the eye, like boxers do, and stand my ground. When he looked away, I knew I had him and I gently backed him onto the pavement. He walked away cursing and kept staring back at me. I admit I had a few watchful weeks, as he was the type to make a comeback. Eventually he teamed up with Spot and helped oust the Whites. One of the people they 'did' was Eddie Raimo.

Jack Spot would take me for a meal in Jack Isow's restaurant in Brewer Street. Restaurants were allowed to charge a maximum five shillings for a meal in austerity Britain. Drinks could be charged as extras, though most restaurants had a cover charge of a few shillings to provide some sort of profit. With Jack I never had less than the 'full five' as we used to call it. Just remember that five shillings was a lot of money for most people and I certainly regarded this as a generous treat. In recent years, I have heard Jack described as being mean, but he never was with me and I know he also treated others. Often people would come up to his table to talk business, which was the custom in Jewish gaffs, but he would wave them away with a 'Not now, not now'. On one occasion, the cockney comedian Tommy Trinder was invited to join us and found it prudent to do so, although he didn't seem to enjoy his dinner.

When I was flush with money, usually after a tip from a tipsy gent, and only on occasions when a celebration was in order, I would join friends in a favourite Italian or Spanish restaurant. There were some marvellous places to eat and for much less than the full five you could have a wonderful feast and share a bottle of Chianti that cost close on £1. Mostly though, my wages went home with me and we lived pretty well in the council flat we were moved into after our house in Lant Street, Southwark, was bombed during the war.

I was working evenings and weekends at the Gargoyle to top up the wages I was earning as foreman packer at the British Trolley Track in Southwark. At work, part of my duties was to deal with the work-shy brigade. I would winkle them out from behind machines and under tables and tell them they were sacked. Most went quietly but a few benefited from the half nelsons and crooked-arm locks I had learned from my soldier friends. I left the Gargoyle when it went downhill, as much of Soho did in the 1950s.

Jack Spot was keen to install himself as the Boss of Soho. He had a strong team, including Billy Hill, Jock Russo, Johnny Carter, Franny Daniels and others. His main opposition was Harry White, Eddie Raimo and remnants of the Sabinis who looked to Harry Boy Sabini and the fledgling Albert Dimes. In 1947, Jack swept them away to become undisputed king. Sadly, he softened after he got married and the vultures gathered. It must be said that when Jack was running the show there was a lot less liberty taking. If only Italian Albert Dimes hadn't challenged him.

AFTER THE WAR, Spot decided he did not want partners who were not supporting his tough stance, necessary to keep off challengers. He added Billy Hill to his team and together they subdued the White brothers' King's Cross gang, led by Alf's brother-in-law, Charlie Wooder, and the Italian gang led by Italian Alec Dimes and his younger brother Albert, who were keen to take over the racecourses. It was then that Billy Hill overstepped the mark and got himself glassed by King's

Cross hard man Eddie Raimo. Spot took care of this by beating up Raimo, Harry White, Billy Goller and Johnny Warren in a night of violence on 5 January 1947.

Jack Spot has never said who was with him in the final attack on the Whites in Al Burnett's Nut House in Piccadilly. Johnny Carter claimed to be one of them, and it is probable that he was, before taking a sabbatical from Jack's gang due to being banged up for attacking one of the south London Brindle family. Carter said it was Tommy Benneworth who cut Billy Goller, inflicting a severe wound on his neck from which he nearly died. He was adamant that Billy Hill was not there. The gang went into hiding until it was certain Goller was going to recover and had not named his attackers. Goller's family came from the Walworth district of southeast London, before moving to Islington, and it seems Tommy Benneworth took exception to Billy signing up with the King's Cross Boys. It was Tommy's last fling, at fifty-three, and Goller's too. Throughout January, Spot's men scoured the West End and Islington for any White men they could find. He was now in sole control of racing pitch sales and Soho protection rackets.

Jack Spot put up money for operations he did not wish to take part in. In 1948, Billy Hill was informed of a store of bullion and other valuables in a bonded warehouse belonging to the airline BOAC at London Airport. Billy, who was a dedicated thief, licked his lips and pondered on the prospect of diamonds, gold, booze and other bonded goodies awaiting his attention. Then he turned over and looked at the bars of his cell to remind himself he was not in a position to take advantage of such information, being locked up as he was for breaking open a safe the previous year. He still had two years to go.

Although Billy had a gang that could carry out the job, they were all broke and not able to come up with the readies needed to finance the operation. Franny Daniels suggested Jack as a means of funding, something Billy was not keen on, as Jack was not known for being a thief and would likely demand too large a share of the take. Daniels was sent to negotiate and a deal was done. Jack put up the 'readies' and a plan was hatched. Maybe to get at Jack, or because of too many ears in the wind, word got back to police that something was afoot.

London Airport in 1948 cannot be compared to present-day Heathrow that occupies the same site. The security warehouse comprised two adjoining aircraft hangars dating from wartime use. Within them, safes held precious stones, including loose diamonds destined for jewellers and for industrial use. There were racks containing valuable paintings and lockers containing medical drugs, such as penicillin, and spirits were stored on shelves. A consignment of gold bullion, valued at £250,000, was due on Wednesday, 29 July from South America, via Madrid, information that had somehow come to the attention of Hill. Because the flimsy hangars were not built to withstand a criminal onslaught, the buildings were guarded inside and out by five or six guards, who also worked as loaders.

One of these guards was approached and offered £500 of Jack's money to dope his colleagues' tea on the night of the gold delivery, which was expected to be locked away in the strong room by 10 p.m.; the guard would then let them in so they could take the keys from the unconscious foreman and help themselves to the gold and whatever else they fancied. The scouting activity of the guard drew the attention of a security officer who reported him to the police. When the guard was interviewed by Detective Superintendent Bob Lee, he coughed the whole set-up. He was told to co-operate with the robbers and pass information to an undercover policeman. Soon the guard was given a £100 retainer and a packet of barbiturate, with instructions to dope the drinks during their midnight break.

The storage facility contained an extra van that night, one that contained fifteen policemen. The airport authority had delayed the arrival of the plane from Madrid, and a fake delivery went ahead. The cargo was delivered by a police crew and a large packing case was dragged from the tailboard of the extra van and deposited at the entrance to the warehouse. It obscured the view from an all-night café, where Franny Daniels was watching and waiting to telephone his heavy pals to tell them that it was time to get going. What he did not see was fifteen plain-clothes officers and three airport security guards sneaking around the crate and into the warehouse, and the regular guards sneaking into the van. One police officer, dressed as a security guard, shoved the crate into the warehouse before getting into the van's cab to drive away.

Inside the hangar, police waited tensely for the next move, which was to be the arrival of a canteen van with tea and coffee that was to be drugged by the inside man. The jugs were taken in by an officer wearing a warehouse coat. The drinks, minus the barbiturate, were shared out in small amounts for the ambuscade officers, who were feeling dry-mouthed with apprehension. After twenty minutes, a policeman, resembling the inside man, opened the wicket door and flashed a torch at the café. Four 'warehousemen' draped themselves across a table, while others took up positions behind cases. Minutes went by ... minutes more ... then they heard the noise of a van pulling up outside, followed by footsteps. A security officer spoke quietly into a telephone linked directly to Scotland Yard: they relayed the alert to four squad cars stationed outside the airport and to a van parked in the car park, which contained a dozen sweaty policemen within sprinting distance of the action.

The warehouse door was forced open and eight men wearing stocking masks entered and went to the table to examine the sleeping guards, giving them a good shake, and one a bash on the head. At this time, they should have been greeted by their inside man. When he did not appear, they went through the pockets of the 'drugged' warehousemen searching for keys. Sergeant Hewitt groaned and rolled his eyes as he was pulled off the table and relieved of keys jangling in his coat. Alf Roome, who led the raid, and Teddy Hughes, recently released from prison for his part in a disastrous raid on an Islington postmaster, went to the strong room, where Roome inserted the key in the lock. As he turned the key, all hell broke loose.

Faced with such odds, the gang should have rolled over. They did not. Police and crooks waded into each other, truncheons against crowbars. Heads were split and teeth shed in a desperate battle. Police reinforcements from the car park left the result in no doubt, though several policemen were knocked out. All of the robbers were badly mauled. They were taken to Harlington Police Station where doctors were called to treat wounds and bandage heads.

Eight men were charged with attempting to steal the contents of a safe belonging to BOAC and of assaulting and robbing Sergeant Hewitt and two other policemen of eight keys. Six of them were also charged with wounding and causing grievous bodily harm. Andy Walsh, the guard who was approached, was charged with being an accessory. When the fighting broke out, three robbers, who had been placed outside the warehouse, observed policemen charging from the car park and ran off into the darkness. Franny Daniels was one, Teddy Machin another and the third never let his name be known. A story persists that either Daniels or Machin hung on to the exhaust of a police van and dropped free at some traffic lights. The burns from this would have been critical. Certainly, Franny Daniels did not have scarred hands; I cannot speak for Machin, who was shot in 1973 in some domestic squabble, so we will never know. Jack Spot was questioned after a car number, noted during earlier observations, was traced to him. Whatever excuse he had, it was good enough, for he was not charged.

At the Old Bailey, the eight raiders pleaded guilty to attempted robbery and not guilty to charges of assault. Perhaps because they had the worst of the fighting, being outnumbered as they were, they thought it strange they should be thought guilty of assault when they were only defending themselves. Evidence was given that the men wielded iron bars and wounded a number of policemen. In all, seven crooks and nine policemen had been injured. When they heard the evidence against them and the list of police injuries, they changed their pleas to guilty on the assault charges.

The gang were an example of a London consortium:

South London
Teddy Hughes, forty-eight, Elephant and Castle, twelve years.
George Smith, twenty-nine, Brixton, eight years.
Sammy Ross, thirty-three, Brixton, eleven years.
Franny Daniels, thirty-seven, Elephant and Castle, escaped.

East London
Alf Roome, forty-two, Ilford, ten years.
Bill Ainsworth, thirty-eight, Dagenham, five years.
Sid Cooke, twenty-seven, Stratford, eight years.
Jimmy Wood, thirty-four, Manor Park, nine years.
George Wallis, thirty-six, Manor Park, eight years.
Teddy Machin, forty, Mile End, escaped.

West London
Andy Walsh, thirty-eight, labourer, tried separately, bound over for two years.

Recorder Sir Gerald Dodson pointed out that men who were prepared to use violence and who got the worst of it could hardly complain. Imagine, he said, what would have happened had the robbers and police been carrying firearms. A bloodbath matching anything in American criminal annals would surely have occurred. The main reason British robberies receive less spectacular news coverage is due to the lack of a shootout. In this instance, a robbery failed but no one was killed.

It must be said that the list of police injuries given out to newspapers before a trial commences, and later read out in court, is often interesting. Police are so concerned at being accused of injuring people they have arrested that they find it prudent to get in first: check out any football riot or violent demonstration.

Billy Hill

BILLY HILL, WHOSE rash tendencies worried Jack Spot, was definitely the junior partner of the pair. Hill was given to using a chiv on people who displeased him, something Spot was trying to move away from: instead, he found himself clearing up the mess left by the hyperactive Billy. When Hill slashed Belgian Johnny, between dessert and coffee in Soho's Le Jardin restaurant, it brought a flurry of police activity. Johnny looked set to die and they wanted him to name his killer before it was too late; sadly for them Johnny pulled through with medical help, stiffened by a fistful of fivers from Hill, who Spot had advised to make reparations.

Belgian Johnny was Jean Baptiste Hubert, a West End pimp who ran a string of girls on the game. This included his French girlfriend, Germaine, who was twelve years his senior and had married an Englishman to obtain British citizenship. In return for British hospitality, she set up a call girl racket, which Johnny took over when young muscle was needed. Johnny had been born in Brussels and arrived in Britain in 1940 as a twenty-four-year-old with the Free Belgian Army. He settled into Maida Vale and swiftly set aside any notion of fighting the Axis, preferring a career in burglary. After the war, he gathered several convictions for robbery and decided it was better to have girls working for him, rather than his shinning up drain-pipes or waiting in alleys on cold, dark nights.

One of his girls, Gypsy Riley, gave up street work when she took up with Billy Hill, relegating his wife Aggie to bar work. The altercation came about when Johnny made a remark to Gypsy, who told Billy, who naturally reached for his chiv. When he recovered, Johnny was not popular with police, who would rather he had died and named his attacker on his deathbed. He fled to Belgium where, in 1953, he was jailed for a year for living off immoral earnings. Somehow, he made it back to London where he soon had a wealthy lifestyle and became known as 'Flash Johnny'. He married Germaine in 1957 and, after the nuptials, put her back on the game along with her daughter from a previous marriage. When his stepdaughter failed to achieve her nightly quota, he gave her a black eye and a bruised lip, which did not improve her prospects. She complained to a policeman, who enquired from Johnny what had happened. Johnny answered with a kick, resulting in his getting fifteen months for the girl and three for the copper.

When he came out, he was not cured. He set up a drinking club in Notting Hill, which he stocked with girls and beverages, both being fully utilised after hours in the seedy parlour. In 1960, his club was raided twice in one week and he was fined for allowing after-hours drinking. Investigations revealed he had considerable assets in Britain, France and Belgium, including a sumptuous flat in St. John's Wood. Knocking people about was one thing, getting rich was another, and this time he was deported as an undesirable alien. There is no record of his coming back, but with Johnny, you cannot be certain.

Billy Hill's resort to his finely honed friend was practised with near lethal dexterity on Tommy Smithson. Spot had called Tommy to a meeting to discuss his high profile in a protection racket, which was causing a stir in the newspapers. Tommy had also given one of Spot's acolytes, Slip Sullivan, a razor stripe or two. Tommy eventually agreed to meet Spot and Hill behind the Black Cat Cigarette Factory in Camden Town, a striking, Egyptian-styled building inspired by the discovery of Tutankhamen's tomb and fronted by two seven-foot-high bronze cats. He arrived with a minder and a gun. Before either could be used, a van pulled up and more men leapt out. Hill, who was a close friend of Sullivan, slashed Smithson's left cheek so deeply that blood erupted in a great gush: the others slashed away at his arms and legs. The attackers drove away leaving Spot and Moisha Blueball trying to stem the bleeding, which they did by tying Spot's tie around Tommy's face. They put him over the wall of the railway embankment on the corner of Mornington Terrace and called an ambulance.

Smithson was a real loser. No one but he could have counted the number of times he had been beaten up. In 1953, he graduated from the East End and started throwing his weight around in small Soho spielers, until he got a severe come-uppance when he demanded money from a club backed by Jack Spot and minded by Johnny Carter. It is likely he was expected when he turned up to collect money from the club's manager. What he got was a severe kicking from Carter and he was lucky not to have been badly cut. Most likely Spot had designated a warning. The next time would be as close to a near death experience as was possible.

The attack at the Black Cat Factory was all of that. Not only did Hill cut his face, others chopped and sliced away at his body, almost severing a hand and doing their best to stop him walking, by slashing at nerves in his back and legs. Smithson never grassed and for this he received £500 from Spot, who made sure Hill supplied the readies. These were not his first or last beatings. He was laid out with a billiard ball-wielding Elephant Boy he had been hunting after a previous scrap. It is probable that Tommy was carrying a knife or gun, or both. As in 'the case of the black cat', he was not given a chance to use them.

Smithson was born in Liverpool in 1920, the sixth of eight children. When he was two years old, the family moved to Shoreditch, east London, where he grew up among the likes of Dodger Mullins and Arthur Harding. His early career amounted to probation for theft and six months in Borstal for fighting. He received a further probation, which he declined to attend and was sent to Reform School, where an effort was made to redeem him. When he left, he was fitter and tougher and took his part in the war by joining the Merchant Navy, serving on ammunition ships voyaging to Australia. In Reform School, he had taken lessons in self-defence, becoming a passable amateur boxer.

As the war came to a close, he reverted to crime by taking part in a robbery in Bow, for which he received eighteen months. As ever, prison was a training ground and he got to know people who ran gambling clubs, something that took his particular fancy. He also continued his fitness training. When released, he found work minding small East End spielers and became a serious gambler, going from flush to bust and back again in a series of large bets, always looking for the big one that never quite turned up.

By 1954, he had his own little gang that included Ronnie and Reggie Kray and he caught the eye of Jack Spot, who employed him as a team member. Smithson, who never exhibited much good judgement, doubled by protecting George Caruana, something that would bring him into conflict with Spot and Hill. Gypsy Riley was upset that Caruana would not allow her the bar concessions she was receiving at other clubs, mainly free drinks for her, then for her friends, then for whole parties. Caruana presented her with a bill at his Cross Club in Berner Street, Whitechapel, sending Gypsy into a rage. She called on the help of party member and Hill crony Freddie 'Slip' Sullivan.

Slip was not the brightest, or toughest, of Hill's associates, coming in way down the list compared to his brother Sonny. Gypsy was not put off by this. She thrust Slip into action and he made the mistake of threatening first. Before he could back his threats with action, Smithson striped him with an open razor, which missed his cheek and sliced down his throat; two more strokes laced Slip's arm as he protected himself. In the scrimmage, Caruana lost part of an ear. This attack was what led to Smithson's appointment behind the Black Cat Factory and several large blood transfusions.

The money he got from Hill in reparations was used for bets and this time he won enough to buy into a club in Soho, the Publishers in D'Arblay Street, a name designed as a futile pretence that the club was for writers. The club was once owned by Freddie Ford. Here Smithson set up a different sort of book, one to indulge his gambling tendencies. To support his erratic lifestyle, he started to protect small spielers that did not come under the auspices of Spot and Carter. Gambling dens came and went and it was easy to find unprotected dice and card games. With the exception of the 49 Club, where Carter did him, Spot was not bothered at Smithson's dealing, especially as he leaned on small Maltese operations. The Maltese were inveterate gamblers and street girl ponces, who were so frugal that they used only the sleaziest of places and ill-favoured of women. Tommy prospered enough to take part ownership in several clubs. For once things were going right. The Publishers folded, but Smithson's protection business flourished after he took hold of a Maltese gentleman and rammed his head into a wall mirror, spun him round, and exhibited his bleeding napper as an example of what happens to dissenters.

Early in 1956, Smithson attempted to expand his mini empire by protecting 'English' spielers. In April, he was attacked by two men when he went to collect a payment; all he got was another twenty stitches in a face already resembling the tramlines at the junction of the New and Old Kent Roads. A general hush followed the incident, but a few fingers from those in the know pointed towards the Carter brothers, Johnny and Harry. Apparently, Tommy had once again strayed into Johnny's domain. This is understandable, as so many spielers and clip joints were springing up that there was bound to be conflicts of interest and Smithson probably did not know he was encroaching. This time, without Spot's magnanimity, the Carters felt no need for restraint.

The Maltese fraternity were on the receiving end from Smithson, Spot, Carter and numerous others. They held a meeting and decided to make a stand. They selected Smithson for a number of reasons: he was taking most from them; he was less equipped to make a comeback, the recent cutting confirmed his weakness; and he was currently demanding money for a defence fund for his girlfriend, Fay Richardson, who was due in court for the misuse of cheques. Tommy Smithson, Wally Downs and Chris Thomas had recently attacked Caruana and threatened his Maltese pal, Phil Ellul, with 'a bullet up the bracket' if he did not cough up. Ellul was a frightened man.

Two weeks later, on 25 June 1956, Smithson was invited to a tawdry lodging house owned by George Caruana in Carlton Vale, a turning off Maida Vale. Caruana had gone from being friend to money machine and was not happy about it. Smithson probably thought he was there to collect a payoff. While he was waiting, he stepped into a room rented by 'Blonde Mary' Bates and probably was unaware of the gathering of wolves downstairs. Into the room burst Phil Ellul, Vic Spampinato and Joe Zammit. Ellul immediately shot Tommy in the arm. Then he was held down while Ellul shot him a second time. This bullet hit him in the neck and did the business. He staggered into Carlton Vale and died sprawled on the pavement.

At the Central Criminal Court, Ellul admitted the shooting, claiming he was defending himself against Smithson, who attacked him with a pair of scissors. Even so, he was sentenced to death, later commuted to life. He served eleven years. Spampinato was acquitted and charges against Zammit were dropped. What saved Ellul was evidence given at the trial by Blonde Mary, who supported the scissors story. It emerged later that she was the girlfriend of Spampinato. Seventeen years later, police charged 'Big Frank' Mifsud and Bernie Silver with Smithson's murder and achieved a conviction for Silver, which was overturned on appeal. Big Frank, who was the wealthiest of the Maltese sex-exploiting machine, was acquitted. The story was that he had worked on Ellul to do Tommy in and had supplied the gun to do it.

THE INEVITABLE RIFT between Spot and Hill came in 1954, when Hill began cosying up to Albert Dimes. This shows how time changes things. Not many years before, the Camden Town gang, under George Sage, had been constantly at loggerheads with the Italians, and it was their younger members who now comprised much of Hill's gang. Hill also snuggled up to the King's Cross remnants of the White brother's outfit. This brought into line the Hoxton crowd, who had made an alliance with the Finsbury gang, who thought about it and decided to team up with Hill. Spot was left with allies at Elephant and Castle and the East End.

Spot should have cultivated friendships. He did not. First, the Elephant and Castle gang deserted him, then the East Enders, who looked towards the Kray twins. Veterans on the scene, such as Frankie Fraser and Teddy Machin, turned against Spot when he reneged on promises made to them. Hill saw his power growing and Jack's businesses were appealing to him. He decided he no longer needed to thieve for a living and decided to double-cross Spot.

WILLIAM CHARLES HILL was born on 13 December 1911. Contrary to popular biographies, he was not born in the Seven Dials district, between Leicester Square and Holborn. The house where Billy was born still stands at 126 Cleveland Street, which runs parallel to Tottenham Court Road in the heart of the West End. The district is on the borders of St. Marylebone and St. Pancras, a catchment area for many of London's most notorious criminals. Nearby is Warren Street, where Hill had an interest in second-hand car firms in that street of automobile infamy.

His parents were Septimus James Hill, known as Jimmy, a house painter – and drunk – of Irish descent, and Amelia, nee Sparling, a sometime receiver of stolen goods, who was born in Dublin. Septimus and Amelia married in 1895. In 1914, the family moved to Netley Street, a hotbed of criminal activity in Camden; here Billy mixed with villains of all sorts, brought to the three-storey Victorian house by his parents and siblings, particularly his sister Maggie, who was eleven years his senior. A number of the twenty-one children the Hills brought into the world were a burden to it. It is probable Maggie knew George Sage, who lived not far away in Mornington Place.

Maggie was a friend of Alice Diamond and as such became acquainted with the Forty Elephants team of shoplifters. She took over leadership in the 1930s, when her husband, Alfred Hughes, was a fence for the gang. Apart from his membership of the Elephant and Castle gang, Alfred was part of a Regent's Park team of warehouse burglars, specialising in the theft of high-quality dresses and fur coats. In 1929, police ambushed the gang while they were raiding a furriers in Green Lanes, Harringay, and followed it with a raid on a flat at Regent's Park, where they found piles of stolen clothes from a wide spread of burglaries. Alfie escaped by nearly running down a policeman with his car, leaving others to take the rap. In 1930, he was arrested by two Flying Squad officers who became suspicious of his peculiar build. Under his overcoat, he had a bundle of fur stoles stolen from a Soho furrier, which he was taking to a bent dealer in the East End. He was described in court as a go-between for shoplifters and receivers.

Hill's father used to hang about the same clubs as Billy and could be counted on to get drunk and start a fight. Thrown out, he would wait in the street to start up again, and then attack any copper who arrived. He died in 1939, aged sixty-four, when Billy was serving time in Chelmsford Prison. A story went around that Billy refused compassionate leave because he had disowned his old man as an embarrassment.

As a youngster, Hill worked for Wal McDonald as a book-ies' lookout and runner. Jim McDonald remembered Maggie bringing her cheeky younger brother to Lambeth, from where the McDonald family operated a network of street pitches spread throughout Waterloo, Blackfriars, Elephant and Castle, Walworth, Kennington and Vauxhall. Hill's criminal convic-tions started when he was fifteen with a spell in Borstal for thieving, something he did for most of his life, racking up thirteen convictions. He became as expert as it is possible to be at burglary, safe-blowing and smash-and-grab, learning much from Alfie Hughes and Ruby Sparks. He also developed a vicious streak learned from the razor gangs he mixed with.

Hill's most lucrative period was at the onset of World War Two, when he embarked on a series of motor car smash-and-grab raids on jewellers and furriers across west London, some-times with Ruby Sparks. It must be said that, although his gang got away with much swag, they were caught far too often and though Hill put money away, which served him well in later life, he paid for it through years in prison. He spent most of the war locked up, before resuming a career in robbery at the end of hostilities, followed by more sentences. It was the path of an incorrigible rogue.

In 1947, after helping to destroy what remained of the White gang, he was arrested on suspicion of theft and left the country for South Africa. There he opened a gambling club, the Mil-lionaire, in Johannesburg. In August of that year, he was forced into a fight with four of Jo'burg's mobsters, who tried to turn his club over. On Billy's team was ex-professional lightweight boxer Bobby Ramsey, who had remained in South Africa after his final bout: they cut several of the attackers, Ramsey taking the top off one of their heads with a machete. Hill, who had fired a revolver into the midst of the four, missed only because Ramsey knocked his arm aside, forcing him to go to work with his razor. They left two men badly damaged on the pave-ment, and one of them, retired wrestler Arnold Neville, nearly died. Hill was arrested, skipped bail, and returned to London, leaving Ramsey to stand trial.[1] Hill's brief spell of freedom ended when he was jailed for three years for blowing a safe.

Billy's memoirs, *Boss of Britain's Underworld*, were published in 1955, just before the eruption of violence following Spot's attack on Albert Dimes in Soho. The book shows that the relationship with Spot had broken down. Hill uses his pages to ridicule his previous benefactor whenever he can. One reason is that the book was ghosted by *People* crime reporter Duncan Webb, who despised Spot. The Sunday newspaper had been running stories on Hill and consequently found opposition in other newspapers that chronicled Spot's career. The culmination was Spot breaking Webb's writing arm.

Hill's book, published by Naldrett Press and promoted through a series of parties attended by prominent criminals and some senior police officers, at the cost of their jobs and pensions, ranges from fact to fantasy. Because many of Hill's gang and enemies were still alive and working, he uses pseudonyms. If you can find a copy, substitute the following:

The Blacks – Whites
Benny the Kid – Jack Spot
Brownson – Tommy Smithson
Frazer – Frankie Fraser
Carter – Johnny Carter
Scarface Jock – Victor Russo
Moisha Blueball – Maurice Goldstein
Italian Albert – Albert Dimes

---

1 Ramsey, whose career covered over eighty bouts, served a short jail sentence before being deported. Born in Limehouse, he saw service with Jack Spot, Billy Hill, the Nash brothers and the Krays. He was jailed with Ronnie Kray after a series of gang fights. Later Ronnie turned on him and gave him a beating after he had knocked about a boxer friend of his. Ramsey took his chastisement without fighting back. He died in 2004.

Franny the Spaniel – Thomas Francis Daniels
Jock Wyatt – John Wyatt
Moshe Cohen – Maurice (Moisha) Cohen
Odd Legs – Teddy Hughes
Taters Portsmouth – George 'Taters' Chatham
Jack Delight – Jackie Sangers
Belgian Johnny – Jean-Baptiste Hubert
Sam Ferryboat – Sammy Josephs
Horrible Harry – Teddy Machin
Tommy Bird – Billy Howard
Flannel Foot – Harry Vicars
Tom Thumb – Tommy Brindle

In his book, Hill compares himself to bank robber John Dillinger and reckons the American's exploits would have looked like a Boy Scouts' jamboree compared to his. He dismisses Dillinger as a killer, although it is doubtful he killed anyone. Dillinger's notorious, but brief, burst of activity lasted little more than a year, yet he was the sensation of crime-torn America and the Federal Bureau of Investigation's first Public Enemy Number One. Yet his most successful bank raid brought a disappointing $52,000 to share between six men and, soon after that, Dillinger and his gang were lying dead.

BILLY HILL HAD his failures and spent many years in prison. Then came the Eastcastle Street job. When the information reached the ears of Billy Hill that a Post Office Royal Mail van, carrying sacks of untraceable used bank notes, was travelling regularly from Paddington Railway Station to the Post Office at St. Martin's-le-Grand in the City of London, with only a handful of guards, he decided he was going to have its contents. The information was dropped in the Yorkshire Grey, near Mount Pleasant Sorting Office, Clerkenwell, by a part-time Post Office employee looking for a drink and a cut of the proceeds. A deal was reached. To gain more details, Hill had himself introduced to an inside man brought to him by the tip-off.

What he found was that the mail van travelled a set route from Paddington Railway Station, into Praed Street, along Edgware Road to Marble Arch, then into Oxford Street, through Oxford Circus, along to New Oxford Street, then into High Holborn, carrying on to Holborn Circus, Holborn Viaduct and Newgate Street, to left to its destination at St. Martin's-le-Grand. There the mail sacks were openly transported from the van, through the delivery bay, into the Post Office back room. Six or seven cashiers would there count the contents. The amount of cash ranged from £30,000 to £45,000. Further details described the van's alarm system and the security instructions given to the driver and two guards. The van was alarmed by a siren which, once switched on from the cab or the interior of the van, could not be switched off without a special key held at the Post Office.

Hill's first inclination was to follow the mail sacks into the room and overwhelm the staff in a sudden rush of power. This meant a team big enough to subdue perhaps as many as a dozen employees. In his mind, large teams divided into maybe only £30,000, equalled small returns. He decided to attack the van. The number of raiders he settled on was seven. Hill would put up expenses and take most of the profit, while his team would have to settle for wages. He was powerful enough not to have problems of extra demands if proceeds exceeded expectations. Thieves liked working for Hill, they knew he not only kept quiet if things went wrong for him, he would also help look after them and their families if the need arose.

To check for ambush sites, Hill needed to be certain the same route was followed every time. He spent hours travelling the route and following the van from Paddington, a journey along well-travelled main roads, which he assessed would be difficult for his objective. Luck had it that part of Oxford

Street was obstructed by road works, making a diversion seem not unusual or suspicious.

The raid took place at 4.15 a.m. on Wednesday, 21 May 1952. Diversion signs were placed in Oxford Street to divert the red van down Newman Street and into Eastcastle Street, where a black Riley 2.5 swerved to a stop in front of it, causing it to brake sharply. A bottle-green Standard Vanguard screeched to a halt close behind the van, shutting it in. Three masked men jumped from the first car and raced to the van driver's cab, wrenched open the doors and dragged the three occupants from the front seat. As the men dropped to the pavement, three robbers from the second car joined the ruckus, pummelling the three Post Office men with fists and coshes: one was knocked unconscious. Three robbers climbed into the van, which still had its engine running, and drove away. Another ran to the Riley and it roared away with him and the getaway driver. The Vanguard departed with the two other raiders. The robbers' cars were abandoned in Covent Garden and no one saw what became of the occupants.

The mail van was driven to a rundown and seldom used builder's yard in Camden Town, where the rear door was opened with a key and nineteen sacks were removed, leaving thirteen in the van: the gang may have been disturbed in some way. It was revealed later that the van's alarm system had been switched off before the raid. It turned out that the siren had developed a fault and been immobilised awaiting repair, probably by arrangement with Hill. The total take was over £287,000. Police soon found the van and robbery vehicles but that was all they found, with the exception, some time after, of several discarded mail sacks. Some money, believed to have been part of the haul, was recovered in someone's house; however, nothing could be proved, so he kept it. The robbery vehicles had been stolen from lock-up garages in Paddington, indicating the gang was a local one.

Billy Hill was interviewed by police, as was Jack Spot, and

both were eliminated from enquiries. Before long, Hill was virtually calling press conferences to disclose how he planned it. Was he telling the truth? Certainly the van was found in Hill territory in Camden Town, not far from where he grew up and went to school. Gangsters generally supposed to have been on the raid were associates of Hill. And two years after the raid, when he was under renewed suspicion, he departed on his yacht, Flamingo, bound for Tangiers.

However, it is possible that he lied about his involvement. Jack Spot was fabled to have been behind the 1948 London Airport Robbery, a raid that went horribly wrong. Hill was eager to rubbish Spot and promote himself, and what better way than to adopt a successful robbery, compared to a failed one? Hill's boasting also had much to do with promoting his biography, penned on his behalf by journalist Duncan Webb. And the police never took Hill seriously: at best he was mildly interrogated, though there was a rumour that he had something on the chief investigating officer.

So who were the robbers? George 'Taters' Chatham was born in Fulham in 1912. In 1938, he was jailed for five years for possession of explosive substances. He immediately lost his share of the take from the Eastcastle Street job in one of Hill's spielers. Chatham was a prolific burglar and safe blower who once broke into the Victoria & Albert Museum and stole two jewel-encrusted, gold-inlaid ceremonial swords, once presented to the Duke of Wellington. He prised out the jewels to sell over a period of time and sold the gold to be melted down. After the Eastcastle Street job, he was imprisoned for receiving stolen goods and made a spectacular escape while on remand in Brixton Prison, being recaptured three weeks later. He never became rich, having an uncontrollable gambling habit. In 1954, with others, he broke into H.A. Byford's diamond mounting premises in Regent Street, and stole £37,000 of gold leaf, platinum and jewellery. His ten year sentence broke his health: even so, he lasted until 1997.

Thomas Francis 'Franny the Spaniel' Daniels, denizen of Elephant and Castle and Soho, was a friend of Jack Spot and Billy Hill. He was born in 1910 in Wandsworth, but soon moved to Walworth. Franny escaped from the 1948 London Airport fiasco. After the Eastcastle Street job, his lifestyle picked up considerably and it was generally supposed in the taverns around Elephant and Castle that he had been involved in a profitable venture. It was a long way from his first adult conviction in 1931, when as a twenty-one-year-old labourer, he served a short sentence for housebreaking. That was followed in March 1933 by twenty-two months for receiving a gold cigarette case and other items stolen from Atherton Grange, in a well-heeled community adjacent to Wimbledon Common. He then became a specialist country house thief. In 1935, he collected three years for stealing jewellery from Lord Plender's home near Sevenoaks. Later sentences included ones for robbery. Franny was aboard Hill's Flamingo when it departed Britain – and when it sank in mysterious circumstances.

It is said that Hill paid the robbers £15,000 each, but this is not certain. It does seem likely that they were working on a percentage basis. If so, and if the £15,000 is correct, each man received five per cent. After expenses, and probably another five per cent to each of his tip-offs, Hill would have pocketed around £150,000. There is a rumour that Hill gave Jack Spot £15,000, indicating he may have put up some of the expenses.

The Eastcastle Street mail van robbery was the first British robbery to receive massive police and newspaper attention. It was a record British tally. Over 1,000 police were allocated to clearing the matter up and Prime Minister Winston Churchill became personally involved. It was six years after World War Two had ceased and Britain was still a pretty dull place, eager for some colour and excitement. Although clothes rationing had ended in 1947, food rationing would not be abolished until 1954. The public welcomed a vicarious treat.

Because Hill remained at large, he was free to mastermind the hijacking of a KLM Dutch Airlines bullion van and its contents, valued at around £46,000. The raid occurred in Jockey Fields, Clerkenwell, in September 1954, and re-focused attention on Hill, not least because he had his affairs chronicled in the *People*. It would be eleven years before the Great Train Robbery eclipsed the memory of the Eastcastle Street job.

South London Villainy

SOUTH LONDON PROVIDES many interesting examples of gangs. The original 'hooligans' came from Borough, a stone's throw from Elephant and Castle, where Patrick Hooligan, born in Limerick, in 1863, caused enough havoc to establish his name in social history. This was despite the fact that the 1898 conviction that made him a focus for particular police venom was of a petty nature: stealing a horse and cart, for which he received eighteen months' hard labour. The word became established in the 1890s when reports of 'hooligan gangs' infesting Southwark and Lambeth appeared in newspapers. According to a *Times* report of November 1900, a large batch of street roughs, aged seventeen to thirty, led by incorrigible youth Henry Roberts, paraded Friar Street, Southwark, pushing people off the pavement and insulting women. In Bermondsey, a similar incident occurred in which several respectable women were grabbed round the waist and tickled under the chin. In 1927, police reported that hundreds of hooligans, led by Robert Hanks of Borough, plagued the Bankside area of the river Thames, some armed with air pistols, turning it into a battleground.

The Bermondsey Boys, also known as the Brick Boys, were an early gang from the Long Lane/Bermondsey Street area of southeast London. They could often be found at the Brick Layers' Arms public house that nestles at the junction of Old Kent Road, New Kent Road, Tower Bridge Road and Great Dover Street. Over the years their luminaries included Frankie Chapman, Brian Kemp, Lucky Fred Smith, Puncher Hooper, the Jackson Brothers and, in his early days, Tommy

Benneworth. The Jacksons, Benneworth and Smith moved on to become substantial players in the Elephant and Castle gang. The Bermondsey Boys' pastimes comprised of fighting other gangs and generally terrorising their local patch. They had affiliations with the Borough Boys and Rotherhithe Boys and had a sporadic war with their stronger neighbours, the Elephant and Castle gang, or Elephant Boys as they were more familiarly known, in which the Bermondsey crowd suffered badly.

Further along Old Kent Road was perhaps the largest of London's 1950s teenage gangs, the New Cross Boys, who roamed from Canal Bridge to Deptford, causing mayhem at Millwall Football Ground, youth clubs, cinemas and dance halls. The only noted puncher among them was Freddie 'Ginger' Simmonds, who gave a creditable performance in a stand-up fist fight with future gangster Eddie Richardson. This occurred on a snow-filled pavement outside the Trocadero cinema at Elephant and Castle, after a snowball fight got out of hand. The gang would follow around local terrors like the Roff and Carter brothers. In a clash with rivals from Peckham's Goose Green, over 200 teenage youths fought running battles over a period of three days in 1956. The Goose Green Boys proved to be no pushover, even when Waggy was recruited from Elephant and Castle to lead the final expedition. The event ended in a draw. An earlier Deptford gang, the Red Hands, so named for the red armband that identified members, came unstuck in 1926 when one of their team was stabbed to death after attacking a rival Rotherhithe Boy. William Shillibeer, aged fourteen, was convicted of the manslaughter of thirteen-year-old Albert Hannah.

The success of gangs could depend upon alliances. A small team calling themselves the Balham Boys, because it sounded catchy, was severely crushed by their Brixton neighbours and subjugated into membership. The main gang from Clapham, however, which had allied itself to the superior Elephant and Castle gang, was pretty much left alone. The stand-alone Wandsworth Boys attached themselves to professional gangs for robberies: in later years the Great Train Robbery owed much to the Wandsworth manor. The Lambeth Boys, who became momentarily famous after a television documentary in the 1950s, were nothing more than a youth club crowd. Sensibly, they pulled in their horns when confronted by other gangs that looked like taking them seriously.

The Brixton Boys ranged over Brixton, Clapham, Stockwell and Balham when they were truly desirable parts of London's suburbs, before they degenerated dramatically in the 1950s. Their criminality could be seen as mild by today's standards. They inhabited illicit gambling halls and drinking clubs and were constantly being fined for their activities. November 1925 saw a typical police raid on a Brixton club resulting in the arrest of several Brixton Boys, who were brought up before the magistrates at Lambeth Police Court. They were charged with using the South London Sporting Club, a billiard hall managed by Leon Kalf of Golders Green, for illegal gambling. A number of sporting clubs and billiards halls were managed by residents of Golders Green, including the notorious Imperial Billiards Hall at Elephant and Castle. They usually employed tough assistants to keep control while they sat in their snug safe houses in northwest London. Among those fined after the raid was Elephant and Castle luminary Angus Gordon. Magistrates bemoaned the fact that fines did not deter persistent gambling. The police sought a different solution by challenging the club's licence, causing it to close. It made little difference: those in the know knew where to go for a night's gambling and saw a court appearance as just another roll of the dice.

In July 1953, elements of the Brixton Boys showed a violent side of their nature, when they were involved in the Clapham Common affray that resulted in the death of seventeen-year-old Johnny Beckley and the wounding of several others. The fight

321

started over the trivial matter of Beckley and others refusing to walk around the Brixton crowd, who were sprawled across a pathway on the common. In the running battle, Beckley was surrounded and stabbed and Matt Chandler received a serious knife wound. The *Daily Mirror's* headline blamed 'Flick Knives, Dance Music and Edwardian Suits.'[1] Beckley was associated with the Elephant and Castle gang and was given a large south London send-off. Hundreds of mourners lined the streets and a mass of floral tributes decorated the hearse. Elephant Boys made several expeditions to Brixton in search of the boy they knew was responsible, but he had gone to ground. Police charged twenty-year-old Michael John Davies and he was jailed for murder, followed by a long campaign by his friends and family to get him out. He was released seven years after being reprieved from a death sentence. Nobody thought the police had the right man.

There had always been conflict between the two gangs. The final battle occurred in 1955, when the Brixton crowd were badly mauled by the Elephant Boys, led on this occasion by Eddie Richardson. This was a fight of which I had personal experience. Richardson had fallen out with Brixton's Joey Dunn. I can't recall what the argument was about, but word reached me that Eddie wanted back-up for a visit to the Locarno dance hall in Streatham to sort it out. I turned up at Elephant and Castle, beneath the Guinness Clock, where Eddie was waiting with Tony Connors, Peter Reuter and Big Tipps (I never knew his first name) and two of the New Cross Boys. Eddie decided not to wait for more support and we boarded a number 95 bus.

---

1 Teenagers' choices of music and clothing have always exercised the minds of newspaper editors. In the 1920s and 1930s, it was the decadent age of the charleston; in the 1940s, jiving and jitterbugging to blaring jazz music; and in the 1950s, the surrender of swing to rock and roll, combined with the arrival of the Teddy Boy. In fact all of the lads involved in the Clapham Common fight were smartly dressed in hand-tailored suits, ties and polished shoes.

Inside the dance hall, Joey was accompanied by a large contingent of Brixton Boys, and it seemed to me that the fight was off. I should have known better. A messenger came up to Tipps and announced that they had counted theirs as twenty-six and ours as seven, something that should have postponed matters. I was standing to the left of Connors, at the end of the line, and he whispered to me, 'When it starts, grab a chair.' At that moment Eddie hit the messenger and he landed, spark out, with his head at my feet. A wall of moving flesh and bone headed my way: I grabbed a flimsy wicker chair and flung it into the midst of them.

I quickly lost track of what was going on. I remember lashing out at a group that rushed at me. Others went by me and attacked the others. Patrons waiting to get on the floor to dance scattered, tables and chairs went up in the air and bodies tumbled over each other. I grabbed a hard Pyrex ashtray and cupped it in my hand. It was as hard as a stone, and I knocked down a giant of a fellow who was trying to reach over the crowd attacking Reuter, to hit him with a figurine he had ripped from a banister.

At some time I was hit with a wooden table, the sharp edge of which caught me across my shoulder blade and sent me to the floor. Desperation brought me to my feet and I continued to fight as best I could. I suppose they thought I was finished. The ones fighting me moved on to Peter and Eddie, who were knocking the crap out of the ones fighting them. Tipps had his back to a wall, a table in one hand and a chair in the other and, rather than chance getting close to him, they lobbed chair after chair until he was covered with them. The fight went out of the Brixton crowd and they picked up their leader and carried him away from Eddie, who walked alongside them peppering the unconscious form with punches.

The Locarno bouncer tried to stop me getting up the stairs towards the exit. My left arm was almost useless and I would have been in trouble, had not Peter seen my plight and knocked the fellow down the stairs. We took a bus home. Back beneath the Guinness Clock, we learned that the two New Cross Boys had legged it at the start of the fight. One had run and the other, who thought we all would, followed him.[2]

After World War Two, the Elephant and Castle gang's leadership never settled on any one person. The gang, which totalled hundreds of members, was made up of small groups that found leaders when they were needed: Johnny Carter, Frankie Fraser, Waggy Whitnall, Tony Reuter, Billy Howard, Franny Daniels and the Rosa brothers were all prominent in their ranks.

Notable names who can trace their loyalties to the Elephant gang include Buster Edwards, Tommy Wisbey, Charlie Wilson, Jimmy Hussey and Bob Welch of Great Train Robbery fame; John Palmer and Ken Noye of Brinks Mat notoriety; Eddie and Charlie Richardson; dock warehouse raiders Jimmy and Lennie Garrett; fence Dave Morbin; Billy Howard and Frankie Fraser. Over the years, the gang kept West End gang bosses in power. When Jack Spot lost their goodwill, he also lost London.

The gang ceased to be when the Elephant and Castle district lost its prospective members to London's suburbs: the area changed with an influx of immigrants in the 1950s, which swiftly altered its culture. Its villainy still exists in the expatriate gangsters who operate today in the Kent suburbs and in the descendants of immigrants who have their own havoc to wreak.

The Garrett brothers and their in-law, Dave Morbin, were at the heart of the Green Van Gang that carried out a rash of raids on bonded warehouses after World War Two. They supplied a

---

2 One of those who ran away was Johnny Daly, a leader among the New Cross Boys (sometimes called Daly's Boys) in the 1950s. Somehow, he later joined with actor David Hemmings to form Hemdale which promoted Evel Kneivel's Wembley spectacle and the Ali-Foreman fight in Zaire. He became a Hollywood film producer and died from cancer in Los Angeles in 2008.

hungry blackmarket, supervised by Jack Spot. The gang, so named by police who rated them as 'most wanted', rigged a headlamp in the rear of their van to dazzle pursuers. Both Garretts were jailed for other offences, Jimmy for burglary, and Lennie for knocking out a constable with a pair of Stillsons' when he interfered in a dispute with his girlfriend. Lennie had convictions from a young age, mostly for motor theft. In 1938, aged seventeen, he was spared Borstal when boxing manager, Ted Broadribb offered to supervise him. He believed Lennie could become a champion. Dave Morbin was the son of John Morbin, the villain captured in 1920 by the Flying Squad.

THE CARTER FAMILY were well-known denizens of the Elephant and Castle. They were cousins of Mickey and Ronnie Roff and uncles of Danny Roff, who almost certainly killed Great Train Robber Charlie Wilson and was himself shot to death in Bromley. South London hard man Tony Reuter married a Carter sister. The Carter brothers ran protection rackets in southeast London and made enough money to become bookmakers with pitches at New Cross and Catford and several illegal street pitches. It was a risky business, requiring tough responses to violent punters, who resented not being paid disputed winnings.

They were the progeny of Henry Carter and Minnie Roff. The eldest of the brothers, Eugene, called Euey or sometimes Buey, was born in 1912 during Minnie's first marriage to Eugene Edward Hill. He was killed while serving with the Royal Irish Rifles in the Flanders mud, during the Third Battle of Ypres. Minnie then married Henry in Camberwell in 1921, a month or so before their son Harry was born. John followed on 23 September 1923, at Kinglake Street, Southwark, a turning out of Old Kent Road.

The Brindles were another wild family, all boys: Willy, variously called Whippo or Whippet, Tommy (Tom Thumb),

Georgie, Bobby and Jimmy. All were born Southwark, to Billy, a Walworth boy, and Ellen, from the Borough. Their feud with Euey, Harry and Johnny Carter began in the early years of World War Two, when they fought each other rather than the Germans. Before that, they were all in the same street gang based at Elephant and Castle, where they were the local terrors, running street bookmaking, point-to-point rackets, crown and anchor, dice schools, dingy gambling joints and black marketeering. They were quintessential spivs during the war.

Inevitably, with such uncompromisingly tough nuts, they fell out. Whippet, the leader of the Brindles, hit Euey, his opposite number, with a car-starting handle and went to jail for it. The Carters responded with attacks on the remaining brothers and anyone siding with them. This brought reciprocal attacks by the Brindles. Fierce fighting made it impossible for members of either family to travel alone around the Old Kent Road, East Street market, Walworth Road and Elephant and Castle. One terrific fight outside the Mason's Arms in East Street market involved over twenty men wielding starting handles, tyre levers, bottles and fists.

The Brindles tended to use coshes of one sort or another. Unfortunately, coshes are trumped by razors and swords, something Johnny was particularly adept in the use of. He cut Brindle ally Johnny Parry, who grassed him for a twenty-one month spell in prison. A truce between the families followed. After his release in 1947, Johnny Carter helped Jack Spot clean up the White brothers. The truce was shortlived and Carter gave Bobby Brindle a terrible cut down his cheek, reaching from eyebrow to chin, leaving a thick, white scar. He then stabbed Whippet, for which he received another five years, something that interrupted his work for Spot. These attacks brought Frankie Fraser into the war, as his sister Eva was married to Jimmy Brindle.

When Johnny was released in 1951, he and his brother Harry did Charlie Woodbridge and were joined by their younger cousins, the Roffs, in taking the fight to the Brindles and another Southwark family, the Harris brothers. Benny and Johnny Harris were from a large Elephant and Castle family and had been part of the old street gang. They were drawn into supporting the Brindles when Harry and Euey set about them in one of Billy Howard's south London clubs. It was Mickey Roff going after Jimmy Brindle that escalated the war, but eventually hardly a southeast London family, disposed to villainy of some sort, was not caught up in the Carter-Brindle feud: Fraser, Porritt, Micklewhite, Reuter, Roff, Harris, Dennis, Rosa, Gerard, Garrett and Richardson. Even Johnny Nash from north London and Albert Dimes were drawn in for special appearances.

In 1955, Johnny Carter went back inside for hitting Charlie Hawkins with a starting handle. In prison, he had a row with Frank Fraser, a man with a powerful following who, when released, led attacks on Euey, now past his best, and Harry. The Carters went looking for Fraser, but found instead the Harris brothers and gave them a severe pummelling.

Johnny and Harry Carter became a force in the West End, allied to Jack Spot, while Fraser was by this time allied to Albert Dimes and Billy Hill, who had fallen out with Spot. The climax would come with attacks on Johnny Carter by Fraser, Ray Rosa and Dicky Frett, and on Jack Spot by Fraser and company.

End of an Era

THE RELATIONSHIP between Billy Hill and Jack Spot had broken down. They had begun separating into camps as early as February 1950, when Hill came under attack from some of Spot's 'old guard', who thought he was taking liberties in the East End. Hill made an example of aging Mullins gang veteran Jack Sangers by slashing both sides of his face. In 1954, Hill was acquitted of cutting Freddie Andrews, a friend of long standing, who he believed was reporting to Spot. Jack had married Maggie Molloy, who preferred to be called Rita, an aspiring actress, and soon he preferred domestic bliss to street fighting. Hill and others sensed a weakness and wondered whether the king could be toppled. Hill primed *People* reporter Duncan Webb to write a series of crime exposés that ridiculed Spot and lauded Hill. Spot thought about it, then lured Webb to the Horse Shoe Hotel in Tottenham Court Road, where he set about him, pummelling his agitator to the ground and breaking his arm in the process. He got off with a £50 fine and felt satisfied with his work. Things simmered while Hill went on a sojourn to Australia, aboard *SS Southern Cross,* to avoid questions about the KLM job. The Aussies sent him straight back.

On 11 August 1955, it really kicked off when Spot attacked Albert Dimes in the 'fight that never was' in Soho. It need not have happened. Dimes, a loudmouth show-off but a popular one, moved too quickly to take over Spot's bookie pitches. Spot could walk away himself but could not stomach being driven off. I was there when Jack hit Dimes on the chin and dropped him. Dimes got up only because Johnny

Rice pulled Jack back, meaning I had to wrestle Rice away. At this, Dimes took off for the delicatessen shop on the corner of Frith and Old Compton streets. Jack followed him in, grabbed a four-inch potato knife from sacks inside the door, and stabbed Dimes several times, until the shopkeeper, Sophie Hyams, hit him on the head with a pair of scales. Dimes got the knife away and returned the favour, stabbing and slashing at Spot in a wild panic. Both men were seriously wounded but, outrageously, they were acquitted of affray: Dimes for lack of evidence and Spot on the perjured evidence of the Rev. Basil Claude Andrews, which proved to have been purchased by some of Jack's pals. They were later jailed for perverting the course of justice. Rita was lucky to escape with probation.

Late in the evening of 2 May 1956, Jack was attacked and badly cut outside his Hyde Park Mansions apartment in Cabbell Street, Paddington, by anything from six to a gangsters' dozen, led by Frankie Fraser. His slash and stab wounds required anything from 100 to 250 stitches, according to whoever is telling the story. He was pretty much alone by then and when he recovered he nearly went to prison on a frame-up by Billy Hill and the Italians. Johnny Rice, who worked for Billy Hill as a 'phantom' Warren Street car dealer, slashed the arm of Tommy Falco, one of their own, who said, 'Eh Spotta, he done it.' The plot failed when Vic Russo, now minding Peter Mario's Italian Restaurant in Gerrard Street under the euphemistic title of assistant manager, told the police he had declined the offer of £500 for taking the stripe. No doubt Russo thought he was in danger of being accused anyway.

Much has been written about the fall of Jack Spot. Certainly it did stem from his domestic arrangements; he had money and love and had become soft, something unforgiving in a world of predatory violence. The Sabini outfit had suffered in a similar way after being taken over by 'soft' Harry White and now, as the Italian gang under Dimes' leadership, they saw a way back.

Spot was on his way out voluntarily. His business interests were run from an office above what used to be the Galahad Club, which had closed after Jack had become a liability. A trio of disgruntled bookies who sensed his weakness had attacked him and only the intervention of Johnny Carter, who took a razor stripe on his arm, saved him. Spot's exit was not soon enough for Billy Hill, who resented Jack's reputation as the King of Soho. Jack still paraded himself in keeping with his image. However, he sidelined his troops and discontinued the practice of looking after their families when their men went inside. The alliance of Hill and Dimes flowed into the void.

Spot's clubs were broken up and his rackets taken over. It was then that Albert Dimes told Moisha Blueball where to go when he demanded his racecourse pitch dues. He also put it about that Spot was finished, which led to Spot's attack on him. Spot's attackers were a mixture of two gangs: Elephant and Castle reprobates Frankie Fraser and Billy 'Ginger' Dennis represented Hill; Bert 'Battles' Rossi, cadaverous Billy Blythe, a vicious razor thug jailed for three years in 1945 for slashing the face of Detective Peter Vibart, and Bobby Warren were Dimes' men. Likely others were Fraser cohorts Ray Rosa and Dicky Frett, who a week earlier had helped Fraser cut up Johnny Carter as part of the Elephant and Castle vendetta. Jack's wife identified Billy Hill as the man who knocked her husband down with a shillelagh she had brought from Ireland, as a present in happier times. She was identifying any of Hill's crowd put in front of her, but she did not convince police that Hill was one of the attackers.

Jack Spot had no comeback. His money was draining away with his power. He was not a saver and his doomed ventures took him from a reputed £3,000 a week to zilch. To add to his woes, Duncan Webb sued for loss of earnings due to his broken arm. Spot was declared bankrupt in 1956, after which he threw in the towel and settled for occasional appearances at boxing tournaments.

On the day of Spot's discharge from bankruptcy in 1958, Bruce Reynolds was jailed, with Terry Hogan, for wounding an unnamed bookmaker and attacking a police constable. Five years later, Reynolds would be a leading light in the Great Train Robbery. London's underworld scene was changing. Although there was no clear-cut successor to Spot and Hill, the rights of passage passed to younger men: the Nash Brothers from Islington, who quickly faded and left the field open to southeast London's Richardson brothers and east London's Kray brothers. This sort of villainy ended with the close of the 1960s after the principals and many of their troops had been jailed.

THE ELEPHANT BOYS hit the headlines on 29 April 1947 with the murder of Alec DeAntiquis. He was a father of six, gunned down when he drove his motorcycle at three young men running away after a botched attempt to rob a jewellery store in Charlotte Street in the West End. The robbery went disastrously wrong from the start, when the gang parked their stolen car without one of them remaining with it for a getaway. The youngest member misunderstood the plan and blundered into the shop before the others were ready, giving staff members an opportunity to react: one of them set off the burglar alarm. This caused the nervous gang to fire a shot and to club the manager with a revolver.

When the gang ran for their car, they found it boxed in by a lorry. Chris Geraghty shot DeAntiquis in the head, and the three made a run for it. A passer-by tripped the younger robber and jumped on him, but Harryboy Jenkins turned and kicked him in the head. The robbers ran into a building at the back of Tottenham Court Road, where Harryboy hid his raincoat and scarf to avoid being recognised, before they crept back to their homes in south London.

The raincoat yielded clues, and two guns found lying by the Thames at Wapping matched the bullets found in the shop and in the murdered man's head. Within weeks, police traced Henry Charles Jenkins to Weller House, Bermondsey, which led them to his associates, Christopher Geraghty and Terence Rolt. Police charged all three with murder. The gang were identified as part of the Elephant Boys and this showed the spread of the gang. Jenkins and Rolt, born at Borough, and Geraghty from Islington, all now lived in the area once called Jacob's Island, in Bermondsey. Rolt escaped the noose because he was only seventeen, but Jenkins, twenty-three, and Geraghty, twenty-one, hanged at Pentonville on 19 September 1947 in a double execution. The crime formed the basis of the classic British police film *The Blue Lamp*.

Harry's brother Tommy was lucky to escape the same fate in 1944, when he and Ron Hedley ran down and killed retired Royal Navy Captain Ralph Binney. They dragged him beneath their car for over a mile, after he tried to stop them driving away from a smash-and-grab at a jewellery shop near the Bank of England. They abandoned their car in Tooley Street, Bermondsey, close to where they lived. Thomas Jenkins was jailed for eight years and Hedley reprieved from a death sentence.

The Carters' brother-in-law, Tony Reuter, born in Southwark in 1931, was well known at Elephant and Castle, where he was generally recognised as leader of the Elephant Boys. He was a colourful character, instantly recognisable by his habit of standing with a slight forward stoop, hands folded behind his back under his open Crombie, passing the time of day with friends and sycophants who liked to be seen talking to him. He was a ferocious fighter with a history of gang violence in his local manor and in the West End. He started out with probation for joy-riding, followed by prison for grievous bodily harm. He soon became leader of the younger branch of the Elephant gang, with a crew of forty or fifty behind him. In 1950, his mob raided the Walworth Road Boys in a youth club opposite East Street market and smashed the place to pieces, upending a snooker table and launching it through a window.

The 'boys' fought other gangs from south London, particularly Bermondsey and Brixton, then took on gangs from the other side of the Thames, in east London and at the Angel, before moving in on the West End. Reuter's greatest solo fight was in the West End in 1954, when his arm was deliberately jogged while playing snooker at the AA Billiards Hall in Leicester Square. He responded by laying out a relative of the celebrated robber and prison escapee Alfie Hinds with his cue. He was chased from the hall by half a dozen men but then launched into them, dropping them all over the place before calmly catching a bus home. The club, where I once laid out Tommy Smithson with a billiard ball, closed shortly after.

In 1955, Tony was rounded up by the *People* newspaper to attend Billy Graham's evangelical mission at Wembley Stadium. They dressed him as a Teddy Boy with a bootlace tie, although he refused to wear the lurid suit so despised by the 'boys'. He then gave a series of interviews to the *People* as 'King of the Teddy Boys', telling the world how reformed a character he was. He failed to complete his tale when he was arrested for a savage attack on PC Anthony Stills, whom he hit with a bottle at the Elephant coffee stall when he tried to arrest Reuter over an argument with two girls. That brought him five years. In 1962, he was given a coming home party in Kennington, which erupted into a free-for-all and a prison sentence for assault with intent to murder.

Mickey Roff, born in Southwark, southeast London, in 1931, was a cousin of the Carter brothers. He received his first conviction in 1943, at the age of thirteen, for store-breaking, for which he was sent to Approved School. This was followed by probation for stealing and three years Borstal for burglary, changed to imprisonment when he was convicted of unlawful wounding in 1950 for attacking two men with a blunt instrument. This was followed by fines for driving while disqualified and assaulting police, and a sentence in 1953 for stealing from lorries. Mickey loved his driving, but not insuring his car, which brought him a fine, three months imprisonment and disqualification in 1954. Soon after release, he was back in prison, this time for twelve months for actual bodily harm and possessing an offensive weapon.

In 1955, he was strolling in the West End when a car driver pulled up to ask directions. Unfortunately for the driver, it was at a time when Roff was on guard against an attack by Frankie Fraser. He shattered the windscreen with his fist and took off. The commotion attracted passers-by and two constables, all of whom struggled for fifteen minutes to overcome him. Roff explained to a magistrate that he came from a tough area where, if a car pulled up beside you, it meant trouble. The magistrate thought about it, then gave him three months for the copper and a fine for wilful damage to the car. A year later came three months and disqualification for life, for driving while disqualified; all rounded off by twenty-one days for assaulting another police officer.

After the attack on the Carter brothers, Roff took charge of matters concerning the family. In Dean Street's 41 Club, he had a stand-up fistfight with Stepney's Mickey Holland, an ally of the Harris brothers and friend of the Krays, in which Holland came off worse. Naturally, Holland returned the compliment. With a dozen others, he engaged Roff's gang in a free-for-all at the 41. Roff and a large southeast London crew then went in search of Holland in east London, targeting a café run by Holland gang member Fred Thompson, who had been involved in the 41 fight and was manager of Berney's café on Commercial Road, Whitechapel.

On 11 November 1956, a convoy of cars carrying up to thirty men mounted two separate onslaughts, tearing the café apart and smashing everything that could be broken. Mickey Roff, brandishing an automatic pistol, led the raid; others wielded swords, crowbars, machetes, axes and hammers. Thompson ran upstairs, where he was cornered by Roff, who tried to get him to disclose Holland's location by shoving the gun into his mouth: at this, Thompson passed out. When he revived, he crawled under a table and listened to the mayhem going on below.

Five came to trial, at which witnesses were given police protection. Roff was cited by police as the 'self-appointed leader of a gang of about thirty hooligans', who had never done any honest work and lived with his mother. He was jailed for three years. Lennie Sexton, an illegal street bookmaker who carried a sword, got twenty-one months; Albert Clark, fifteen months; Reg Gunner, nine months; and Jim Wiggins, a term in Borstal. Most likely, some of the Carters were part of the assault. Leonard Ronald Sexton was jailed again in 1966 for carrying a gun and a stack of forged banknotes.

Mickey Holland, born in 1932 in Finsbury, was a typical young tearaway, constantly in trouble over trifling matters before progressing into more serious activity. On 25 January 1958, he and his hooligans visited the Vincents Club in Batty Street, Commercial Road, Stepney. They had the usual drinks, got drunk and turned on a group of men who were at the bar. Pushing and shoving turned into a fight, which only stopped when the Maltese owners evicted the men who had been attacked 'to avoid trouble'. Mickey's group were still up for a fight and turned their spleen on the Malts, who were about fifteen strong. Mickey's head was cut open, while his pal George Flay, who went out on the pavement to fight the club's manager, found himself fighting a half-dozen. All in all, Holland's team took a beating and retreated to the Umberstone Billiard Hall to plan a comeback. Someone thought of burning the Vincents Club down and a can of petrol was bought and carried to the club. Bob Woodford poured it on the stairs and Terry Wilson struck a match, lit a piece of paper and dropped it. Whoosh! Terry's eyebrows went up with the stairway and they ran from the scene. The fire reached the bar and burned Anthony Francisca's hands as he tried to put it out.

Six men were arrested. Holland was able to prove he was in hospital having his head stitched when the fire started and was only charged with causing malicious damage. Flay, Bill Fisher and Bill MacFarlane were charged with grievous bodily harm; Wilson, whose singed face gave him away, and Woodford, were charged with arson.

The 1950s were rounded off with the hanging of twenty-five-year-old Ron Marwood at Pentonville, on 8 May 1959. Marwood and his Angel gang had been drinking heavily and got into a number of fights, culminating in a brawl with the rival Finsbury Park gang, outside Grey's Dance Academy in Seven Sisters Road, Holloway. When PC Raymond Summers tried to arrest him, Marwood stabbed him to death.

The Angel gang were notorious at the time for serial gang fights and for welcoming battles with gangs from all parts of London, including a brawl in Old Street with the Elephant Boys. Knives, axes, knuckledusters and coshes of all sorts were liberally used, often causing severe injuries. Six-foot four Marwood revelled in his reputation as a 'top man'. Both the Krays and Nashes claim to have hidden Marwood, until he gave himself up to explain how he accidentally killed PC Summers. As it was friends near Holloway Road who harboured Marwood, the Islington Nash family's claims are the more likely ones. When it was shown the knife was a ten-inch stiletto and that PC Summers had been stabbed in the back with considerable force, the jury rejected a plea of manslaughter. There were disturbances inside and outside Pentonville on the day of his execution.

Final Bows

BERTHA WEINER, who headed the gang of thieves and receivers reminiscent of Fagin's brood, died in Mile End in 1925, aged seventy-five. Her brother, Ludvig, and his sons were deported.

The Bidwell brothers complained bitterly about their incarceration in British prisons, a case of doing the crime and carping about doing the time. George was released in 1887, due to ill health, and Austin pardoned in 1892. They pegged out pretty much together, in March 1899. Both were described as paupers and it has been suggested that George topped himself. George MacDonnell, also released in 1892, went to France, where he was arrested for forgery. After that he went nuts.

Eddie Guerin, once described as a soft spoken, tall, distinguished criminal of the gentlemanly type, went from flamboyant international bank robber to snivelling petty thief. He lived in hovels in the Hoxton district and was arrested for numerous thefts in London and seaside towns, where he targeted hotels. In Portland Prison he was beaten by a friend of Charlie Cubine, who was given a reciprocal beating by Elephant Boy Charlie Gordon (Eddie at least had one friend). He was sentenced to jail in 1931 for forging cheques, but won an appeal after stating he had only two fingers on one hand. He was convicted in 1932, aged seventy, for stealing a handbag. He pleaded for leniency on the basis of being penniless and married with four kids, but his record was so dire, Sir Percival Clarke said he must go to prison for twelve months. His last conviction was in 1939, aged seventy-seven, when he was jailed for one month as a suspected person at Epsom racecourse.

Guerin was evacuated during the early days of the London Blitz and died on 5 December 1940 in Bury, Lancashire, aged seventy-eight. He was buried in a pauper's grave. His brother Paddy served many years in American prisons for bank robbery. Chicago May served over ten years of her sentence and Charlie Cubine fifteen: both were deported to America on their release. In 1928, the year before her death, May Churchill Sharpe penned *Chicago May: Her Story*. Not to be outshone, Eddie Guerin wrote his version in 1929: *Crime: The Autobiography of a Crook*, (published in America as *I Was A Bandit*). May passed away in Philadelphia that same year.

Jim Lockett, of pearl necklace fame, was another who fell from the lofty height of international thief and criminal mastermind. He was born in Southwark in 1861 and had an association with the Elephant and Castle gang, before transferring himself and his jemmy to Holborn for a career in burglary at home and abroad. He led a gang of burglars in a rash of raids across Hampstead and Highgate, which only stopped when he was recruited by Kemmy Grizzard to assist in finding a buyer for the pearls. He became a jeweller and a commission agent and owner of a fine house at Golder's Green, from where he squandered riches harvested through the investment of his ill-gottens. In 1938, aged seventy-six, he was jailed for six weeks for loitering at West End Post Offices with the intention of stealing from women's handbags. He died in the 1940s. Lockett is often regarded as underworld nobility, but in reality he was a chancer who lived off women, before deserting them for richer pastures.

Arthur Harding, stalwart of the East End Vendetta, died in 1962.

Joseph 'Kemmy' Grizzard was born as Grisaard, in 1867 in Whitechapel, and by 1900 was known to be a prolific dealer in 'hot' jewellery. During his prison sentence for the theft of the pearl necklace, he turned from master criminal to supergrass, supplying police with information on thieves and receivers. A final prison sentence broke his health and he died in 1923.

Edward Spencer, one-time leader of the Titanic, was acquitted of manslaughter in 1936, at age fifty-four, after knocking William Hageloch under a bus in Shoreditch High Street. Hageloch was a public house busker who pestered Spencer for money. Spencer died shortly after from cancer. Leading light in the Titanic, Harry Bargery, gave way to the stresses of villainy and bareknuckle fighting: he died in 1926, aged forty-three.

Freddie ford is sometimes confused with Frederick Henry Ford, who was acquitted of manslaughter in 1924. However this fellow was eight years younger, lived at a different address and had a different occupation. Freddie eventually gave up his nightclub enterprise and went into the restaurant and hotel business. In 1946, he ran a popular fish restaurant in Soho. In 1951, he was approached by Jack Spot and Billy Hill to put up money for yet another drinking club in Ham Yard. He invested but refused to front the club, which folded very quickly leaving all concerned out of pocket. His opinion of Spot and Hill was that they were nothing more than spivs. Freddie died soon after, still a wealthy man.

Alice Diamond served her time for the Lambeth riot in Holloway Prison, which did not cure her: she was convicted on numerous occasions, under different aliases, including Alice Blake, which may have been her birth name. She lived an unashamedly lavish lifestyle, splashing money around and being generous to her friends: she also tutored a future Queen of the Forty Thieves, Shirley Pitts. Her last traceable conviction was in 1929 as Alice Evans, when she was arrested with Billy Hill's sisters, Maggie Hughes and Dollie Mays, after they were seen going from shop to shop in Oxford Street, with Bert Pitts following in a motor car. She died in the 1950s.

Maggie Hill (Hughes) spent much of her life in jail. According to Billy Hill's memoirs, Maggie married burglar Reuben 'Brummy' Sparkes, who is shown in a photograph visiting Billy in Borstal. As Billy was in Borstal in about 1927, this places the photo at about 1928: a time when Maggie was due for release from prison for her part in the Lambeth riot, and when she was still the wife of Alfred Hughes. The answer to this conundrum must surely be that the man in the photo is Alfred Hughes and that Billy had followed his practice of using pseudonyms. Alfred was born in 1887 and was therefore eleven years older than Maggie, whom he married when she was seventeen and possibly regarded him as a protector. Billy says that her husband took to beating Maggie and flogging off the family furniture, for which he was beaten by Archie Hill. Maggie's last sentence was in about 1938 for stabbing a policeman in the eye with a hatpin, which is ironic as, by this time, Maggie had only one eye herself. In her latter years she was reduced to working as a prostitutes' maid and a police informant, putting violent pimps away on behalf of girls who did not dare do it themselves. She died in the 1970s, possibly by suicide.

Otavio 'Darby' Sabini was working as a turf commission agent when he died from splenic anaemia at his home at Old Shoreham Road, Hove, Sussex, not far from Hove Greyhound Stadium, on 4 October 1950. He was registered as being sixty-two years of age. His name is recorded as Ollovia Sabini due to the illegible handwriting of the Registrar, something not uncommon in birth, marriage and death records. His wife, Annie, reported his death. Darby's nickname probably stemmed from being left-handed; Jim McDonald, who was left-handed himself, was puzzled when sometimes he was referred to as 'darby', until told it was a term applied to southpaw boxers. The Sabini chieftain boxed as a welterweight. Annie died in 1978 and she and Darby are buried in Hove Cemetery.

Fred Sabini died, aged sixty, in central London in 1942; John Sabini in Paddington in 1964; Joe in Enfield in 1970; George in Haringey in 1977; and Harry in Islington in 1978. Sabini associate Alf Solomon died in central London in 1947, aged fifty-five. His pal Eddie Emanuel checked in his bucket and sponge in Edmonton, north London, in 1943. Emanuel's partner Gershon Harris died in Willesden, in 1952.

Pasqualino Papa, who boxed as Bert Marsh, was born in 1894, in Islington, to Giuseppe Papa, an ice cream vendor. As a young man, he took part in 'ice cream wars', battling for best sites for a prosperous living. Fights for street pitches, for everything from ice cream to baked potatoes, were commonplace. It was a simple step from there to racecourse pitch warfare, which he engaged in for most of his life. He died in Islington on 3 October 1976.

Big Alf White was not destined to make old bones. He made a brief comeback in 1938, when he led a riot that wrecked Harringay Greyhound Stadium, after two dogs tied for first place. But his star had become a white dwarf by which time Jack Spot was a rising sun and not at all sentimental about old-timers trying to do a bit of business in his firmament. Spot wound up some East End tearaways to take Alf down a peg; they gave him such a beating at Harringay Stadium that he never fully recovered. His energies and will sapped, he died at his son's home in Camden in late 1942, aged fifty-four. His son, Alf Junior, died in the same period. Alf's other son, Harry, died in 1972 at his home in Copenhagen Street, Islington, the street where his father had been born. Alf's daughter, Caroline, married Albert Dimes' brother, Victor (one year after he was sentenced to eight months with hard labour for pocket-picking).

Michael McCausland died in 1933, aged forty-three; his wife Julia in 1936, aged forty-six; and elder brother Matt, in 1953, aged sixty-eight. Tommy Mack died in Bethnal Green in 1953, aged fifty-seven. George Sage died from tuberculosis in Archway Hospital in June 1947. His wife Ellen died in 1967, aged eighty.

Frederick Arthur Gilbert, in spite of his many traumas, lived to a ripe eighty-two years. He died at his home near King's Cross in early 1975. His adherent, John Thomas Phillips, died in St. Pancras Hospital in 1970, aged seventy. Arthur 'Toddy' Phillips died in about 1985.

Jack 'Dodger' Mullins, also known as Jacob Cohen, and described as a retired bookmaker's clerk, died from cancer of the bowel on 2 September 1967 in a hospice for the terminally ill at Donisthorpe Hall, Shadwell Lane, Leeds, Yorkshire, aged seventy-four. I believe the hospice was primarily for the use of elderly Jewish persons, hence Jack emphasising his Jewish half.

Harry Distelman, born in Mile End in 1905, was a lowlife pickpocket and racecourse pest with six convictions for assault: he was killed in a Wardour Street club fight with Antonio Mancini, Albert Dimes and others, in May 1941. Mancini hanged at Pentonville Prison five months later, aged thirtynine. In later years, it emerged Mancini was given an opportunity to plead guilty to manslaughter. He was so confident of acquittal, on the grounds of self-defence, that he turned the offer down.

Andrew Towey, Eddie Emanuel's opposite number with the Brummagems, died at Ilkley, Yorkshire, in 1969. Kimber enforcer Tommy Armstrong died in Birmingham in 1931, aged fifty-six, and Jack Allard in Southwark in 1925.

Billy Kimber continued to wage war on the Sabini-Solomon-White alliance with the assistance of Wal McDonald, George Sage and Tommy Benneworth. In 1927, he and Bert McDonald fled to the United States after firing shots into the Sabini headquarters at Clerkenwell. In America, hinted at in later years by Wag McDonald, it is probable Kimber that killed a man in Phoenix, Arizona, who had failed to come up with money owed for a favour. Kimber and Bert left Phoenix in a hurry to meet up with Wag in Los Angeles. Bert became connected to the Los Angeles Mafia through Wag.

Kimber quickly fled to Chicago, where he was hidden by Capone lieutenant Murray Humphreys, until he was smuggled back to England. In September 1929, Bert McDonald was killed on orders of Nick Licata, who had been humiliated by the McDonald brothers on behalf of Los Angeles mob boss Jack Dragna. Kimber was joined back home by Wag, who fled America after killing his brother's assassin. They operated a series of land and securities swindles organised by Jake Factor, the Briton who had left England for the States and returned to take the stock markets apart. Factor, the half-brother of cosmetics genius Max Factor, skipped back to America, where he is part of gangster folklore. *Elephant Boys – Tales of London and Los Angeles Underworlds* gives the full account of Wag McDonald's ten-year stay in the United States. He was a minder there to Dragna and bodyguard to Charlie Chaplin and other Hollywood film stars, such as Colleen Moore, Barbara Kent and Neva Gerber, when silent movies were giving way to talkies.

Billy Kimber is said to have been on the managerial staff at Wimbledon Greyhound Stadium in 1931. The business has no record of this, however some of its records were destroyed when the stadium was bombed in World War Two. It appears Billy never married and he disappears from sight, and records, in the early 1930s. Billy could well have died overseas – perhaps he returned to America. Ada McDonald believed he had gone to Chicago and never returned; Australia has also been suggested. It must be remembered that he was suspected of a murder in Arizona and might have changed his name.

Wag and Wal McDonald died in the same month in 1940; Wag on 3 October at Union Street, Borough, and Wal on 22 October at his home in Old Kent Road. They are buried side-by-side in Streatham Park Cemetery. Wag remained unmarried, but Wal married a widow with five children a few years before his death. Tom McDonald, using the alias Tom King, had his career cut short when he drowned overseas somewhere around 1919 while returning from Australia, after serving in the Royal Navy during World War One. The circumstances are unknown. Jim McDonald died on 26 April 1972, at Charlton, southeast London.

Tommy Benneworth narrowly missed death on 8 September 1940, when his father's print workshop, under the arches in

Silwood Street, Bermondsey, was bombed. His brother William and eight-year-old nephew Terence were killed. In 1945, when first his mother, then his father, passed away in the middle of the year, Tommy went on a rampage around Elephant and Castle pubs. This was followed by a visit to the Yorkshire Grey in Theobalds Road, a prime seat of the White family. Harry White, who had taken over the reins from his tougher father Alf and was reeling from attacks by Jack Spot's gang, fled to his business premises in Farringdon Road and stayed there until he was assured Tommy had gone home to Walworth to sober up. Tommy supported Jack Spot in the 1947 destruction of the White brothers' gang.

In his latter days, Tommy, who was overweight and permanently saturated with alcohol, must have had difficulty keeping up with the action. He finally succumbed to bronchial pneumonia and cancer of the throat in King's College Hospital, Camberwell, on 21 December 1958, aged sixty-four. Some say his body was so well pickled internally that little needed doing to his carcass to ensure it lasted 1,000 years.

When he was released from Dartmoor in the 1940s, Ruby Sparks retired from a life of crime, settling for a new life as a minor celebrity. He died in 1991, and is remembered as the doyen of organised smash-and-grab on a grand scale.

In 1974, Franny Daniels was acquitted of the gangland murder of 'Scotch Jack' Buggy, after which he went to live with family in New York. He returned to London to die in 1992. Buggy was shot dead in 1967: the initial suspect was Franny's nephew Charles 'Waggy' Whitnall, but attempts to extradite him from France were dropped on the basis of insufficient evidence.

Jack Spot decided to immigrate to Canada and got as far as a jail cell in Quebec, where he sat for two weeks until deportation. He remained bitter at his treatment by Billy Hill and his Clerkenwell cronies. Sadly, Rita left him when he became too difficult to live with. He lived out his last days in Hounslow, west London, under the Heathrow flight path: he died in a residential care home in Isleworth on 12 March 1995, as John Colmore. He had the consolation of knowing that first, Albert Dimes in 1971, and then Billy Hill, who went out to the echo of Auld Lang Syne on the first day of 1984, had preceded him to wherever retired gangsters go when they fade away. Rita Comer/Colmore died from cancer in 1988.

Albert George Dimeo was born in Hamilton, Lanark, in 1914, to Nicola and Louisa Dimeo, who had married in 1910 in Glasgow. He left Scotland as a young man. His 1945 Holborn marriage to Rosie Southey has two entries, under Dimeo and Dimes. He backed Eddie Richardson financially in his Atlantic Machines enterprise, which also employed Frankie Fraser to help push sales of their one-armed bandits. This endeavour ended when Eddie and Frankie were jailed for the fight at Mr Smith and the Witchdoctor's nightclub and the Richardson gang's downfall in the so-called torture trial, all in the 1960s. Albert succumbed to cancer at River Street, Islington. His death is registered as both Dimes and Dimeo. He is buried in Beckenham, southeast London, where he had another home.

Short, but dangerous, Vittorio Russo, aka Vic Russo, Scarface Jock, was born in 1918, near Glasgow. He arrived in London in the 1940s and worked for a while for Jack Spot. Because Spot bailed him out when he was in debt, he refused to take a few cuts on his already scarred frame in order to have Spot jailed where Billy Hill's associates could get at him. He took the money, but avoided the stripes. Jock returned to his home in Scotland and died there in 1982.

Billy Hill slipped towards retirement by managing gambling clubs for other backers. In 1959, he was arrested for running illegal gaming clubs, in Walworth Road and Belgravia: two vastly different locations. After that, he settled for celebrity status. He went a bit loopy before he died in his flat in Moscow Road, Bayswater, where he lived alone. Haunted by the thought that old enemies were waiting for him in the street, he did not go out much and had his comestibles left outside his door. He is buried in the outer reaches of City of London Cemetery, Manor Park, close to the international rail line trundling its wares into Stratford, and many miles from his north west London turf. No peace for the wicked, Bill.

Freddie 'Slip' Sullivan was stabbed to death by his girlfriend, Mary Cooper, in January 1955, after an argument over a bowl of stew. He was forty-three. Mary was not charged with any offence, even bad cooking. Jock Wyatt died in King's Cross in 1973 and his pal Eddie Raimo, the hard Alan Ladd lookalike, in Islington in 1980.

Mickey Roff continued as an incorrigible rogue until his death in 1991. Danny Roff, born in 1960 to Mickey's brother Daniel, almost certainly killed Great Train Robber Charlie Wilson in 1990, and was himself shot to death at the second attempt in 1997. Mickey Holland died around 2000. Tony Reuter passed away in Southwark in 2004.

Johnny Carter, who had remained loyal to Spot, began his decline on 15 April 1956, when he was badly cut in a savage brawl in Hutton Road, Lambeth. Frankie Fraser, Dicky 'Dido' Frett, Ray Rosa and one other, had tracked him to the Tanker-ville Arms, where he was drinking with his wife and a friend. When he saw them enter, he jumped over the bar, ran through the pub and out of another door, where they caught up with him. He fought them for 200 yards, before running into a garage and locking himself in the toilet. When his attackers smashed through the door with hammers and a three-foot stopcock, he wrested a sharpened piece of metal from Frett and drove them off, leaving him requiring sixty stitches. Fraser, Frett and Rosa were charged with assault. In court, Carter was described as the leader of the Elephant and Castle gang. Frett and Rosa received seven years apiece: Fraser's case was not proceeded, with as he was about to stand trial for the attack on Jack Spot that had taken place two weeks after the attack on

Carter. For that attack he too received seven years, Blythe five years, and Dennis and Rossi four years apiece. William 'Billy' Blythe died in a prison hospital in 1957.

Harry Carter was attacked outside his fruit and veg shop in Trundley's Road, Deptford, a few days after his brother Johnny had been slashed. Harry took on six attackers in a fight that spilled into his shop, cucumbers and cabbages against crowbars; even so he fought them off, suffering only minor damage. The two south London scallywags Johnny and Benny Harris went to jail: the others were not caught. An attack outside the World Turned Upside Down, in Old Kent Road, saw Harry with a broken leg and a chase after Johnny, who escaped in his car only to run out of petrol: he was forced to jump into the Grand Surrey Canal, at that time a stinking ditch.

On 21 July 1958, Johnny Carter was in the Highball Club in Lancaster Gate, part owned by Spot's wife Rita, when the Harris brothers and a dozen others smashed their way. They intended to wreck the place – and Jack Spot with it. Johnny Harris was knocked down by Carter, while Spot stood there screaming at the invaders. Carter then chased Benny Harris from the club and saw him knocked down by another of Spot's minders. Police put a guard outside the Highball after hearing it was to be attacked by a 'Soho gang'; it failed when a gang broke in during the night, piled furniture in the middle of the large lounge and set fire to it. The club closed for repairs, but did not reopen when Rita refused to continue financing it. Johnny and Benny Harris were acquitted, together with Finsbury tearaway John More.

In September 1958, Johnny Carter was mentioned in the trial at the Central Criminal Court of Ronnie Dimond, John Flanaghan and Luigi Fraser: three north London villains, who were jailed for threatening hoteliers and restaurateurs with a vicious assortment of bicycle chains, hatchets and the like. It was suggested the three were associates of Jack Spot and were contending to take over protection rights in Paddington, currently enjoyed by Carter. Dimond, who was born in Finsbury, followed in the footsteps of Gilbert and Phillips as the leader of the Finsbury Boys and their allies the Angel gang.

In an interview in the *Star* newspaper, Johnny Carter denied being a protection racketeer known as 'Top Johnny'. He pointed out he worked as a barrow boy, selling his wares in the streets of Victoria, and that his only desire was to own his own fruit shop: readers may have noted how often purveyors of fruit appear in the annals of London's gangland. He did admit to earning £20 a week as Spot's bodyguard, making him a 'thousand a year man', the out-of-reach desire of working class men in the late 1950s. As usual with such interviews, he had a selective memory and was able to bemoan his lot in life, starting with his first arrest at twelve, followed by seventeen years of sporadic custody. He could not recall just how many men he had cut, and was very sorry he had been so nasty.

Carter continued to mind and manage a number of West End drinking and gambling clubs for Spot and continued as a bookie. His last cut was from his surgeon, who removed his larynx (and his voice), leaving smoke to billow from under his shirt collar every time he took a drag: but throat cancer still got him. He died in Lewisham Hospital in 1991, the same year as his cousin Mickey Roff. His father, Henry, had been attacked in 1925 in a Bethnal Green brawl involving Dodger Mullins. Harry Carter died in the 1980s and Euey in 1988. Tommy Brindle died in Kent in 1984, Bobby in 1987 and Jimmy in 1990, both in Southwark.

THIS ACCOUNT OF the gangs of London ends with the 1950s. By the close of this period, improved regulation of racecourses and point-to-point tracks had put an end to racing gangs. Protection demands on restaurants and clubs continued through the Fifties and Sixties, gradually receding as large-scale crime: today, corner shops are targeted by street gangs seeking money to feed drug habits. The 1960s belonged to the Richardson, Kray and Nash gangs, followed by other families in south and north London, before London's gangster elite moved to the suburbs: this left the inner city to teenage gangsters fighting over street territory. There are more gangs now – in some parts of London every street seems to have one – but the romance has gone.

Today, Islington and Camden Town struggle to maintain their earthiness in the face of growing occupation by political and media classes; even Hackney and Bethnal Green resound to the clink of wine glasses in the hands of the chattering classes. Borough, once the grimmest of places, now has delightful wine bars: on Thursdays, Fridays and Saturdays, the public are welcomed in Borough Market to sample a wide assortment of delicatessen foods. Elephant and Castle, always a challenging environment, became more so in the 1950s when a grotesque shopping centre scarred this historic landmark. It awaits promised regeneration but, as always, south London endures its position at the bottom of the list of the Mayor's priorities.

Contemporary Gangsters

Born:

1860s   Eddie Guerin, Charlie Pitts, Albert and James
               Gorman, Jim Lockett.

1870s   Freddic Ford, George Sage, Wag McDonald,
               Jack Allard, Arthur Phillips Snr, Moey Levy,
               George Moss, Tommy Armstrong, Geor-
               gie Wooder, George West, Chicago May
               Churchill.

1880s   Hymie Eisenberg, Arthur Harding, Eddie
               Emanuel, Gershon Harris, Johnny McCarthy,
               Alf White, Edward Spencer (Emms), Darby
               Sabini, Billy Kimber, Wal, Bert and Jim
               McDonald, Henry Byfield, Charlie Gordon,
               Sam Sheldon, Bill Beach, Tommy Ingram,
               Sam Garvin, George Mooney, Alfie Hughes,
               Danny Driscoll, Charlie and Freddie Wooder,
               Matt McCausland.

1890s   Freddie Gilbert, John Phillips, Tom McDon-
               ald, Jack Mullins, Timmy Hayes, Tommy
               Benneworth, Joe and Johnny Jackson, Alf and
               Henry Solomon, Joe Sabini, Antonio Mancini,
               Tommy Mack, Jim Ford, Mike McCausland,

1900s	Alice Diamond, Maggie Hill, William Plommer, Ed Rowlands, Arthur Phillips, Harry Sabini, Pasqualino Papa (Bert Marsh), Eddie Raimo, Jock Wyatt, Georgie Spain, Teddy Hughes, Teddy Machin, Ruby Sparks, Lawrence and Wilfred Fowler, Jimmy Wooder, Jimmy Spenser, Gert Scully.
1910s	Jack Spot, Billy Hill, Franny Daniels, Freddie Sullivan, Vic Russo, Alec and Albert Dimes, Billy Blythe, Bert Rossi, Jimmy Spinks, Eugene Carter, Billy, Tommy and Georgie Brindle.
1920s	Frankie Fraser, Tommy Smithson, Johnny and Henry Carter, Bobby and Jimmy Brindle, Billy Dennis, Ray and Jackie Rosa.
1930s	Reg and Ron Kray, Charlie and Eddie Richardson, Jimmy and Johnny Nash, Mickey and Ronnie Roff, Mickey Holland

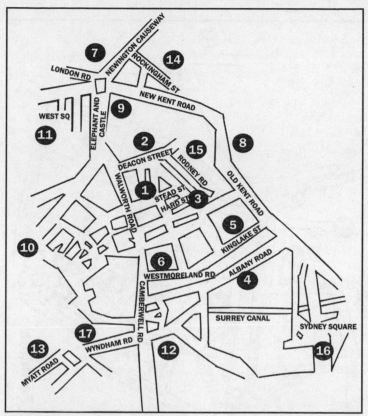

Southeast London Families

1. Frankie Fraser and Ada McDonald.
2. Dicky Frett.
3. Brindle Family and George Moss.
4. Mickey Roff.
5. Carter Family.
6. Reuter Family.
7. Pitts Family and Len Winter.
8. Callaghan Family.
9. Garrett Family and Rosa Family.
10. Dennis Family and Morbin Family.
11. Alice Diamond, Fred Sabini, McDonald, Fraser and Gorman families.
12. Porritt family and Watson (Ruby Sparks).
13. Tommy Benneworth.
14. Bobby Brindle.
15. Harris family.
16. Johnny Carter.
17. Richardson Family.

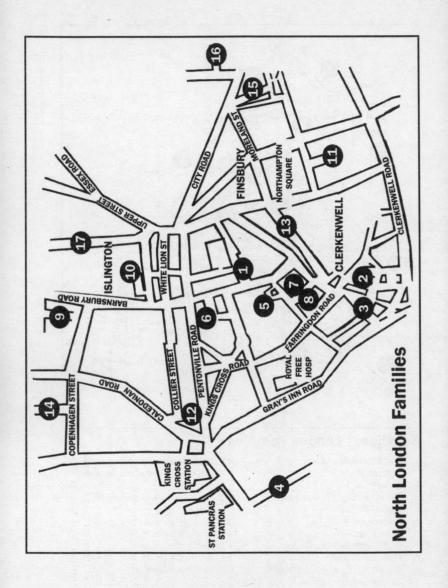

North London Families

North London Families Key

1. River Street, home of Albert Dimes.
2. Bakers Row, Joe Sabini born at number 10.
3. Mount Pleasant, George and Harry Sabini born at number 29.
4. Judd Street, home of Fred Rye.
5. St. Helena Street, home of Darby and Annie Sabini in 1913.
6. Cruickshank Street, home of Pasqualino Papa (Bert Marsh).
7. Easton Street, home of Harry Sabini.
8. Easton Place, home of Fred and Darby Sabini (1890s).
9. Gainford Street, home of Eddie Raimo.
10. Grant Street (Warren Street), Billy Kimber's home at the time he was shot. Clerkenwell Boys.
11. Malta Street, home of Jock Wyatt.
12. Northdown Street, Sam Baws, licensee of Prince of Wales.
13. Myddleton Street, home of Billy Blythe.
14. Bemerton Street, Bemerton Boys.
15. Macclesfield Road, Michael McCausland attacked by White Gang. Home of John Phillips.
16. Nile Street, centre of the Titanic.
17. Liverpool Street, home of John Cheesewright.

Farringdon Road	Alf and Carrie White's florist shop.
Grays Inn Road	Scene of a number of incidents including the Portpool Road shooting.
Barnsbury Road	Barnsbury Boys.
Collier Street	Darby and Annie Sabini at number 70. Scene of shooting of Billy Kimber.
Copenhagen Street	Alf White born.
Northampton Sq.	Home of Alf and Carrie White and their sons Alf, Harry and Billy in 1935.
White Lion Street	White Lion Street Gang.
Moreland Street	Home of Freddie Gilbert in 1920s.
Essex Road	Home of Arthur Phillips.
Upper Street	Spanish Gang.

Bibliography

Bean, J.P., *The Sheffield Gang Wars* (1981), Sheffield, D. & D. Publications.

Bell. L., *Bella of Blackfriars* (1961), London, Odhams Press.

Bidwell, A., *From Wall Street to Newgate* (1895), Hartford, Conn., Bidwell Publishing.

Butler, J. and F., *The Fight Game* (1954), The World's Work: Kingswood.

Cheyney, P., *Making Crime Pay* (1944), London, Faber & Faber.

Churchill, M., *Chicago May: Her Story* (1928), London, Samson Lowe.

Clark, N., *All In The Game* (1935), London, Methuen & Co.

Cornish, G.W., *Cornish of the Yard* (1935), London, John Lane.

Deyong, M., *Everybody Boo* (1951), London, Stanley Paul.

Divall, T., *Scoundrels and Scallywags* (1929), London, Ernest Benn.

Fabian, R., *London After Dark* (1954), London, The Naldrett Press.

Felstead S., *The Underworld of London* (1923), New York, E P Dutton.

Felstead S., *Shades of Scotland Yard* (1950), London, John Long.

Firmin, S., Scotland Yard – The Inside Story (1948), London, Hutchinson.

Gamman, Lorraine, *Gone Shopping* (1996), London, Signet.

Greeno, E., *War on the Underworld* (1960), London, John Long.

Gordon, C.G., *Crooks of the Underworld* (1929), London, Geoffrey Bles.

Guerin, E., *Crime: The Autobiography of a Crook* (1929), London, John Murray.

Hart, E.T., *Britain's Godfather* (1993), London, True Crime Books.

Higgins, R. *In the Name of the Law* (1958), London, John Long.

Hill, B., *Boss of Britain's Underworld* (1955), London, The Naldrett Press.

Horan, J.D. and Swiggett, H., *The Pinkerton Story* (1952), William Heinemann Ltd.

Ingram, G. and Mackenzie, D., *Hell's Kitchen* (1930), London, Herbert Jenkins.

Jackson, S., *An Indiscreet Guide to Soho* (1946), London, Muse Arts.

Kingston, G., *Dramatic Days at the Old Bailey* (n.d.), London, S. Paul.

Leach, C.E., *On Top of the Underworld* (1933), London, Sampson Low & Co.

McDonald, B., *Elephant Boys – Tales of London and Los Angeles Underworlds* (2000), Edinburgh, Mainstream.

Macintyre, B., *The Napoleon Of Crime: The Life and Times of Adam Worth* (1997), London, HarperCollins.

Morton, J., *Gangland Volume 2* (1994), London, Little, Brown.

Samuel, R., *East End Underworld* (1981), London, Routledge & Kegan Paul.

Sharpe, F. D., *Sharpe of the Flying Squad* (1938), London, John Long.

Smithson, G., *Raffles in Real Life* (1930), London, Hutchinson.

Spenser, J., *Limey* (1958), London, Transworld Publishers.

Walter, G., *White Ties and Fisticuffs* (1951), London, Hutchinson's Library of Sports and Pastimes.

Wensley, F., *Detective Days* (1931), London, Cassell & Co.

Other sources are *Daily Mirror*, *The Times*, *The Star*, *Hackney Gazette*, *Islington Gazette*, *South London Press*, *Brixton Free Press*, records of the Central Criminal Court at the Old Bailey, Metropolitan Police Records, National Archives.

Index

Weiner, Ludvig 259–260, 339

Weiss, Hymie 95

Welch, Bob 324

Wellman, Ada 222, 224

Welsh, Freddie 139

Wensley, Det. Ins. Fred 47–48, 49, 91–92, 141, 260

West End gang 125, 140, 167, 257

West, George 172, 175, 181, 352

West, Robert 68

Westbury, Billy 157

Wheeler, Bob 91

Wheeler, John 75

White, Alf 34, 46, 100–102, 104, 107, 124–125, 139–140, 146–147, 151–152, 156–157, 159, 163–164, 167–169, 172–176, 179–180, 191, 200–203, 218, 231, 271, 274– 278, 285–287, 343, 346, 352

Alf White, Jnr. 274, 277–278, 343

White, Alf, Snr. 100–101

White, Billy 276, 277

White, Caroline 101, 277, 343

White, Frederick 217

White, George 82

White, Harry 274–275, 278–279, 285, 295–296, 330, 332, 343, 346

White Lion Street gang 80–81, 101, 159

Whitnall, Charles 'Waggy'

320, 324, 346

Wiggins, Jim 336

Wilcox, William 94

Wild, Jonathan 15–18

Wilkins, Bert 256–257

Wilkins, Harry 256

Williams, Arthur 141

Williams, David 63

Willis, Harry 86

Willmore, Frederick 60–62

Wilson, Charlie 324–325, 348

Wilson, Georgie 73

Wilson, Terry 336–337

Winter, Len 155, 194, 199, 202, 204, 211

Wisbey, Tommy 324

Witton, Joe 119, 129, 162

Wonderland, Stepney 137

Wood, Jimmy 300

Woodbridge, Charlie 326

Wooder, Charlie 101, 105, 107–108, 203, 295, 352

Wooder, Freddie 101–102, 105, 352

Wooder, Henry 105

Wooder, Jimmy 166, 270, 278, 285, 353

Wooder, Georgie 101, 105, 352

Woodford, Bob 336–337

Woods, William 141

Woolgar, One-eyed Charlie 87, 89, 253

Worms, Alfred 69

Worth, Adam 18–25